Franchise Value and the Price/Earnings Ratio

**The Research Foundation of
The Institute of Chartered Financial Analysts**

Research Foundation Publications

Active Currency Management
by Murali Ramaswami

Canadian Stocks, Bonds, Bills, and Inflation: 1950–1987
by James E. Hatch and Robert W. White

Closed-Form Duration Measures and Strategy Applications
by Nelson J. Lacey and Sanjay K. Nawalkha

Corporate Bond Rating Drift: An Examination of Credit Quality Rating Changes Over Time
by Edward I. Altman and Duen Li Kao

Default Risk, Mortality Rates, and the Performance of Corporate Bonds
by Edward I. Altman

Durations of Nondefault-Free Securities
by Gerald O. Bierwag and George G. Kaufman

Earnings Forecasts and Share Price Reversals
by Werner F.M. De Bondt

The Effect of Illiquidity on Bond Price Data: Some Symptoms and Remedies
by Oded Sarig and Arthur Warga

Equity Trading Costs
by Hans R. Stoll

Ethics, Fairness, Efficiency, and Financial Markets
by Hersh Shefrin and Meir Statman

Ethics in the Investment Profession: A Survey
by E. Theodore Veit, CFA, and Michael R. Murphy, CFA

The Founders of Modern Finance: Their Prize-Winning Concepts and 1990 Nobel Lectures

Initial Public Offerings: The Role of Venture Capitalists
by Joseph T. Lim and Anthony Saunders

The Modern Role of Bond Covenants
by Ileen B. Malitz

A New Method for Valuing Treasury Bond Futures Options
by Ehud I. Ronn and Robert R. Bliss, Jr.

A New Perspective on Asset Allocation
by Martin L. Leibowitz

Options and Futures: A Tutorial
by Roger G. Clarke

The Poison Pill Anti-Takeover Defense: The Price of Strategic Deterrence
by Robert F. Bruner

Predictable Time-Varying Components of International Asset Returns
by Bruno Solnik

Program Trading and Systematic Risk
by A.J. Senchack, Jr., and John D. Martin

The Role of Risk Tolerance in the Asset Allocation Process: A New Perspective
by W.V. Harlow III, CFA, and Keith C. Brown, CFA

Selecting Superior Securities
by Marc R. Reinganum

Stock Market Structure, Volatility, and Volume
by Hans R. Stoll and Robert E. Whaley

Stocks, Bonds, Bills, and Inflation: Historical Returns (1926–1987)
by Roger G. Ibbotson and Rex A. Sinquefield
(Published with Irwin Professional Publishing)

Franchise Value and the Price/Earnings Ratio

ISBN 0-943205-21-2

Printed in the United States of America

January 1994

Mission

The mission of the Research Foundation is to identify, fund, and publish research material that:
- expands the body of relevant and useful knowledge available to practitioners;
- assists practitioners in understanding and applying this knowledge; and
- enhances the investment management community's effectiveness in serving clients.

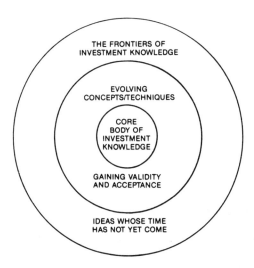

The Research Foundation of
The Institute of Chartered Financial Analysts
P.O. Box 3668
Charlottesville, Virginia 22903
U.S.A.
Telephone: 804/977-6600
Fax: 804/977-1103

Table of Contents

Foreword

The traditional securities analysis approach to valuing a share of common stock is to multiply an estimate of the underlying company's earnings per share by a forecasted price/earnings ratio (P/E) of the company. Typically, analysts laboriously forecast future corporate earnings, but the predicted P/E often receives less attention. Yet studies reveal that many major stock price changes result from a movement in the P/E. Thus, understanding the key ingredients that combine to affect P/Es is of crucial importance.

In this monograph, Martin L. Leibowitz and Stanley Kogelman tackle the imposing task of determining what really has an impact on P/Es. The monograph collects Leibowitz and Kogelman's research on this topic conducted over a period of several years. The authors subscribe to the conventional logic that the P/E gauges the market's assessment of the firm's future. They then introduce the franchise-value approach to analyzing the prospective cash flows that determine a company's P/E. The franchise-value approach is original, insightful, and even daring, but it has a practical bent that should appeal to investment practitioners.

The motivation behind this new valuation approach comes from the rapid changes that have occurred in the business and financial communities. As a result of the dynamic nature of business today, investment analysts cannot depend solely on traditional valuation models and tools. Often, the techniques that served the analyst so well in the past have been rendered obsolete by the new business dynamics.

The authors contend that the current investment environment also poses many new challenges to the modern equity investor. Because of the increasing global competitiveness of markets, an investor can no longer rely on past history to indicate future prospects. Companies with sustained levels of high profits now face fierce competition that can eradicate their superior earnings performance. As Leibowitz and Kogelman point out, "earnings momentum" has become an oxymoron.

Possibly the most often cited model for forecasting P/Es is the familiar dividend discount model, which was first proposed by John Burr Williams in 1938. The DDM's underlying assumptions have become increasingly untenable, however, in today's rapidly changing markets. In particular, the DDM suffers from the assumptions of stable return on equity (ROE), smooth earnings growth, and the financing of new initiatives through retained earnings. The appeal of the franchise-value approach is that it is not dependent on such increasingly unrealistic assumptions. At the same time, it retains the simplicity and intuitive appeal of the DDM.

At the foundation of the franchise-value approach is the belief that the following three aspects of a company interact to affect value: (1) the sustainable returns that can be expected from current businesses, (2) the prospects for growth through the pursuit of new investments, and (3) the return level that can be achieved from those investments. Of course, a firm's ROE on existing businesses is unlikely to match exactly its ROE on new investments. Yet the DDM model uses a blended-ROE approach that produces a difficulty, if not an impossibility, in discerning between these two ROEs.

The initial appeal of the approach developed in this monograph occurs as a result of the franchise-value approach's differentiation of the firm's value into value from existing business and value from prospective new investments. In this sense, the approach separates the ROE of existing business from the ROE of new businesses. In effect, the franchise-value approach enables the analyst to break the firm into two key component parts and to value those components. The first component is the *tangible value* of existing businesses and the earnings they are likely to generate over time. The second factor, the *franchise value*, is derived from prospective new investments and is subdivided into two components: a *growth equivalent* that captures the present value of the opportunities for productive new investment, and a *franchise factor* that captures the return levels associated with those new investments.

In a series of ten chapters, the authors introduce and develop the franchise-value approach to the determination of P/Es. Some of their observations conform to conventional beliefs. For example, it should come as no surprise that a no-growth firm will have a low "base P/E" that is simply the reciprocal of the firm's equity capitalization rate or that high P/Es result only from growth opportunities that consistently exceed the market rate of return.

On the other hand, several of the authors' findings tend to belie accepted wisdom. In particular, they reveal that high P/Es are especially fragile and can be maintained only if the firm continues to uncover high-return investment opportunities of ever greater magnitude. The differences in price growth and earnings growth, and the reason for the difference, may also come as a surprise to analysts. In addition, the analysis of varying impacts of inflation on the P/Es of different firms represents a novel approach to P/E valuation.

When all considerations are combined, this monograph provides a valuable framework for the determination of price/earnings ratios. The monograph leaves the analyst with a renewed appreciation for the difficulty confronting firms that are striving to maintain an above-average P/E. The difficulty is compounded as the firm becomes larger, because the magnitude of required high-return projects grows exponentially. Consequently, as a result of the increased competitiveness of world markets, high P/Es will be increasingly difficult to sustain. The prudent analyst, therefore, must comprehend the myriad of factors that can lead to major and sudden changes in P/E valuations. Fortunately, Leibowitz and Kogelman provide a working format for understanding and evaluating those important determining factors.

The Research Foundation is pleased to sponsor this collection of works on the franchise-value approach to P/E valuation. Without a doubt, benefits from these studies will accrue to investment analysts for many years to come.

John W. Peavy III, CFA

Preface

We developed the research and ideas in this monograph during a period of several years and with the support of Salomon Brothers Inc, for which we are most grateful. Pieces of the work have been published elsewhere, but this monograph presents the first opportunity to publish the concepts pertaining to the franchise-value model together as a whole. In doing so, we have made substantial changes to the presentation of the ideas but not to the ideas themselves.

The chapters that form the body of this monograph (Chapters 2–10) were originally published as papers by Salomon Brothers Inc (SB). Later, the articles that provided the bases of Chapters 2, 5, 6, 8, and 9 were published in slightly revised form in the *Financial Analysts Journal* (*FAJ*) or *The Journal of Investing*. The published titles and dates are as follows:

Chapter 2:	"Inside the P/E Ratio: The Franchise Factor," *FAJ*, November/December 1990.
Chapter 3:	"Inside the P/E Ratio (Part II): The Franchise Portfolio," SB, January 1991.
Chapter 4:	"A Franchise Factor Model for Spread Banking," SB, April 1991.
Chapter 5:	"The Franchise Factor for Leveraged Firms," *FAJ*, November/December 1991.
Chapter 6:	"Franchise Value and the Growth Process," *FAJ*, January/February 1992.
Chapter 7:	"The Growth Illusion: The P/E Cost of Earnings Growth,"SB, April 1993.
Chapter 8:	"Inflation-Adjusted ROEs: Strong Effects Even with Low Inflation," *The Journal of Investing*, Winter 1993.
Chapter 9:	"Resolving the Equity Duration Paradox," *FAJ*, January/February 1993.
Chapter 10:	"Theoretical P/Es and Accounting Variables," SB, June 1992.

The authors wish to express their appreciation for the helpful comments and suggestions from Edward Altman, Lawrence Bader, Peter Bernstein, James Farrell, Robert Ferguson, Ernest Frohboese, John Goldsberry, Michael Howell, Cal Johnson, Geoff Kieburtz, Kim Leibowitz, Eric Lindenberg, Robert

Salomon, David Shulman, Eric Sorensen, Jack Treynor, and William Van Harlow. We are also grateful for the support of the Research Foundation of the Institute of Chartered Financial Analysts in publishing this monograph.

Martin L. Leibowitz
Stanley Kogelman
New York
July 1993

1. Introduction

This monograph introduces the *franchise value* (FV) approach to analyzing the prospective cash flows that determine a company's price/earnings ratio. The FV technique provides more flexibility and greater insight than the standard dividend discount model, particularly in light of the dynamic character of today's financial markets.

The decade of the 1980s brought remarkable changes to the business environment not only in the United States but also throughout the world. Products, capital, and expertise began to flow across corporate and national boundaries at an unprecedented pace, and this fluidity of resources breached the traditional constraints on growth and development. New enterprises and regional economies surged into prominence. For investors and entrepreneurs, opportunities to facilitate and participate in this growth were exceptional.

Ironically, the same factors that created investors' successes in the 1980s are adding to their headaches in the 1990s. In this new decade, all economic processes have shifted into fast forward. Product cycles have shortened. Brilliant innovations are quickly reverse-engineered—and then often surpassed. Wonderful ideas rapidly become accepted knowledge or, worse, stale news. The advantages of firm size are no longer overriding, nor can a well-established firm rely on exclusive access to the capital, technical knowledge, and distribution muscle that in earlier days would have ensured continued market dominance.

The global economic machine is working in high gear day and night to reduce everything that was once unique and precious into broadly distributed commodities. Among the first casualties of this global leveling has been the ability of many companies to sustain and compound their historically high levels of profitability. "Earnings momentum" has become an oxymoron.

This environment creates many difficulties for a modern equity investor. Because newly empowered global competitors can challenge the champions in any market, the bridge between a company's past success and its future prospects is increasingly fragile. Today's investor cannot follow the custom of extrapolating past levels of return to tomorrow's investments. The investor must carefully assess each of the following aspects of a firm: (1) the sustainable returns that can be expected from current businesses, (2) the prospects for growth through the pursuit of new investments, and (3) the return level that can be achieved from those investments.

Just as basic earnings measures indicate the reward that existing businesses offer, the price/earnings ratio (P/E) gauges the market's assessment of the firm's future. To merit a high P/E, a firm must have the prospect of significant earnings growth. Moreover, to the extent that this growth is fueled by new investment, the firm must have the ability to earn an extraordinary return on that investment. Normal returns on future growth prospects will provide no P/E benefit whatsoever. Indeed, no matter how great its expansion in markets, revenues, or earnings, the firm that cannot generate an above-normal profit on future investment cannot command a high P/E. Therefore, high P/Es will surely be even more difficult to sustain in the new market environment than they were in the old. After all, if normal profits are fragile and short-lived, extraordinary profits become all the more scarce and tenuous.

To be useful, any theoretical P/E model should reflect the realities of the business environment, but the standard dividend discount model (DDM) has its limitations in this regard. Although the DDM has always had great appeal because of its fundamental simplicity, this simplicity belies a complex bundle of assumptions that have become increasingly untenable. In particular, the most common form of the DDM embodies the following assumptions:

- Return on equity (ROE) is stable.
- Earnings growth is smooth—at least for specific time spans.
- The financing of new initiatives is solely through retained earnings.
- All growth is beneficial to current shareholders.

Although the FV approach is founded on a more general framework than the DDM, it retains the original DDM's essential simplicity and intuitive appeal. In addition, the FV approach is in several ways better attuned to today's realities:

- In the FV approach, the return from new investments is differentiated from the current ROE.
- Earnings growth from new investments can follow any pattern, no matter how erratic, over time.
- Growth per se is not viewed as evidence of highly profitable investments.
- Productive new investments are assumed to be a scarce resource, limited by the availability of good opportunities rather than by the financing levels attainable from retained earnings.
- The level of retained earnings may have little to do with the "excess

profit" potential of new investments; if good projects are not available, earnings retention cannot create them.

At the outset, the FV approach differentiates the firm's past from its future by separating its value into two components: the *tangible value* of existing businesses and the earnings that they are likely to generate over time, and the *franchise value* derived from prospective new investments. The franchise value is then further divided into two factors: a *growth equivalent* that captures the present value of the opportunities for productive new investment, and a *franchise factor* that captures the return levels associated with those new investments. This decomposition provides an intuitive and simplifying framework for separating past, current, and future cash flows and for isolating the different effects that size and achievable returns have on the firm's P/E.

The FV approach allows a much clearer focus than the DDM on how corporate and economic events affect the different components of firm value. Building on this foundation, models are developed that address several important investment issues: reinvestment policy, capital structure, taxes, accounting practices, inflation, and duration.

The analysis leads to the following observations, some rather surprising, about the determinants of the P/E ratio:

- A no-growth firm will have a low "base P/E," one that is simply the reciprocal of the equity capitalization rate appropriate to the firm's risk class.
- High P/Es result only when growth comes from new projects that provide sustainable above-market returns.
- The P/E impact of new investments depends on the size of those investments relative to current book equity. Consequently, enormous dollar investments may be necessary for a significant effect on the P/E of large companies.
- The P/E-producing power of any new investment can be approximated from a knowledge of its internal rate of return and the duration of the payouts.
- Leverage changes the P/E in different directions, depending on the firm's preleverage P/E. This effect is surprisingly modest, however, within the range of conventional debt ratios.
- High P/Es have an intrinsically fragile character. To maintain a high P/E, a firm must continue to uncover new and previously unforeseen investment opportunities of ever greater magnitude.
- When franchise investment opportunities are limited in both scope and timing, the P/E will decline toward the base P/E.
- During a finite franchise period, price growth and earnings growth will

differ. The gap between the two growth rates can be approximated by the rate of P/E decline.

- Three factors contribute to a price-to-book premium: (1) a *market-to-book premium,* which results when economic book value exceeds accounting book value; (2) a *going-concern premium* attributable to an above-market economic return on the current market value of assets; and (3) a *future franchise premium* based on the income-producing power of new investments.
- The ability to pass along inflation increases, even partially, can dramatically enhance a firm's P/E.
- A firm's future investments are likely to be far more adaptive to unexpected inflation than its existing businesses. Consequently, when the value of a firm's equity is derived primarily from prospective businesses, its interest rate sensitivity (equity duration) is likely to be low.
- The FV approach helps explain why equities have much lower observed durations than the high levels suggested by the standard DDM.

All these findings are included in the nine studies that form the body of this monograph. In a sense, these studies represent the evolution of our thinking as we attempted to piece together the ingredients of high P/Es.

Chapter 2 develops the basic FV model and provides definitions and examples of the franchise factor and the growth equivalent. Chapter 3 shows how to compute the franchise P/E when a firm has a range of investment opportunities with different return patterns. A key ingredient in this analysis is the development of perpetual streams of "normalized earnings" having the same present values as the more erratic paths of projected earnings. Normalized earnings naturally lead to normalized ROEs, which can be used to test the reasonableness of long-term earnings projections. Chapter 4 applies the FV model to the spread-banking activities found in commercial banks, insurance companies, investment banks, brokerage firms, and many other financial enterprises.

To this point in the monograph, the model makes the simplifying assumptions that firms are tax free and financed solely with equity, and it focuses on the P/E at a single moment in time. The next three chapters address these issues directly.

Chapter 5 explores the effects of debt and taxes on the P/E. To a certain extent, the results are counterintuitive. Informal polls reveal that practitioners and academics hold strong but widely divergent views on the directional effects of leverage. Surprisingly, this study finds that either view is correct—under the right conditions. For firms with meager growth prospects and low P/Es, leverage further reduces P/Es. In contrast, for firms with already high

P/Es, the introduction of leverage actually elevates those P/Es.

The situation of a firm that has a prescribed set of future franchise opportunities is the subject of Chapter 6. This firm's P/E will be greatest when projected investment opportunities are at their maximum present values. In time, as new investments are made, franchise value is depleted and converted into tangible value. Because tangible value is fully reflected in the base P/E, the P/E will decline toward the base level. After the prescribed franchise is fully consumed, earnings, dividends, and price will all grow at a single rate determined by the firm's retention policy, but the P/E will remain at the low base level.

Chapter 7 continues the discussion of growth. Its value-preservation line illustrates the continuum of combinations of year-to-year earnings growth and P/E growth that can lead to equivalent levels of price growth. This line enables one to distinguish growth that is value enhancing from growth that is merely value preserving or, worse, value depleting.

The next two chapters are devoted to two key issues in a dynamic marketplace: inflation and changing interest rates. Even in a low-inflation environment, long-term investors are under pressure to achieve positive real returns. Companies that can increase earnings to keep pace with inflation tend to be more valuable than otherwise comparable firms that lack this flow-through capacity. Indeed, in countries with very high inflation, high flow-through capability is a prerequisite for survival.

In Chapter 8, an inflation adjustment factor that reflects a firm's flow-through capacity is developed. This factor permits a simple modification of the earlier formulas that shows how inflation flow-through can lift the base P/E and boost the franchise power.

Chapter 9 demonstrates how inflation flow-through can dramatically change the interest rate sensitivity of equity. Although the standard DDM predicts an extraordinarily long equity duration, 25–50 years, statistical analyses indicate that equity duration is closer to 2–6 years. This paradox is resolved by considering separately the durations of the franchise value and the tangible value. For discount rate changes driven by inflation, the FV approach argues for a very low franchise-value duration and a tangible-value duration of 6–10 years. This finding leads to a low overall firm duration, which is consistent with observed market behavior. Armed with an understanding of the nature and level of equity duration, portfolio managers can readily calculate their total portfolio durations and, if necessary, adjust their asset mixes to create better matches between the rate sensitivities of assets and liabilities.

As yet, the discussions have made no distinction between economic and accounting measures of earnings, book values, and returns. To facilitate comparisons between observed and theoretical market multiples, therefore, the final chapter introduces a "blended P/E" computed from a theoretical franchise-factor-based price and the reported accounting earnings.

In summary, the concepts and methodology of the FV approach lead to fresh insights into the building blocks of value. By working backward from an observed P/E, one can isolate the assumptions for growth and return implicitly embedded in the P/E and assess their reasonableness.

Capital expenditure and product development plans can be the starting point for estimating a firm's franchise opportunities and its appropriate P/E ratio. When the plans include a limit to the franchise opportunities, the P/E projections should generally reflect an ultimate erosion down to base levels. This sobering insight highlights the fragility of franchises and the unrelenting pressure on companies to seek out new avenues for profitable future growth.

2. The Franchise Factor

Equity analysts use a combination of judgment, understanding of an industry, and detailed knowledge of individual companies plus an arsenal of analytical models and measures to help them assess value. These measures include cash flow, return on equity, dividend yield, and such financial ratios as price/earnings, price to book value, earnings per share, and sales per share. Among the ratios, the P/E is one of the most scrutinized, modeled, and studied measures in use today.

The classic approach to estimating a theoretical P/E is the dividend discount model. Originally proposed by Williams (1938), this model has been modified and extended by many others.[1] Despite this abundance of literature, significant insight into the influence of various factors on P/E multiples can be gained from delving more deeply into the DDM-based models. For example, the authors have found that the investment community often does not appreciate the magnitude and type of growth required to support a high P/E multiple.

The problem stems, in part, from researchers' tendencies to model growth in a simplistic manner as proceeding smoothly at a constant rate, self-funded by retained earnings, and generating added earnings with each growth increment. This convenient and appealing concept forms the basis for most standard forms of the DDM; that is, these models are built on the assumption that dividends, earnings, and/or book values grow at the same constant rate. This growth usually is taken either to continue at the same rate forever or to be composed of two or three different growth rates covering consecutive time periods. Most DDMs further assume that the growth in dividends is solely the result of retained earnings.[2]

Despite its appeal, this simple concept of growth can be misleading in several ways. First, not all growth produces incremental value. A simple

---

[1]See for example, Miller and Modigliani (1961), Gordon (1962), and Fruhan (1979). For an update on the DDM, see the *Financial Analysts Journal* (1985).

[2]In addition to its role in DDM models, the smooth-growth concept has had a great impact on our intuitions regarding the value of equity. For an early discussion of the relationships among growth, above-market returns, and firm value, see Solomon (1963).

illustration is the "growth" in the amortized value of a discount bond. This growth does not add to the bond's promised yield to maturity; it is simply one means of delivering on that original promise. The situation is similar for equities: *Growth alone is not enough.* The routine investments a firm makes at the market rate do not add net value, even though they may contribute to nominal earnings growth. (Investments at below-market returns actually subtract from value.) Incremental value is generated only through investment in *exceptional* opportunities that promise above-market ROEs.

Thus, researchers must be careful to distinguish between the different kinds of growth. To do so is often difficult, however, because we are accustomed empirically to viewing the aggregate growth of an overall corporate entity. In the context of total growth, a rate of 8 percent may, on the surface, seem admirable, but in fact, it reveals nothing exceptional about the firm if the firm is obtaining only the market return on all its new investments. Value is added only on that portion of the 8 percent growth that is achieving above-market returns. If the entire 8 percent year-to-year growth is in investments at above-market rates, then this corporation may indeed be offering the investor something special. Only exceptional, "high-octane" growth fuels the engine driving high P/E multiples.

Another point of confusion inherent in the usual growth assumptions is the notion that growth should be self-funded out of retained earnings. This concept is also appealing: The smoothly growing flow of new investments appears to be a sign that the thrifty corporation and its investors will be rewarded. The key issue is not whether the company has retained earnings to self-fund a new investment opportunity, however, but whether that opportunity offers an above-market return. Such exceptional opportunities are, by definition, few and far between. Thus, when a corporation is presented with such a franchise opportunity, it should pursue the investment regardless of whether the funds are in its corporate coffers. In today's financial markets, by issuing new securities, a firm should always be able, theoretically, to participate in an opportunity to earn above-market returns.

This chapter looks inside the DDM-based price/earnings ratio and relaxes the restrictions imposed by assuming smooth growth through retained earnings. The resulting model of the exceptional future investment opportunities implicit in any given P/E is surprisingly simple. By representing all future investments by their present values, the model can capture in a single number the impact of all embedded investment opportunities on a firm's P/E. This number is called the franchise factor (FF).

The focus of this model is narrow. It assumes a stable market in which all stocks are unleveraged and priced according to the DDM. Thus, it does not account for the uncertainty and volatility that are endemic in the equity markets. It also assumes that all earnings are properly reported and that each firm's ROE remains unchanged over time. In fact, in the discussion of the price/earnings ratio, equity investments are treated as if their earnings, growth, and dividends were all certain. In essence, this approach tackles the complex and uncertain cash flows associated with equities in much the same manner as an analysis of the price and yield characteristics of risk-free bonds.

A Spectrum of Illustrative Firms

To explore the interactions between the P/E, the ROE, growth, and the FF, the next sections of this chapter consider the cash flows and reinvestment incomes of four illustrative firms. Relevant financial characteristics of these firms are presented in Table 2.1.

Table 2.1. Financial Characteristics of Firms A, B, C, and D

Characteristic	Firm A: Stable Growth	Firm B: No Growth	Firm C: Market ROE	Firm D: Reinvestment
Book equity	$100.00	$100.00	$100.00	$100.00
ROE	12.00%	12.00%	15.00%	15.00%
Earnings	$12.00	$12.00	$15.00	$15.00
Payout ratio	33.33%	100.00%	100.00%	33.33%
Dividend	$4.00	$12.00	$15.00	$5.00
Market rate	12.00%	12.00%	12.00%	12.00%
DDM price	$100.00	$100.00	$125.00	$250.00
Dividend yield	4.00%	12.00%	12.00%	2.00%
Growth rate	8.00%	0.00%	0.00%	10.00%
P/E	8.33	8.33	8.33	16.67

Firm A: Stable Growth in Earnings and Dividends. Firm A holds to a constant-dividend-payout policy and expects earnings to grow at a steady 8 percent a year far into the future. Now, examine the cash flows to an investor in Firm A under the simplifying assumption that the investment is subject to neither risk nor taxes. The investor's return will have three components: dividend return, price return, and reinvestment return.[3] Because earnings grow at 8 percent and dividend policy remains unchanged, dividends also will grow at 8 percent (see the solid bars in Figure 2.1).

Price appreciation is a consequence of the assumptions regarding the firm

---

[3]For fixed-income securities, the realized compound yield, or total return, incorporates all the components of return. This concept was discussed in Homer and Leibowitz (1972).

and use of the DDM for pricing the stock. The DDM implies that, in a static market, price growth will keep pace with dividend growth. Thus, if dividends grow at 8 percent, the stock price will also grow at 8 percent (see the middle bars in Figure 2.1). A new investor who buys Firm A's stock will realize a 4 percent return from dividends and an 8 percent return from price appreciation. In total, in the course of one year, the investor will experience a return on the stock purchase price that is equal to the market rate, which is assumed to be 12 percent.

Figure 2.1. Growth in Portfolio Value for a Firm with an 8 Percent Growth Rate and a 12 Percent ROE (Firm A)

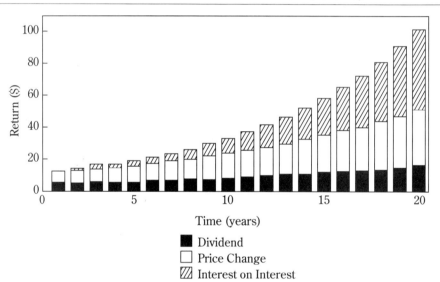

In the absence of risk, the stock of Firm A is equivalent to a perpetual bond with increasing principal and a constant 4 percent coupon. If the principal is initially $100, the first coupon payment is $4. If the principal increases by 8 percent annually, the second coupon will be $4.32 (4 percent of 1.08 × $100). This "perpetual bond" provides coupon payments that are the same as the dividends for Firm A.

The final consideration is the gain from reinvesting all dividends (see the top bars in Figure 2.1). Assume the investor has the opportunity to continue investing in the equity market to earn the 12 percent market rate.[4] If all

---

[4]With fixed-income securities, reinvestment is generally assumed to be in riskless assets, which may offer a lower return than the original investment. In this example, dividends are reinvested in equity assets that offer the same expected return as the original investment.

dividend payments are invested and those investments compound at a 12 percent rate, the investor will build a growing "side pool" of wealth. This pool will consist of all accumulated dividends, "interest" on those dividends, and the further compounding of this additional "interest on interest" (or, more accurately, "dividends on dividends").

At first glance, the overall pattern for the total investment return shown in Figure 2.1 seems to correspond to what would be characterized as a "growth" investment. In the early years, price growth is the dominant component of return. In time, however, interest on interest begins to dominate, which is consistent with the return patterns observed for fixed-income securities.

Firm B: No-Growth. Consider now a second firm, Firm B, that appears, at least on the surface, to be quite different from Firm A. Firm B has the same earnings as Firm A, but it has a 100 percent payout ratio; that is, all earnings are paid out as dividends on a year-by-year basis. Firm B is just the opposite of a growth stock; it has *no* growth in earnings, dividends, or price.

Firm B's dividend remains constant forever, and in the absence of a change in the discount rate, no price appreciation occurs. In fact, the payment stream for Firm B is identical to the payment stream for a perpetual bond with a 12 percent coupon and a principal of $100. Figure 2.2 compares the period-by-

Figure 2.2. Comparison of the Dividend Streams of an 8-Percent-Growth Firm (Firm A) and a No-Growth Firm (Firm B)

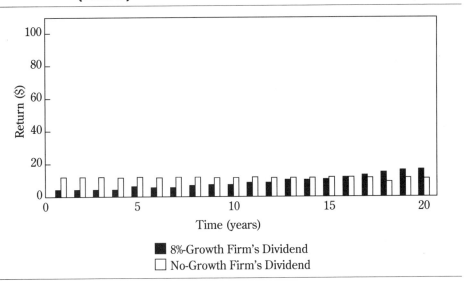

■ 8%-Growth Firm's Dividend
□ No-Growth Firm's Dividend

period dividends of Firm A and Firm B. The dividend stream of Firm B clearly dominates in the early years, but by Year 15, the growth in Firm A's earnings leads to dividends that surpass those of Firm B.

Because of Firm B's policy of paying out 100 percent of earnings in dividends and its consequent lack of growth, its stock price never changes. In the first year, the total of the 4 percent dividend yield plus the 8 percent price gain for Firm A matches the 12 percent dividend payment for Firm B. As time passes, however, both the dividend and the price gain from Firm A grow. The combined gain pulls increasingly ahead of the fixed $12 payment from Firm B.

The growth properties of Firm A enable it to outrun the stable 12 percent return from Firm B. Firm B does have one advantage over Firm A, however. Because Firm B pays out all earnings as dividends, an investor in this firm has the option of either spending or reinvesting those dividends. In contrast, the investor cannot spend the price appreciation from Firm A. By retaining earnings and adding to book value, Firm A is in charge of a major component of the investor's reinvestment decisions.

According to the assumptions of the DDM, 66⅔ percent of Firm A's earnings are retained and reinvested to produce additional income at the same rate as the firm's initial ROE (12 percent). The same investment opportunity is directly available to an investor in Firm B. That investor can invest all dividend receipts into the general equity market and earn the 12 percent rate. Thus, all of the earnings of both firms will be put to work at 12 percent, either by internal investment of retained earnings (Firm A) or through general market investments of dividends received (Firm B). The effect is illustrated in Figure 2.3, where the incremental year-by-year return from interest on interest is layered on top of the dividend and price gains. On the basis of returns alone, a fully compounding investor should be indifferent between Firm A and Firm B.

Figure 2.3 illustrates dramatically the importance of interest on interest for Firm B. The constant high dividend payments offer investors reinvestment opportunities that enable Firm B to provide precisely the same year-by-year increments in portfolio value as Firm A. Thus, as expected, under stable market conditions, both firms produce compound returns equal to the 12 percent market rate.

In summary, from the point of view of the fully compounding, tax-free investor, Firms A and B are equivalent in total return. They are also equivalent in current price, because the dividend streams from both firms, when appropriately discounted, have the same present value of $100. Moreover, because the earnings are the same, both stocks have the same initial P/E of 8.33.

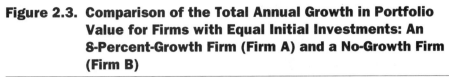

Figure 2.3. Comparison of the Total Annual Growth in Portfolio Value for Firms with Equal Initial Investments: An 8-Percent-Growth Firm (Firm A) and a No-Growth Firm (Firm B)

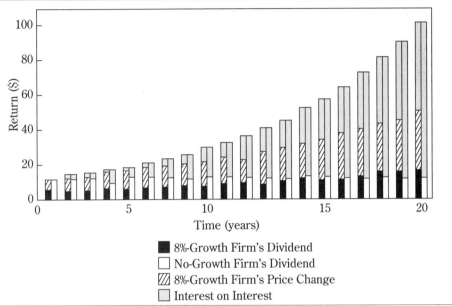

Internal Growth versus External Growth. An analysis of the earnings streams of Firms A and B provides further insight into their P/Es. Both firms start with a book value of $100 and first-year earnings of $12. Hence, both stocks have identical P/Es of 8.33. Firm B continually pays out all its earnings as dividends, and its book value remains constant at $100. For Firm B, neither price nor earnings ever grow beyond their initial values. Hence, the P/E for Firm B always remains 8.33. This figure is called the "base P/E."

Some insight into this base P/E can be gained by again comparing Firm B's stock with a perpetual 12 percent coupon bond. The price of such a bond is found by dividing the earnings (that is, the "coupon" payment of $12) by the yield (the 12 percent market rate). This approach is equivalent to requiring that the P/E ratio be the same as the reciprocal of the yield. Thus, the P/E of 8.33 is the same as 1/0.12.

In contrast to Firm B, Firm A retains 66⅔ percent of each year's earnings and adds this amount to its book value. In the first year, it retains $8 (⅔ of 12 percent of $100), thereby bringing its book value up to $108 (that is, 1.08 × $100) by the end of that year. As book value increases, total dollar earnings rise, because the same 12 percent ROE applies to an ever-larger base. Firm A's earnings will be $12.96 in Year 2 (the ROE of 12 percent applied to a book value of $108), $14.00 in Year 3, and so on.

For the "growth stock" Firm A, the dollar earnings build year by year in direct proportion to the 8 percent growth in the book value of the firm. Under the assumed stable market conditions, the price of Firm A's stock also appreciates by 8 percent a year in accordance with its growth in dividends and earnings: $100.00 in Year 1, $108.00 in Year 2, $116.64 in Year 3, and so on. Accordingly, in Year 2 for Firm A,

$$P/E = \frac{\$100 \times 1.08}{\$12 \times 1.08}$$

$$= \frac{\$100}{\$12}$$

$$= 8.33,$$

and in Year 3,

$$P/E = \frac{\$100 \times 1.08^2}{\$12 \times 1.08^2}$$

$$= \frac{\$100}{\$12}$$

$$= 8.33.$$

In other words, the P/E for Firm A remains at its initial value of 8.33. Thus, Firm A has exactly the same P/E as Firm B in every period.

Because Firm A appears to be a growth firm, one might intuitively expect it to have a higher P/E than Firm B. As discussed earlier, however, a firm that reinvests only at the market rate is not providing any special service to its investors; they could reinvest their dividend receipts at this same rate. Reinvestment at the market rate is thus tantamount to paying out all earnings to the investors: The reinvestment rates are the same; only the labels look different.

Firm A, although a growing enterprise, is simply a full-payout equivalent of Firm B, generating fundamentally the same value for its investors as the literally full-payout Firm B. Any full-payout-equivalent firm has the same price as a perpetual "bond" with an annual coupon payment equal to the firm's current earnings. Moreover, although the stock price of such a full-payout-equivalent firm will depend on its earnings, any such firm will have the same 8.33 base P/E. In short, any firm with a 12 percent ROE is equivalent in P/E value to Firm B, regardless of the firm's dividend payout policy. Furthermore, as the next section demonstrates, any full-payout firm, regardless of its ROE, is also equivalent in P/E value to Firm B.

A key message from this comparison of Firms A and B is that investors will not "pay up" in stock price or in P/E for access to a firm that reinvests at just the market rate. A firm must achieve a return in excess of the market rate on new investments to command a P/E in excess of the base P/E.

Although the focus in this section is on total portfolio returns under stable conditions, note that the stocks of the two firms will exhibit different sensitivities to changes in market assumptions. Because the growth stock of Firm A compounds internally at 12 percent, it may have a longer duration and, hence, a greater sensitivity to declining market discount rates than the stock of Firm B (see Chapter 9). Thus, the stocks are not identical under dynamic market conditions.

Firm C: A Full-Payout Firm with an Above-Market ROE.   Firm C has an above-market, 15 percent ROE but, as does Firm B, a 100 percent dividend payout policy and, therefore, no expectation of future growth. Based on an initial book value of $100, Firm C earns $15 annually in perpetuity. Consequently, the price of its stock must be at a premium to book (that is, at $125) to bring its return down to the market rate of 12 percent (12 percent = [15/125] × 100 percent). Because all earnings are paid out as dividends, the dividend yield for this firm is also 12 percent.

As in the case of Firm B, Firm C's stock is equivalent to a perpetual bond. The difference between the two "perpetuals" is that Firm C's stock is equivalent to a premium bond with a 15 percent coupon, while Firm B's stock is equivalent to a par bond with a 12 percent coupon. From an investor's viewpoint, Firm C offers no advantage over Firm B: Both firms provide the same dividend yield and no price appreciation. The only difference is in their stock prices.

The fundamental similarity between Firm B and Firm C is reflected in their P/Es: Firm C has the same 8.33 base P/E as Firm B (that is, $125/$15). Thus, A, B, and C are all full-payout-equivalent firms.

Firm D: A Reinvesting Firm with an Above-Market ROE. Firm D is significantly different from the full-payout-equivalent Firms A, B, and C and has the same 15 percent ROE as Firm C but a 33⅓ percent payout ratio. It differs from all the preceding firms in that it can apply its above-market ROE of 15 percent to any new investment it funds out of retained earnings. Applying the DDM (see Appendix A for details) indicates that Firm D's greater ROE and higher growth rate (10 percent) lead to an initial stock price of $250, which is higher than the price for the other three firms.

Because the initial stock price is no longer $100, a comparison with results for Firms A and B is facilitated by expressing the three components of return as percentages of their original prices. Although Firm D's dividend of $5 is higher than Firm A's dividend, it represents a lower dividend yield, only 2 percent; Figure 2.4 contains a comparison of the yearly dividends of Firm A and Firm D (as percentages of the original price of each). Observe that, despite the rapid 10 percent growth of Firm D, the dividends of Firm A dominate those of Firm D for many years.

Figure 2.4. Comparison of the Dividends of an 8-Percent-Growth Firm (Firm A) and a 10-Percent-Growth Firm (Firm D)
(percentages of the original price)

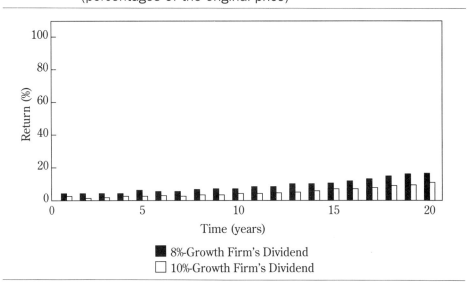

An investor in Firm D would expect yearly rises in stock price, however, to keep pace with the firm's 10 percent growth in book value and earnings. During the course of a year, the 2 percent dividend yield combined with a 10 percent price gain would provide a new investor with the 12 percent market

Figure 2.5. Annual Dividends and Price Appreciation for an 8-Percent-Growth Firm (Firm A) and a 10-Percent-Growth Firm (Firm D)

(percentages of the original price)

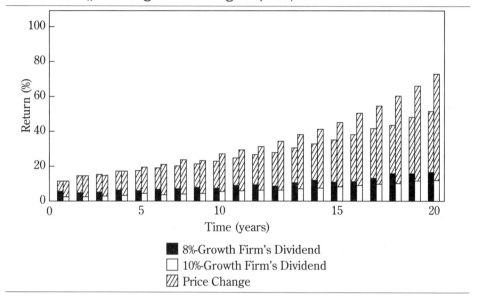

return on an investment in Firm D's stock. As Figure 2.5 shows, the 10 percent annual price return of Firm D is sufficient to bring the combination of its dividends and price increments (expressed as a percentage of Firm D's initial $250 price) to a level that completely dominates the dividends and price increments for Firm A.

As with Firm A, Firm D's stock, in the absence of risk, is equivalent to a perpetual bond with increasing principal. The only differences are that, in Firm D's case, the coupon is 2 percent and the principal increases by 10 percent a year.

To complete the comparison of the two firms, consider the total portfolio growth an investor in Firm D can expect to receive. A fully compounding investor in Firm D will create a side pool of wealth that compounds at the assumed 12 percent market rate. Because dividends for Firm D represent a relatively small percentage of the initial investment, this side pool will grow more slowly than it would for an investment in the other firms. In fact, the side pool for Firm D grows just enough, in comparison with that of Firm A, that when all components of return are considered, the period-by-period returns for the two firms are identical (see Figure 2.6).

Figure 2.6. Comparison of Year-by-Year Returns for an 8-Percent-Growth Firm (Firm A) and a 10-Percent-Growth Firm (Firm D)

(percentages of the original price)

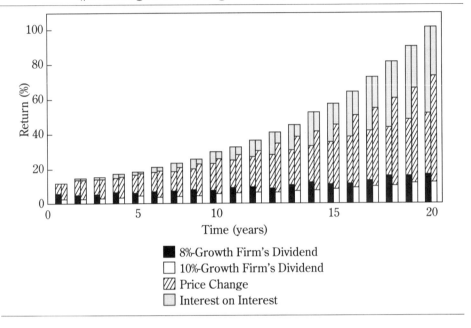

8%-Growth Firm's Dividend
10%-Growth Firm's Dividend
Price Change
Interest on Interest

In the context of the narrow model defined in this chapter, the positive impact of growth combined with a high ROE is not on return, but on the P/E. This ratio reflects both current earnings and future franchise opportunities.

Dissecting the Investment Process

Firm D's stock was priced at $250, whereas the initial price was $100 for Firm A's stock. The $250 reflects both Firm D's high current earnings and the expectation of future above-market investment opportunities. By virtue of its business franchise, Firm D has the special opportunity to reinvest a portion of its earnings at the 15 percent ROE. This opportunity is not directly available to investors, because in the equilibrium model, investors are able to achieve only the 12 percent market return. Thus, the excess 3 percent return Firm D is able to achieve produces a pool of incremental value beyond what the investor could do with an external side pool. This compounding stream of excess returns, therefore, has real value to the investor, who will pay up to access it.

The value of the excess returns is reflected in the P/E for Firm D. Because this firm earns $15 the first year, its P/E is 16.67 (that is, $250/$15), twice the P/E of the other firms. This P/E increment can be interpreted as a premium for franchise opportunities.

As noted previously, when a firm's ROE is the same as the market rate (Firms A and B), the P/E always remains at its base level, regardless of the firm's payout policy or growth rate. A firm with an above-market ROE but no growth also offers only the base P/E (Firm C). A growth firm with an above-market ROE (Firm D), however, will have a higher P/E than the base P/E of 8.33. (Note also that a growth firm with a below-market ROE would have a P/E below the base P/E.)

To see how this premium value is created requires a close focus on the reinvestment process. After one year, Firm D pays out $5 of its $15 in earnings as dividends and retains and reinvests the remaining $10. As a result, the firm's book value grows to $110. The new book value may be viewed as consisting of the original $100, from which earnings were fully reflected at the outset, and a $10 new investment, which will be a source of new earnings. By assumption, this new investment will produce returns at the 15 percent ROE in perpetuity.

The year-end reinvestment of $10 can in itself be viewed as achieving a 3 percent premium return over the 12 percent market rate because of Firm D's special franchise situation. The real added value from Firm D is derived totally from this 3 percent excess return that it earns on its new investments in perpetuity, a compounding stream of incremental earnings. In the second year, the retained earnings available for new investment will grow to $11 (that is, $1.10 \times 10). In the third year, Firm D has $12.10 (that is, 10×1.10^2) to invest.

In time, this sequence of opportunities produces a growing aggregate stream of excess earnings. The present value of this stream of excess earnings will amount to $125 a share—that is, 50 percent of Firm D's price, according to the DDM. The other 50 percent of Firm D's value is derived simply from its full-payout equivalence to Firm C (recall that the price of Firm C's stock was precisely $125). In summary, Firm D can be viewed as a combination of (1) a full-payout-equivalent firm such as Firm A, B, or C and (2) a stream of opportunities for investment at a rate 3 percent above the market rate.

The Present-Value Growth Equivalent

A firm's opportunities to earn returns on new investments in excess of the equilibrium market rate can be thought of as franchise growth opportunities. As discussed previously, the traditional DDM implicitly assumes that a firm has the opportunity at any time to make investments that offer returns equal to the firm's initial ROE. Furthermore, the DDM implicitly assumes that such investments are made according to a smooth growth pattern determined by the firm's sequence of retained earnings. Clearly, franchise opportunities arise in an irregular pattern, however, and the extent of franchise opportunity is not guaranteed to equal the available cash. Nevertheless, the firm will want to take full advantage of these opportunities to earn above-market returns. The lack of cash is not a restriction because, in today's capital markets, a firm should have no problem selling equity to fund projects that offer exceptional returns.

Thus, the assumptions are that the firm will fully pursue all franchise opportunities and that the cost of capital for the firm will be the market rate.[5] Whether the funds are supplied by retained earnings or by raising new funds at the market rate does not matter. (This chapter deals only with the unleveraged firm; the obvious alternative of using debt is the subject of Chapter 5.)

A variable is needed that will measure the total dollar value of all franchise investments regardless of whether those investments occur at irregular intervals or in the smooth stream implied by the DDM. This variable is the present-value *growth equivalent* of the franchise investments.

The value of the growth equivalent can be derived by discounting all future franchise opportunities at the market rate and then expressing the result as a percentage of the original book value of the firm.[6] This growth equivalent enables the stream of future opportunities to be viewed as equivalent to a single immediate opportunity to invest and then earn the ROE in perpetuity. In other words, this approach reduces all growth patterns to the simple model of a single immediate "jump" in book value. Moreover, the growth equivalent can represent any sequence of opportunities; thus, use of the growth equivalent can penetrate the assumption of smooth growth that often obscures the real implications of many DDM models. In this way, the growth equivalent provides insight into the magnitude of investments implicit in any constant-growth assumption.

As an example, recall that Firm D's P/E was at an 8.34 premium to the base P/E of 8.33. Basically, this incremental multiple was the value attached to the growing sequence of opportunities to invest at 3 percent above the market rate. This sequence coincided with Firm D's pattern of retained earnings. By

---

[5]For ease of exposition, we consider only the case in which the return is equal to initial ROE. In Chapter 3, we discuss the more realistic situation in which franchise opportunities offer a range of returns.

[6]For a constant growth rate (g) and market rate (k), the growth equivalent is $[g/(k-g)]$. See Appendix A for a derivation of this formula.

computing the growth equivalent of this series of investments, one can find the magnitude of the single immediate opportunity needed to provide the same present value as the smooth-growth pattern associated with Firm D's retained earnings. This equivalent single immediate investment (G) would have to correspond to 500 percent of Firm D's current book value.[7] In present-value terms, Firm D must have the opportunity immediately to invest an amount equal to five times its current book value and earn 15 percent on that investment in perpetuity.

Figure 2.7 shows the growing increments of book value that Firm D generates through its actual growth, at the 10 percent annual rate, and the hypothetical book value of the corresponding growth equivalent. Both cases start with an original book value of $100, but for the growth-equivalent firm, book value immediately jumps by $500 to $600. It then remains constant at that level.

Figure 2.7. Present-Value Growth Equivalent for a 10-Percent-Growth Firm (Firm D)

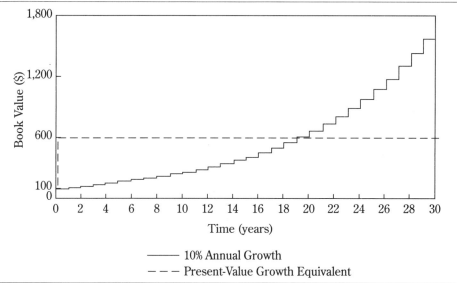

In essence, the growth-equivalent approach creates a hypothetical "alter-ego" for any growth firm. Following the immediate jump in book value, the alter-ego firm has no further growth. It thus retains none of its earnings, and

---

[7]Because $G = g/(k - g)$ and g = 10 percent for Firm D, $G = 0.10/(0.12 - 0.10)$ = 500 percent.

all net flows are paid out immediately as dividends. Consequently, the alter-ego firm can be viewed as an augmented full-payout equivalent of a growth firm.

This view is clarified in Figure 2.8, which compares the dividend flows from the growing Firm D with the constant dividend payments of its full-payout alter-ego. The payouts for Firm D begin with the initial dividend of $5 (that is, 2 percent of $250) and grow at a constant rate of 10 percent forever. In contrast, the growth equivalent provides an annual payout consisting of the original $15 of earnings (the full-payout equivalent), augmented by an additional $15 from the 3 percent excess return (3 percent = 15 percent – 12 percent) on the $500 growth-equivalent investment. Thus, this hypothetical growth equivalent provides a constant annual payout of $30 in perpetuity. When discounted at the market rate, both cash flows have the same present value, $250.

Figure 2.8. Comparison of Cash Flows: A 10-Percent-Growth Firm (Firm D) and a Growth-Equivalent Firm

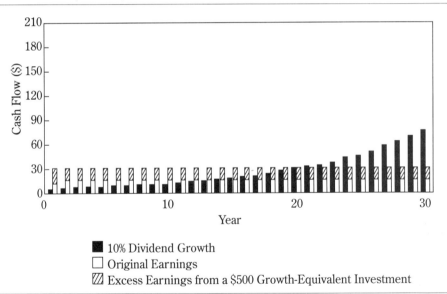

The expected level of above-market investments implicit in a P/E of 16.67 is startling. Perhaps a start-up firm with a new product and an incontestable franchise can expect several years of spectacular investment opportunities, but a large, mature company in a highly competitive market will have difficulty finding investment opportunities that amount to five times current book value and also earn a perpetual above-market return.

The Franchise Factor Model

As demonstrated, firms that offer both growth and above-market ROEs are valued at a premium to the base P/E. The franchise factor (FF) is defined to be a direct measure of the impact of the above-market investments on the P/E. In a stable market, the FF depends only on the firm's ROE for existing and new investments. Computationally, the FF is the return premium offered by new investments divided by the product of the ROE for existing businesses and the market rate (see Appendix A for the derivation of the franchise factor). If the ROE on both old and new investments is the same,

$$FF = \frac{r-k}{rk},$$

where r is the firm's ROE, k is the market rate, and all values are expressed as decimals.

Firm D will be used to illustrate how the franchise factor works. Because its ROE is 15 percent and the market rate is 12 percent, the FF for Firm D is

$$FF = \frac{0.15 - 0.12}{0.15 \times 0.12}$$

$$= \frac{0.03}{0.018}$$

$$= 1.67.$$

A franchise factor of 1.67 means the P/E will increase 1.67 units for each unit gain in book value (in present-value terms). Recall that the present-value growth equivalent for Firm D was 500 percent of book. Thus, the franchise factor lifts the P/E by 1.67×5 (that is, 8.34) units above the base P/E to a total level of 16.67.

The P/E can be expressed in terms of the market rate, the growth equivalent, and the franchise factor:

$$P/E = \frac{1}{k} + (FF \times G)$$

or

$$P/E = (\text{Base } P/E) + (FF \times G).$$

The second term captures the increase in the P/E that results from the combination of growth and an above-market ROE. Recall that, in a stable market, the franchise factor depends only on the ROE, whereas the growth equivalent depends only on the assumed growth rate. Thus, the franchise factor and the growth equivalent fully, but separately, capture the impact of ROE and growth on the P/E.

Figure 2.9 illustrates the franchise factor for a wide range of ROEs. When an ROE is the same as the market rate, the FF is zero. As a result, growth makes no contribution to the P/E. For example, recall that Firm A had 8 percent growth but only a market ROE; thus, its FF was zero, and its growth did not contribute to its P/E.

Figure 2.9. The Franchise Factor

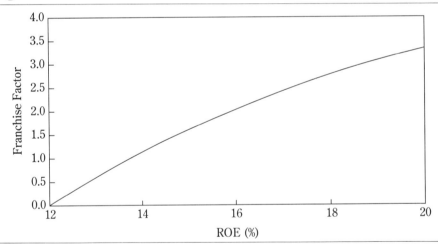

Consider a firm with an FF of 1 (that is, from Figure 2.9, a firm with an ROE of 13.64 percent). For such a firm, an immediate investment equal to 100 percent of its current book value lifts the P/E only by a single unit, from 8.33 to 9.33. With an FF of 4 (that is, an ROE of 23.08 percent), an investment equal to 100 percent of book value raises the P/E only by four units. These examples underscore the difficulty of creating a high P/E.

As the return on equity increases, so does the franchise factor. Thus, as expected, the higher the ROE, the greater the P/E impact of new investment. As illustrated in Figure 2.9, however, this impact levels off as the ROE increases. In particular, as the ROE approaches infinity, FF approaches the inverse of the market rate. With the 12 percent market rate assumed here, this FF implies that a 100 percent increase in book value can never lead to more than an 8.33-unit increase in the P/E.

These findings are summarized in Table 2.2. Because Firms B and C have no growth, their growth equivalents are zero. In contrast, Firm A has a 200 percent growth equivalent, and Firm D has a 500 percent growth equivalent. Firm A's growth fails to add value, however, because its FF is zero (its ROE is the 12 percent market rate). In addition, observe that Firm C has the same FF as Firm D (it has the same 15 percent ROE), but because of a lack of new investments, its potential is not being used. Only Firm D with its combination of positive growth and a positive franchise factor is able to command a premium P/E.

Table 2.2. P/E Ratios and Franchise Factors for Firms A, B, C, and D

Firm	ROE	Growth Rate	Growth Equivalent	Franchise Factor	P/E Increment	P/E
A	12%	8%	200%	0.00	0.00	8.33
B	12	0	0	0.00	0.00	8.33
C	15	0	0	1.67	0.00	8.33
D	15	10	500	1.67	8.34	16.67

Figure 2.10 is a graphic view of how the franchise factor and growth equivalent explain the P/E level of the four example firms. When the P/E is plotted against the growth equivalent, all firms that have the same ROE will plot along a straight line. This line will always start at the base P/E (8.33 here), and the slope of the line will be the FF for that ROE. Thus, firms with a 12 percent ROE have an FF of zero and plot along a horizontal line; firms with a 15 percent ROE plot along the line with a slope of 1.67.

In Figure 2.10, Firm A has 200 percent growth, but it is on the horizontal (FF = 0) line. Thus, it commands only the base P/E ratio of 8.33. Because Firms B and C have no growth, they too can obtain only the 8.33 base P/E. Only Firm D has the right combination of growth (a 500 percent growth equivalent) and an above-market ROE (15 percent) to enjoy a high P/E. It lies on the line with a slope of 1.67.

Figure 2.10 also shows how firms with 20 percent ROEs plot in such a diagram: A high ROE certainly makes growth valuable, but to obtain a high P/E, even with an ROE that is significantly above the market, the firm must possess some sizable growth prospects.

Figure 2.10. Interpreting the P/E through the Franchise Factor

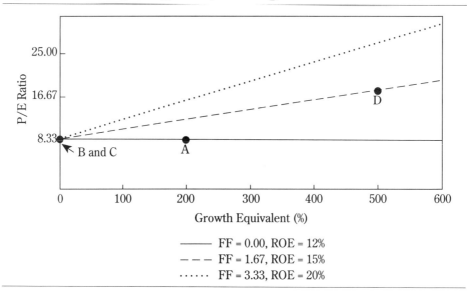

Summary

The analysis in this chapter was based on the simplifying assumption of a static market in which stock prices are at their theoretical values according to the DDM. Under these market conditions, when the three components of return are taken into account, all investments produce the same market return. The relative importance of each component of return is, however, directly related to a firm's return on equity and growth prospects. Analysis of the cash flows that a fully compounding, tax-free investor realizes shows how each component of return contributes to the cumulative growth of the investor's portfolio.

In the context of the dividend discount model, the combination of growth and an above-market ROE can have a significant impact on the price/earnings ratio. Growth alone is not enough, however, to boost the P/E above a base level. When a firm can invest only at the market rate, it provides no advantage to investors, because an investor can also reinvest all dividend payments at the market rate. Similarly, if a firm has a high ROE but no opportunities to earn that rate on new investments, the firm's stock is essentially equivalent to a high-coupon bond that makes payments equal to the firm's earnings in perpetuity. Thus, a high-ROE, no-growth firm can command only a base P/E.

Firms that have opportunities to invest and earn above-market returns may be said to possess embedded franchise opportunities. The impact of such opportunities can be captured in a franchise factor, which depends only on the firm's ROE. It is a measure of the impact on the P/E of all future investments that provide a return equal to the firm's ROE.

One surprising result of the analysis is the small size of the franchise factor. When the ROE is 15 percent, for example, the FF is only 1.67. Thus, a series of investments that is equal in terms of present value to the initial book value of the firm is necessary to raise the P/E by 1.67 units. A firm with a 15 percent ROE and a 16.67 P/E, for example, must have investment opportunities equivalent to 500 percent of its current book value.

The requirement for such large investments raises the question of what types of firms can sustain above-market P/Es. To be sure, the market has seen many a new company that offered an exceptional product in a rapidly developing market, and such companies have often grown many times in size in a fairly short time. Mature companies with significant market shares, however, face substantial obstacles to growth.

By representing above-market investment opportunities by their present values, this analysis was able to look beyond the pattern of smooth, constant growth implied by the DDM. Thus, this analysis can be readily extended to an entire portfolio of investment opportunities. Each investment could have its own (possibly irregular) capital schedule, return pattern, and life cycle.

The FF approach can provide valuable insights into the structural relationships that lie inside the price/earnings ratio. The results presented in this chapter were derived under highly simplified assumptions, however, and must be interpreted with appropriate care. In reality, taxes, leverage, and uncertainty do exist, prices do not coincide with their theoretical values, and market rates, investment opportunities, and year-to-year ROEs change constantly. Later chapters in this monograph deal with some of these issues.

3. The Franchise Portfolio

This chapter presents a methodology for estimating the theoretical impact on the price/earnings ratio of the portfolio of investment opportunities available to a firm. The analysis makes the highly restrictive assumptions of a world without taxes, leverage, or uncertainty.

A franchise opportunity has two components: the magnitude of investments and the pattern of payments that evolves over time. The magnitude of a given investment opportunity is measured by the present value of the total amount of funds that can be invested in it. Because the accumulation of these investments constitutes the growth in the firm's book value, this measure, the growth equivalent, is the first component of the franchise opportunity.

The second component, the sequence of payments the investment generates, is the return pattern. Return patterns exhibit a wide variety of shapes. Annual returns may increase rapidly at first, for example, and then level off; ultimately, a period of deteriorating returns may result from the declining value of the franchise. The P/E-producing power of a given return pattern is captured in the investment's franchise factor. The incremental P/E value of a specific investment opportunity is given by the product of its FF and the size of the investment as measured by its growth equivalent. An infinite number of combinations of franchise factors and growth equivalents can give rise to the same P/E increment.

The first section of this chapter examines fairly general return patterns for new investments and develops a duration-based formula that can be used to approximate the franchise factor.[1] The approach to finding the exact FF that corresponds to any pattern of investment returns is to compute the investment's *perpetual equivalent return*. This return is simply a constant annual payment that has the same present value as the payment pattern. After the tools of analysis are developed, the methodology is applied to a portfolio of franchise investment opportunities.

---

[1]The observations presented here are consistent with the usual capital budgeting considerations. See, for example, Rao (1987).

A Duration-Based Approximation

To develop a formula for computing an exact FF for any return pattern, a formula for approximating FF is needed. For the approximation, consider a choice between two investment opportunities: Investment A provides annual earnings equal to 20 percent of the investment for 10 years. At the end of 10 years, both the returns and the salvage value of the investment drop to zero. Investment B offers a lower return (16.06 percent) than Investment A, but this return is sustained for 20 years. Because the returns for both investments are constant over a fixed interval, the earnings flows from these investments are level-payment annuities.

The evaluation of the two investments begins with computation of their net present values (NPVs) per $100 of investment. This computation is done by discounting the returns back to the time the investment is made, subtracting the original $100 investment, and dividing by 100. The results for a range of discount rates are illustrated in Figure 3.1. Observe that the 20-year investment has a higher NPV than the 10-year investment when discount rates are low. When the discount rate reaches 15.1 percent, the NPV for each investment is equal to zero. For discount rates above 15.1 percent, the NPV of the 10-year investment is higher than that of the 20-year investment.

By definition, the internal rate of return (IRR) is the discount rate at which the NPV of an investment is zero. Thus, Investments A and B each have a 15.1

Figure 3.1. Net Present Value per $100 Investment for a 10-Year and a 20-Year Investment

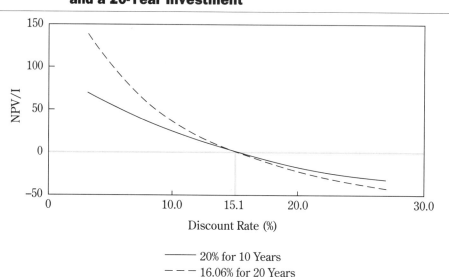

percent IRR. If the only measure of the relative worthiness of investments were the IRR, one would conclude that Investments A and B are of equal value to investors. The problem with the IRR is that it accounts for neither the timing of returns nor the sensitivity of returns to changes in the discount rate. For example, at the 12 percent market rate, the NPVs of the 10- and 20-year investments are $13.00 and $19.98, respectively. Clearly, at this rate, the 20-year, 16.06 percent annuity adds significantly more "present value" than the 10-year, 20 percent annuity.

The greater slope of the NPV curve for the 20-year annuity compared with that of the 10-year annuity indicates that the value of the longer annuity is more sensitive to changes in the discount rate. This variation in sensitivity is consistent with the well-known duration concept for bonds: All other things being equal, bonds with longer maturities have longer durations than bonds with shorter maturities. As a result, the price (present value) of a long-maturity bond will be more sensitive to changes in interest rates than the price of the bond with a shorter maturity. The duration concept applied here is referred to as *investment duration*.

The importance of both investment duration (D) and IRR in providing additional P/E is captured in the approximation formula for FF (which is derived in Appendix B):

$$\text{FF} \approx \frac{D(\text{IRR} - k)}{r},$$

in which k is the discount rate and r is the return on equity (ROE). This formula has general application; it applies to any pattern of investment payoffs, not solely to annuities.[2]

Observe that when the IRR is the same as the market rate, the franchise factor will be zero. In that case, the investment will not add value, regardless of its duration. When the IRR is greater than k, however, duration is critical, because FF is computed by multiplying the difference between the IRR and the market rate by the duration. In both example annuities, the IRR is 15.1 percent. Thus, both investments offer the same 3.1 percent IRR advantage over the 12 percent market rate. Yet, the investments have different durations: The duration of the 10-year annuity is 4.09 years, while the duration of the 20-year annuity is 6.27 years. If the firm has a 15 percent ROE (r) on its initial book value, the FFs for the 10- and 20-year investments are approximately 0.85

---

[2]In the approximation formula, "duration" (D) is the modified duration of the investment computed at a discount rate equal to k.

and 1.29, respectively. Thus, each unit of investment in the 20-year annuity contributes 1.29 units to the P/E; whereas each unit of investment in the 10-year annuity contributes only 0.85 units. The greater duration of the 20-year investment makes its IRR advantage count more in terms of P/E expansion.

The duration of an annuity increases with the term of the annuity but is independent of the magnitude of the cash flow (assuming a constant discount rate). In addition, as the term increases, the annuity approaches a perpetuity. Thus, the duration of the annuity approaches the duration of a perpetuity (which is simply the inverse of the discount rate). Because the duration is evaluated at the market rate, the perpetuity duration in the examples here is 8.33 (that is, 1/0.12).

The relationship between duration and the term of the annuity is illustrated in Figure 3.2. The duration initially increases rapidly as the number of years of earnings increases; the rate of increase slows as the duration approaches 8.33.

Figure 3.2. Duration versus Term of the Annuity
(at a 12 percent discount rate)

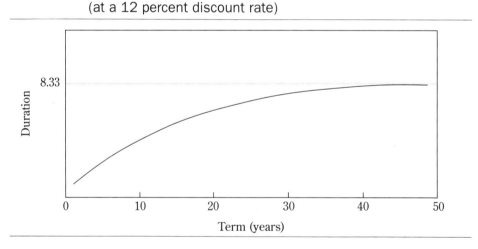

Consider now the other component of FF estimation—the IRR advantage. As indicated earlier, the IRR is an incomplete measure of value, because an infinite number of combinations of annual payment rates and payment periods will result in the same IRR. The combinations of payment rate and period required to maintain a constant IRR are illustrated for IRRs of 15 percent and 20 percent in Figure 3.3.

The approximation formula states that, for a given IRR, the FF increases with duration. Because the duration of an annuity lengthens with its term, the

Figure 3.3. Annual Payment Rate versus Term of the Annuity for IRRs of 15 Percent and 20 Percent

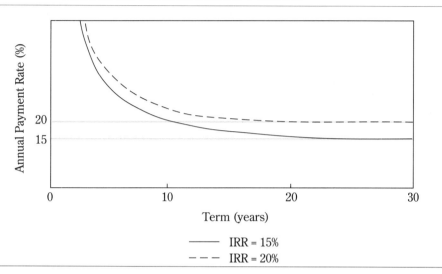

franchise factor also increases and, eventually, reaches a maximum value for a perpetual annuity—that is, for a duration of 8.33. In addition, at a given duration, FF increases with the IRR.

These results are illustrated in Figure 3.4. Observe that the franchise factor is zero when the IRR is 12 percent; it would be negative for an IRR of less than 12 percent.

A further insight into the approximation formula can be gained by noting that, as the number of years of returns increases, the duration approaches $1/k$ and the annual return approaches the IRR. Thus, as the term of the annuity increases, the approximation formula,

$$\text{FF} \approx \frac{D\,(\text{IRR}-k)}{r},$$

approaches the exact FF formula,

$$\text{FF} = \left(\frac{1}{k}\right)\left(\frac{R-k}{r}\right).$$

To illustrate the accuracy of the FF approximation formula, Figure 3.5 plots

Figure 3.4. Approximate Franchise Factor versus Annuity Duration
(ROE = 15 percent)

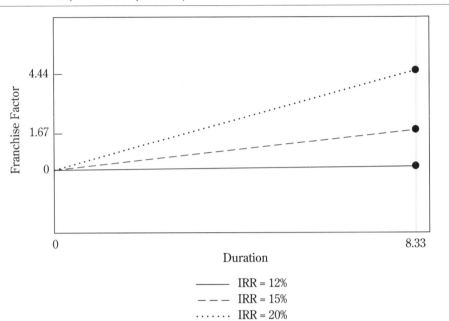

the actual and approximate FFs for 20-year annuities with a range of IRRs.[3] Note that the FF approximation is quite accurate for IRRs within about 400 basis points of the 12 percent market rate. For example, if the IRR is 17 percent, the error in this approximation is slightly more than 4 percent of the FF value.[4]

When all new investments generate the same pattern of payments, the theoretical P/E is given by the following formula:

$$P/E = \frac{1}{k} + (FF \times G).$$

In this formula, the base P/E (that is, $1/k$) can be interpreted as the duration of a perpetuity that corresponds to level earnings on the firm's initial book value. The franchise factor is approximately equal to the duration of the new investment payment multiplied by the investment's IRR advantage. Conse-

---

[3]For investments with payoffs in the form of 20-year, level-payment annuities, higher annual returns lead to higher IRRs.

[4]Appendix B shows that the approximation formula holds for arbitrary payment patterns.

34

Figure 3.5. Approximate versus Actual Franchise Factors
(for 20-year, level-payment annuities)

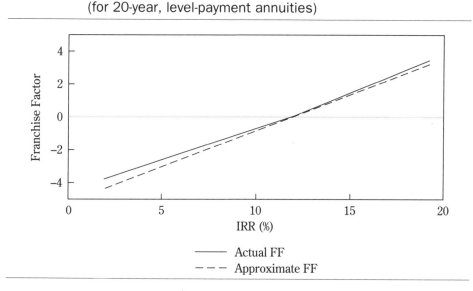

quently, the P/E can be written as

$$P/E = \frac{1}{r}\left[\left(\begin{array}{c}\text{Duration of}\\ \text{base earnings}\end{array}\right)r + \left(\begin{array}{c}\text{Duration of}\\ \text{new investment}\end{array}\right)(IRR-k)G.\right]$$

This formula shows that the P/E builds from duration-weighted net earnings (expressed as a fraction of base earnings, r). In the first term in the brackets, the net earnings are the same as the base earnings (per $100 of book value), because no financing costs associated with the firm's basic book of business are being considered. The duration can be roughly interpreted as the present-value weighted-average time at which earnings occur.[5] In the second term in brackets, net earnings on new investment are measured by the investment's IRR advantage over the market rate, multiplied by the magnitude of the investment as measured by the growth equivalent.

[5]It is actually the Macaulay duration, rather than the modified duration, that precisely measures the weighted-average time of payments. The two are sufficiently close, however, that the intuitive interpretation of the modified duration as a weighted-average time is valid. The relationship between the two durations is $(1 + k)D_{MOD} = D_{MAC}$.

The Perpetual-Equivalent Return

In the standard dividend discount model, all new investments are assumed to provide the same return in perpetuity. This perpetual-return model allowed the development in Chapter 2 of a simple formula for the exact franchise factor. In a certain sense, the perpetual-return model turns out to be general, because any pattern of payments can be converted to an equivalent perpetual return (see Appendix B). An exact franchise factor can be computed for any return pattern by using the perpetual-equivalent return in the original FF formula.

The perpetual-equivalent return is the return on a perpetual investment that provides the same present value (at the market capitalization rate) as a given return pattern. For example, an investment that provides an annual return of 20 percent for ten years (Investment A) is equivalent in present value to an equal investment that provides a 13.56 percent annual return in perpetuity.[6]

Figure 3.6 shows the behavior of the perpetual-equivalent return as the years of constant annual returns increase. At first, the perpetual equivalent grows rapidly. After 15 or 20 years, however, the perpetual equivalent begins to level off and, as the period extends to infinity, slowly approaches the constant

---

[6]The present value of $20 a year for ten years at a 12 percent discount rate is $113. The present value of the perpetual equivalent is the perpetual return (R_p) divided by 0.12. Thus, R_p = 0.12 × 113 = 13.56.

Figure 3.6. Perpetual-Equivalent Returns for 20 Percent and 15 Percent Annuities with a Range of Terms

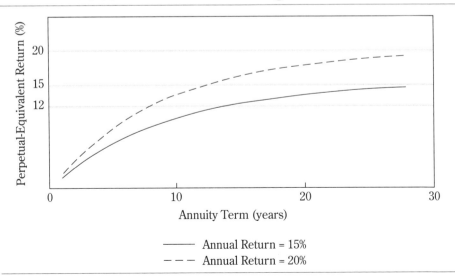

annual return. For example, an investment that returns 20 percent annually for 20 years has a perpetual equivalent of 17.93 percent.

Because investments that provide 20 percent returns for 20 years are not easy to find, perpetual equivalents above 18 percent are clearly difficult to attain. Furthermore, with the more "normal" patterns of rising and declining returns, the perpetual equivalents will be even lower than 18 percent. Figure 3.7 depicts such a normal return pattern. The annual investment returns increase steadily for five years until they reach the 20 percent level; these superior returns then continue for ten years, after which the payments decline to zero. The IRR for this investment is 12.62 percent, and the perpetual equivalent is 12.55 percent. This perpetual equivalent represents only a 55-basis-point advantage over the market rate, and because such an investment has an FF of only 0.31, it contributes little to the firm's P/E.

Figure 3.7. Rising-and-Falling Pattern of Returns

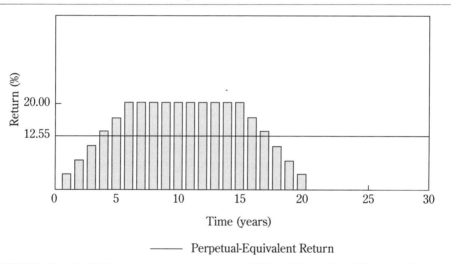

The exact FF can be computed from the perpetual return (R_p) according to the previously provided formula:

$$FF = \frac{R_p - k}{rk}.$$

The linear relationship between the franchise factor and R_p for a firm with a 15 percent return on its initial book equity is illustrated in Figure 3.8. The

37

Figure 3.8. Franchise Factor versus Perpetual-Equivalent Return

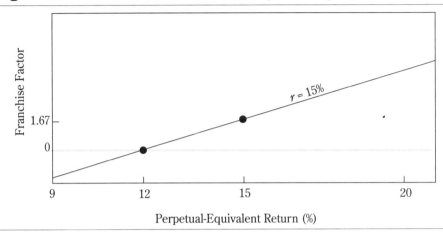

franchise factor is zero when the return on investment is the same as the market rate, and it increases by 0.56 units for each 100-basis-point increase in R_p.[7] Thus, when R_p is 15 percent (300 basis points above the market rate), the franchise factor increases to 1.67 (3×0.56). In addition, the franchise factor is negative if R_p is less than the market rate.

Perpetual-equivalent returns can be used to evaluate investment opportunities. If a firm has a fixed amount of capital to invest and must choose between several different potential projects, the project with the highest perpetual equivalent will make the greatest P/E contribution. This result is both intuitively reasonable and consistent with the FF approach. It is also consistent with the NPV approach to project valuation. That is, the ranking of projects by the magnitude of their NPVs will be the same as the ranking of projects by the magnitude of their perpetual-equivalent returns.

The Growth Equivalent

Recall from Chapter 2 that, if two investments have the same G, the one with the higher FF will have the greater impact on P/E. Similarly, the magnitude of investment required to raise the P/E by one unit will decrease as FF increases (see Figure 3.9). For perpetual-equivalent returns above 16 percent, the growth equivalent tends to level off, but even at high perpetual-equivalent returns, a substantial investment is required to raise the P/E. At a return of 18 percent, for example, an investment equal to 30 percent of book value is

---

[7]The slope of the FF line is $1/rk$. Because $r = 15$ percent and $k = 12$ percent, $1/rk = 55.56$. If the change in R_p is 100 basis points, the change in FF will be $0.01 \times 55.56 = 0.56$.

required to raise the P/E by one unit. When the perpetual-equivalent return drops below about 16 percent, the growth required to raise the P/E increases dramatically. If the perpetual-equivalent return is 14 percent (200 basis points above the market rate), an investment equal to 90 percent of the current book value is needed to raise the P/E by just a single unit.

Consider now the factors that influence the growth equivalent. Suppose that, by virtue of its business franchise, a firm expects to have a 9 percent annual growth rate for the next ten years. The firm thus expects to be able to

Table 3.1. Firm with a 15 Percent ROE Growing at a 9 Percent Annual Rate

Year	Book Value at Beginning of Year	Amount of New Investment at Year End	Present Value of New Investment at 12 Percent Discount Rate
1	$100.00	$ 9.00	$ 8.04
2	109.00	9.81	7.82
.	.	.	.
.	.	.	.
.	.	.	.
10	217.19	19.55	6.29
Total			$71.33

make a new investment at the end of each year equal to 9 percent of its book value at the beginning of the year (see Table 3.1). Assume also that the firm will achieve a perpetual-equivalent return on each new investment equal to the firm's current ROE. Recall that if the ROE is 15 percent, the franchise factor

Figure 3.9. Required Growth Equivalent per Unit of P/E

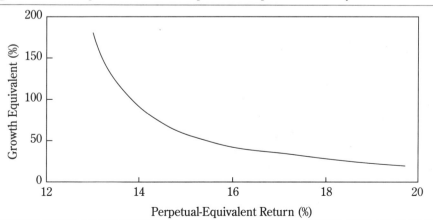

for each such investment will be 1.67.

If the firm has an initial book value of $100, it is assumed to have a $9 investment opportunity (9 percent of $100) at the end of the first year, and the book value will increase to $109. At the end of the second year, the investment opportunity is $9.81 (9 percent of $109). This pattern of growth continues for ten years. The growth equivalent is found by computing the present value of all future investments and expressing that present value as a percentage of the current book value. This computation indicates that G is $71.33.

Now suppose that the firm could, as an alternative, invest $71.33 immediately and earn the same 15 percent a year in perpetuity. Under these conditions, the immediate investment and the series of investments are of the same value to current stockholders, which is why G is called the growth equivalent.

Table 3.2 presents values of the growth equivalent for three different growth rates. Growth is assumed to continue for a fixed number of years and then stop. For a given number of years of growth, the higher the growth rate, the greater the value of G. As the number of years of growth increases, so does the value of G. If the growth rate is less than the market capitalization rate, however, the value of G levels off as the number of years of growth approaches infinity. This result is illustrated in Figure 3.10. Observe that although a 9 percent growth rate may sound modest, it represents 300 percent of book value in present-value terms.

Table 3.2. Growth Equivalents at a 12 Percent Discount Rate for Three Growth Rates

Years of Investment	8 Percent	9 Percent	10 Percent
5	33.25%	38.08%	43.08%
10	60.98	71.33	82.44
15	103.36	125.70	151.29
50	167.54	222.81	296.90
∞	200.00	300.00	500.00

Note: Growth rates are amounts invested annually as percentages of book value.

If the growth rate is the same as the market rate, the growth equivalent will increase linearly with the years of growth. If the growth rate is greater than the market rate, the growth equivalent will increase exponentially with time. Clearly, growth rates at or above the market rate can be sustained for only a few years.

40

Figure 3.10. Growth Equivalents for Various Growth Rates

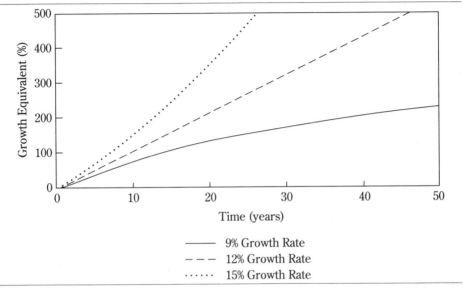

——— 9% Growth Rate
– – – 12% Growth Rate
· · · · · 15% Growth Rate

Multiphase Growth

The FF model can be extended to firms experiencing different types of growth and return opportunities. Because the growth equivalent incorporates both magnitude and time of occurrence, any pattern of investment opportunities and returns is accommodated by computing the sum of the products of franchise factors and corresponding growth equivalents to obtain the total above-market P/E increment. This general result, which is derived in Appendix B, is summarized in the following formula:

$$P/E = \frac{1}{k} + (FF_1 \times G_1) + (FF_2 \times G_2) + \ldots$$

As an example of the general methodology, consider the two-phase growth example described in Table 3.3. During years 1 through 10, the firm invests

Table 3.3. Two-Phase Growth Example

Phase	Years	Growth Rate	Perpetual Return	Franchise Factor	Growth Equivalent
I	1–10	10%	18%	3.33	82.44%
II	11–∞	5	15	1.67	59.65

10 percent of book value each year and earns 18 percent in perpetuity on each investment. The franchise factor for these investments is 3.33, and the growth equivalent is 82:44. During the final investment phase, the firm grows at a 5 percent annual rate and earns 15 percent on each investment. In this case, FF and G are 1.67 and 59.65 percent, respectively.

Phase I growth contributes 2.75 units to the P/E (FF × G = 3.33 × 0.8244), while Phase II growth contributes just 1 unit to the P/E (1.67 × 0.5965). Thus, the P/E of this two-phase growth firm is 12.08 (that is, 8.33 + 2.75 + 1.00).

The accumulation of the additional P/E provided by the firm's growth can be illustrated in a vector diagram as shown in Figure 3.11. The first vector, corresponding to Phase I growth, raises the P/E from 8.33 (the base P/E) to 11.08. The slope of this vector is 3.33 (the franchise factor for Phase I), and the vector extends over 82.44 units of Phase I growth. The slope of the second vector, 1.67, is the franchise factor for Phase II, and this vector extends over an additional 59.65 units of growth, bringing the P/E up to 12.08. The timing of the investments matters only to the extent that it affects the value of the growth equivalent. Thus, although Phase II follows Phase I in this example, once the phases are reduced to their G and FF values, the sequence is irrelevant.

The Portfolio

A firm with a unique business franchise will have a range of current and

Figure 3.11. Vector Diagram of Two-Phase Growth

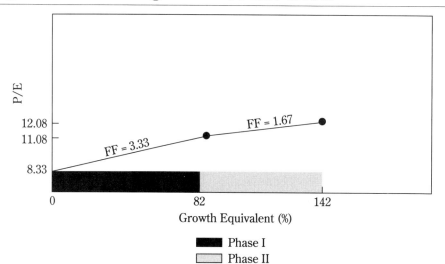

Table 3.4. The Franchise Portfolio: Example for a Firm with $100 Book Value

Investment	Perpetual Return	Franchise Factor	Growth Equivalent	P/E Increment
1	20%	4.44	50%	2.22
2	15	1.67	100	1.67
3	13	0.56	150	0.83
4	12	0.00	200	0.00
Total			500%	4.72

expected investment opportunities. If the company's sole objective is to maximize P/E, the FF model can be a guide in choosing among investments. Consider the franchise opportunities for the firm described in Table 3.4. The firm has an initial book value of $100, can invest $50 (in present-value terms, representing a G of 50 percent), and can achieve an extraordinary 20 percent return in perpetuity. Other investments provide successively lower returns and, therefore, have lower franchise factors.

Although the third investment is three times as large as the first ($G = 150$ percent), it contributes less to P/E than the first because of its low FF. The fourth investment has a zero FF because it provides only the market return. Only the first three investments, with their combined growth equivalents of 300 percent, will add value. The accumulated P/E value is shown in the vector diagram of Figure 3.12.

Suppose the firm in this example expects to build up its cash holdings by retaining a portion of its earnings year after year. This cash then becomes

Figure 3.12. Vector Diagram of P/E Growth

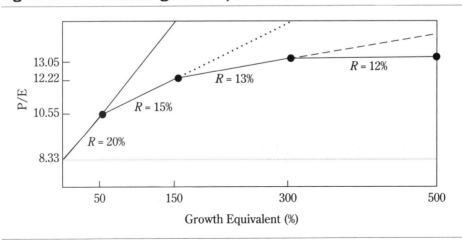

available as a source of financing for franchise opportunities. The present value of all such future cash generation is the *G* available from retained earnings. Ideally, if the firm expects to have available less than $300 (300 percent of the $100 book value), it should raise the necessary capital to achieve its full P/E potential. Funds beyond $300 will not add to P/E and should be returned to investors in the form of either increased dividend payments or stock buy-backs. Of course, these idealized conclusions neglect the fact that, in the real world, the firm must consider factors other than P/E gain. It must, for example, take into account the signaling effect that increases in dividends have on stock prices.

Finally, note that the FF model can accommodate the general situation in which an investment phase is followed by an earnings phase. For example, suppose a firm needs four years to build a new plant; the firm must continue to add to its investment during each of the four years, and payoff on the investments begins in Year 5. (The inflows and outflows are illustrated in Figure 3.13.) The payoff grows to a maximum level that is sustained for ten years before it begins to decline. Determination of the P/E impact of such a pattern of investments and payments can be accomplished, as before, by computing appropriate franchise factors for the annual payments and growth equivalents for the investments.

Figure 3.13. Schematic Diagram of Investments and Payments

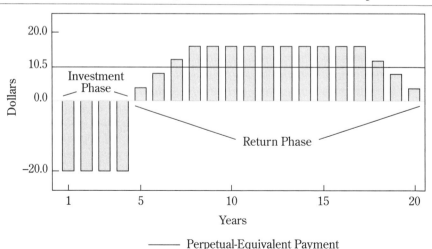

—— Perpetual-Equivalent Payment

Summary

A firm with an exceptional business franchise should have a variety of opportunities to make investments that provide above-market returns. Both the timing of investments, however, and the pattern of payments on those investments may vary considerably. This chapter introduced a general methodology to assess the P/E impact of a portfolio of franchise opportunities with different payoff patterns.

The procedure involves three steps. The first is to calculate a perpetual return that has the same present value as the actual flow of returns on investment. Although this step is not crucial, the perpetual-equivalent return does simplify the computation of the franchise factor, and it provides a convenient measure to use in comparing investment returns. The second step is to compute the franchise factor that measures the P/E impact per unit growth in new investment. Finally, when the magnitude of investment is represented by its growth equivalent, the impact of new investment on the P/E can be determined as the product of the franchise factor and the growth equivalent.

Despite the restrictive assumptions of no volatility, leverage, or taxes, the model provides insight into the inherent difficulty in raising a firm's P/E. Furthermore, if a firm's only goal is to maximize its P/E, the model suggests that the managers consider dividend increases and/or stock repurchases in lieu of below-market investments.

The franchise factor is essentially the product of the excess annual return that the investment generates (compared with the market rate) and the duration of its payments. Because the franchise factor emerged as a fundamental measure of the P/E impact of new investments, the chapter provided a simple formula for its estimation involving the IRR of the new investment and the duration of its payments. A high franchise factor alone cannot elevate the P/E, however; it must be combined with a growth equivalent that represents a substantial percentage of current book value.

In general, franchise situations tend to erode over time, although certain business enterprises are apparently able to continue capitalizing on their basic strengths. They seem to "compound" their franchise positions—as if they had a *franchise* on the generation of new franchise opportunities. In the terminology of this monograph, these firms have what it takes to justify exceptionally high P/Es, namely, a superior franchise factor working on large growth-equivalent investments.

4. A Franchise Factor Model for Spread Banking

Spread banking is borrowing money at one rate and lending it out at a higher rate in order to profit from the "spread" between the two rates. Although the term spread banking is most commonly associated with commercial banks and thrift institutions, many other financial firms, such as insurance companies, also engage in such activities. In addition, many nonfinancial firms have important activities that can be viewed as essentially spread banking.

This chapter offers a theoretical model for relating a spread-banking firm's price/earnings ratio to the franchise factors that characterize returns on the firm's *prospective* new books of business. In theory, a firm should try to expand its asset base (called "footings" in the banking industry) to include all opportunities that provide a positive franchise factor (even if doing so means reducing the overall return on book equity). At this point, the firm will have reached its optimal size and should resist temptation to expand.

To some extent, the profitability of spread-banking firms depends on their ability to seize opportunities by quickly shifting resources from businesses with tightening spreads to fast-growing new businesses with ample returns. Such opportunities cannot always be fully and rigorously pursued, however, because of explicit regulatory constraints. In addition, implicit regulatory constraints may limit the magnitude and sustainability of large spread opportunities. In contrast, industrial concerns may have virtually unlimited growth prospects, at least in theory, because they can create entirely new markets through, for example, discoveries and patents. For these (and other) reasons, the equity of spread-banking concerns is not usually placed in the category of growth stock.

The subject of growth is never simple, however. In the case of footings, U.S. commercial banks have certainly demonstrated an ability to sustain substantial growth over the years. In spread banking, however, as in all businesses, asset growth alone guarantees neither earnings nor price performance. Despite an almost sixfold increase in bank assets during the past two decades, bank P/Es have remained chronically and significantly below average market levels. The theoretical extension of the FF model in this chapter provides some insight into why such low P/Es have persisted.

Most spread-banking lines of business look best at the outset. The initial spreads are booked into the earnings stream immediately; the prospect of negative surprises lurks in the future. In response to such events as a sudden rise in market interest rates, a change in credit quality, or increased competition, the effective spread between borrowing costs and lending income can quickly narrow. Thus, the net spread structure of current and prospective businesses may be quite vulnerable. Questions about the reliability and/or sustainability of spread businesses lead to low franchise factors, which may partly explain the banking industry's below-market P/E.

This chapter uses the simple FF model to clarify the relationship between market forces and the P/E valuation of spread-banking firms. The model does not pretend to address the complete spectrum of issues, complexities, and interrelationships that must be considered when analyzing specific firms or sectors. However, even in its simple form, the FF model can prove helpful in illustrating and sharpening the insights derived from more traditional analyses of spread-banking problems and opportunities.

Building Return on Equity through Leverage

With its equity capital as a base, a bank can borrow up to some maximum multiple *(L)* of the equity capital and make loans or investments with those borrowed funds. If the net spread earned on leveraged funds is positive, leverage enables the bank to add to its return on equity. The net spread *(NS)* is defined here as the after-tax difference between the marginal cost of borrowed funds and the net return on those funds (that is, the net return after expenses). Also, the assumption is that a bank always earns a risk-free rate on funds that correspond to the equity capital. The formula for the ROE is as follows:

$$\text{ROE} = \text{Risk-free rate} + (\text{Leverage multiple} \times \text{Net spread})$$

$$= R_f + (L \times NS).$$

For example, consider a bank that has $100 in equity capital and a 5 percent after-tax cost of borrowing.[1] If the bank is allowed to borrow up to 20 times

---

[1]If the borrowing rate is 7.58 percent and the bank's marginal tax rate is 34.00 percent, the after-tax borrowing rate is 66.00 percent of 7.58 percent, or 5.00 percent.

capital, it will be able to borrow an additional $2,000 by paying 5 percent interest. The lending rate that can be earned on these borrowed funds is assumed here to be 5.75 percent after taxes and expenses.[2] This combination of lending and borrowing rates is illustrated in the region to the left of the dotted line in Figure 4.1. This region represents current borrowings.

Figure 4.1. The Lending Rate and the Cost of Funds

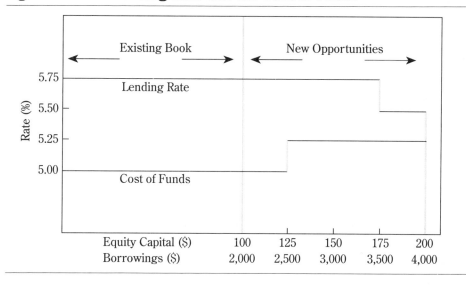

The bank believes that it will have the opportunity to extend another $1,500 in loans (beyond the initial $2,000 in loans) at 5.75 percent. To take advantage of this opportunity, the bank must raise an additional $75 in equity capital (at the assumed 20:1 leverage ratio), which will bring its total equity capital to $175. Beyond this level, $500 in lending opportunities exist at a lower, 5.50 percent, rate. This final opportunity would require another $25 addition to the capital base.

The cost of borrowed funds follows a different path from that of the lending rate (see Figure 4.1), namely, 5.00 percent for the first $2,500 in borrowings and 5.25 percent for the next $1,500 in borrowings. By calculating the difference between the lending rate and the cost of funds, one can see that a 75-basis-point net spread is earned on the $2,000 in current borrowings (see Region A in Figure 4.2). This same 75-basis-point net spread is also expected

---

[2]If the bank earns 9.71 percent on borrowed funds and it estimates expenses at 100 basis points, earnings after expenses and taxes equal 66.00 percent of (9.71 percent – 1.00 percent), or 5.75 percent.

for the first $500 in new borrowings (Region B). The next $1,000 in new borrowings (Region C) produces a net spread of 50 basis points, and the final $500 in new borrowings (Region D) yields a spread of only 25 basis points. At this point, the simplifying assumption is added that each net spread can be earned in perpetuity. As indicated in Figure 4.2, the new borrowings of $500, $1,000, then $500 will require $25, $50, and $25 in new equity capital, respectively.

Figure 4.2. The Net Spread on Borrowed Funds

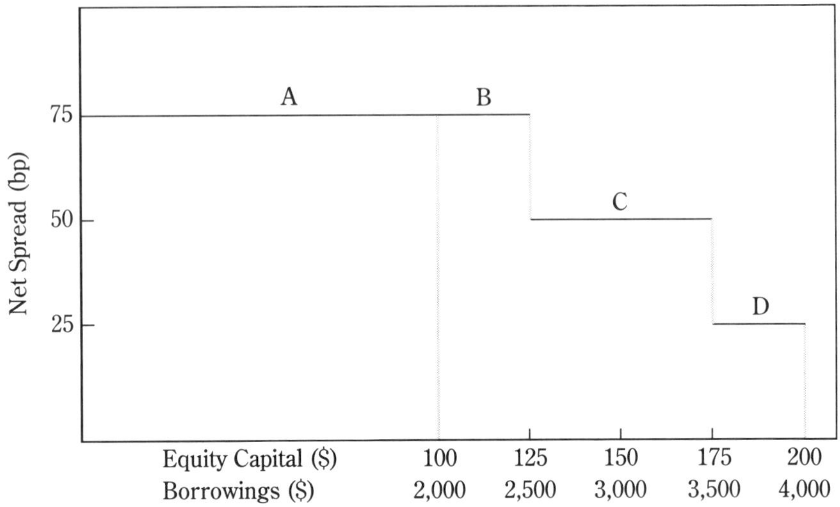

Note: bp = basis points.

Now consider the return on equity for the current book of businesses and the prospective ROE for the investments related to the new businesses, labeled B, C, and D. In general, earnings on equity capital are distinguished from earnings on borrowings. Assume that equity capital is invested in risk-free instruments that can earn 5 percent after taxes. The ROE for both the current $100 in equity capital (Region A) and the first $25 in new equity capital (Region B) is computed as follows:

$$\text{ROE} = R_f + (L \times NS)$$

$$= 5.00 \text{ percent} + (20 \times 0.75 \text{ percent})$$

$$= 20.00 \text{ percent}.$$

50

The relationship between ROE and net spread is illustrated in Figure 4.3. Point A corresponds to the 20 percent ROE on the current book. Because the first incremental expansion of the equity capital base also generates a net spread of 75 basis points, the new capital provides the same 20 percent ROE (Point B in Figure 4.3). Continued expansion leads to lower spreads of 50 basis points (Point C) and 25 basis points (Point D), with ROEs of 15 percent and 10 percent, respectively. At the limit, if the net spread were zero, leveraging would gain nothing and the ROE would be the same as the 5 percent risk-free rate.

Figure 4.3. Return on Equity versus Net Spread
(leverage = 20)

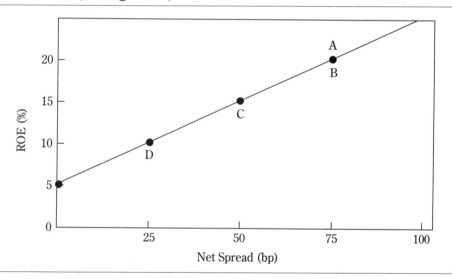

A Perspective on Bank Asset Growth

Although the generic structure of spread-banking entities is the focus of this chapter, a look at the rate at which commercial bank assets have grown since 1950 is illuminating. Figure 4.4 is a comparison of the compound annual growth rates of nominal gross national product (GNP) and bank assets for three-year periods from December 31, 1949, to December 31, 1988, and for the final two-year period ended December 31, 1990. During the 1949–52 period, GNP grew almost twice as fast as bank assets, but that period was the last to exhibit such extreme dominance. In most nonoverlapping three-year periods until the early 1980s, bank assets grew somewhat faster than GNP. Since then, growth in both GNP and bank assets has slowed, but GNP growth has again

Figure 4.4. Growth in Nominal GNP and Bank Assets, 1949–90
(compound growth rate over three-year periods)

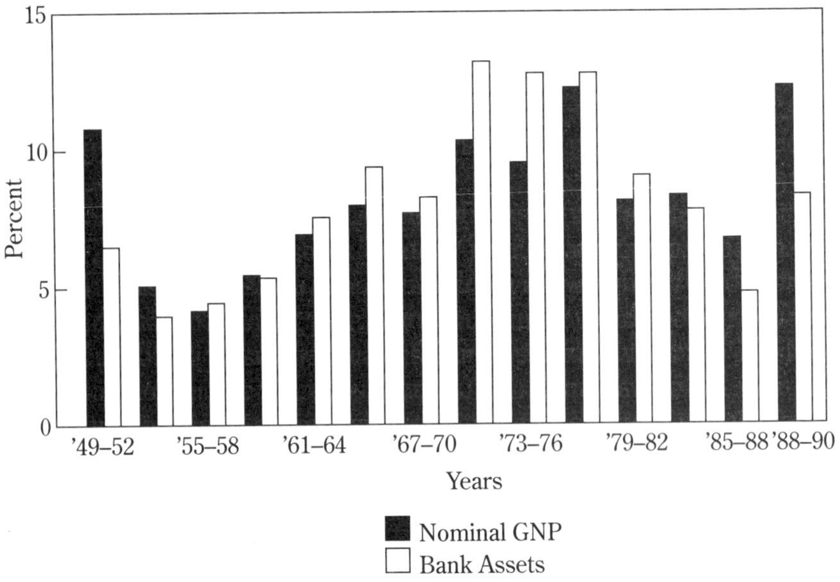

Note: The banks are commercial banks insured by the Federal Deposit Insurance Corporation.

dominated bank asset growth.

Because bank assets are geared to the transactional flows of the economy at large, a correspondence between the growth in nominal GNP and the growth in bank assets would be expected, but the closeness of that correspondence over a 41-year period is surprising, given the dramatic changes in the financial markets during that time period. Figure 4.5 compares the cumulative growth in GNP and bank assets. For the comparison, the value of GNP and the value of commercial bank assets were each assumed to be $100 on December 31, 1949. The rapid rise in GNP during the early 1950s enabled GNP to stay ahead of commercial bank assets until the 1970s. By 1973, however, the steady dominance of bank asset growth through most of the 1960s had allowed cumulative bank asset growth to overtake cumulative GNP growth. For the entire 41-year period ended December 31, 1990, the compound annual growth rate of bank assets was 7.8 percent, and the rate for GNP was 7.7 percent.

If asset growth alone were enough to ensure high P/Es, one would expect the shares of banks during this period to have sold at ample P/E multiples. Bank P/Es, however, have for many years (even prior to the well-advertised

Figure 4.5. Cumulative Growth in Nominal GNP and Bank Assets, 1949–90

(relative to a base of $100 on December 31, 1949)

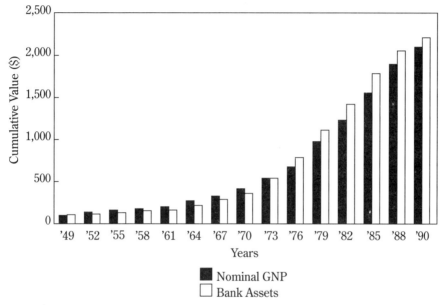

troubles in the banking sector in the early 1990s) been consistently below average market P/Es.[3] Some of the causes of this underperformance can be understood by looking at the franchise factors that are applicable to spread investments.

The Franchise Factor in Spread Banking

This section focuses on the impact on P/E of new investment opportunities presented to spread-banking entities. When computing the P/E, the base earnings (*E*) will represent the (sustainable) earnings from the firm's current book of business. If the firm experiences neither growth nor contraction and if current earnings are maintained in perpetuity, the investor's sole source of return will consist of *E*. In equilibrium, this perpetual stream of earnings would be capitalized at the general market rate (*k*). This earnings capitalization results in a theoretical price (*P*) that is equal to *E/k*, and as in previous chapters, this price/earnings relationship implies a base P/E equal to *1/k* for all firms.

---

[3]See Salomon Brothers Inc (1990).

If current earnings are fully and properly reflected in the base P/E, an above-market P/E can be realized only if, by virtue of the firm's business franchise, the market foresees future opportunities for the firm to invest in new projects with above-market returns.[4] Recall from Chapters 2 and 3 that the formula for computing the theoretical P/E that explicitly incorporates the impact of future earnings expectations is as follows:[5]

$$P/E = \text{Base P/E} + (\text{Franchise factor} \times \text{Growth equivalent}).$$

Recall also that, in general, each new investment opportunity will have its own franchise factor and growth equivalent. In the case of multiple investment opportunities, the P/E is computed by adding in the $(FF \times G)$ term for each new investment. Without any new investment opportunities (and assuming the 12 percent market rate), all firms would sell at a P/E multiple of 8.33.

The FF for an investment is computed according to the formula,

$$FF = \frac{R-k}{rk}.$$

In the current context, r is the return on equity that applies to the existing book of business (20 percent in the bank example) and R is the ROE on the new investment opportunity (20 percent for Business B, 15 percent for C, and 10 percent for D). For investment in Business C, for example,

$$FF = \frac{0.15 - 0.12}{0.20 \times 0.12}$$

$$= 1.25.$$

Because the total equity investment in Business C was \$50 (that is, 50 percent of the existing \$100 book), C adds 0.625 units to the P/E (that is, $FF \times G = 1.25 \times 0.50$).

Figure 4.3 illustrated that, if the degree of leverage is fixed, ROE increases with net spread. Consequently, FF will also increase with net spread. If the market capitalization rate is 12 percent, the relationship between the franchise

---

[4]If current earnings are believed to be understated as reported, a corrected earnings estimate may be used in place of the current earnings. See Chapter 10 for further details.

[5]Fruhan (1979) provides a similar structure for tracing out the relationship between firm value and future investment opportunities.

factor and the net spread is as illustrated in Figure 4.6 (for the incremental new Businesses B, C, and D).

Figure 4.6. The Franchise Factor versus the Net Spread
(leverage = 20)

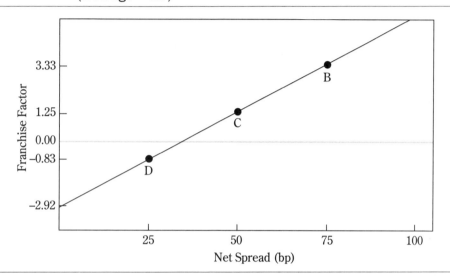

Business D has a net spread of only 25 basis points (and a 10 percent ROE), and its FF is –0.83. (A negative FF results whenever the ROE of an investment falls below the 12 percent market capitalization rate.) A prospective investment with a negative FF, such as Business D, will reduce both the firm's P/E and its value to shareholders.

The Impact of Future Franchise Opportunities

To see the dynamics of the P/E impact of prospective projects, consider a firm that has only one future investment opportunity. When the time comes to implement this final anticipated project, the firm will find the needed capital (possibly through the issuance of new shares) and begin to reap the project's promised returns. Once these returns are fully implemented, however, the firm's overall earnings will stabilize at the higher level. At this point of equilibrium, the firm can be viewed as providing this new earnings stream on an ongoing basis with no further prospect of change. When these conditions are realized, the P/E must return again to the base P/E of 8.33. Thus, although the anticipation of additional earnings from a new project will raise a P/E, the complete realization of the project will bring the P/E (relative to the expanded earnings) back to the base level.[6]

Figure 4.7 illustrates the P/E gains (or losses) that result from expectations that the bank in this section's example will pursue various new business

Figure 4.7. P/E Gain versus Size of Investment
(with varying franchise factors)

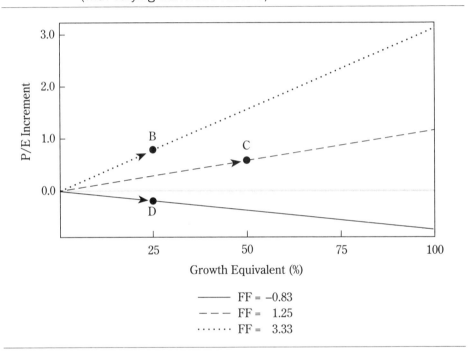

opportunities. The horizontal axis is the growth equivalent available for a given investment opportunity. The slope of each line in the figure corresponds to the franchise factor for a new business activity. Each line represents the relationship between the expected P/E increment attributable to a new business and the size of that business. For example, the P/E impact of Business B can be read as 0.83 units, which corresponds to a size limit of $25 (that is, 25 percent of the $100 current equity capital) and an FF of 3.33. Although Business C has a lower FF than Business B, it provides almost as much P/E

[6]Chapter 6 shows that, if a firm is to maintain a P/E greater than the base P/E while "consuming" its previously known franchise opportunities, the firm must be able to replenish expectations by generating new future franchise opportunities that are of the same magnitude as those that have been consumed.

enhancement because of the greater magnitude of Business C's opportunity. Business C can accommodate an equity investment that is twice that of Business B. On the other hand, Business D's negative FF results in a reduction in the P/E.

The P/E of this bank is illustrated in Figure 4.8's vector diagram of P/E increments. If all of these businesses are expected to be undertaken, the P/E ratio is 9.58. If the firm's goal is to maximize value to shareholders, however, it will not undertake Business D; without Business D, the P/E is 9.79.

In the example, the footings of the bank have almost doubled (from $100 to $175), but the P/E has improved only from 8.33 to 9.79. Even a full doubling of the bank's size, if additional opportunities existed at the 20 percent ROE level, would not lift the P/E above 12.

Figure 4.9 is a comparison of the relationships between the P/E and the ROE at various levels of expansion of the bank's capital base. The 20 percent ROE on the current book of business does not provide P/E enhancement, because the share price should already have adjusted upward to drive the base P/E to its equilibrium value of 8.33. The prospect of undertaking Business B is attractive to current shareholders, however, because it holds out the promise of gain *beyond* the current level of earnings. Business B's 20 percent ROE represents an 8 percent return advantage over the cost of new equity capital (assumed here to be 12 percent). This incremental value is reflected in the

Figure 4.8. Vector Diagram of P/E Value

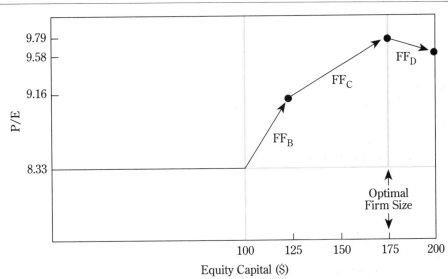

Figure 4.9. Comparison of Return on Equity and P/E

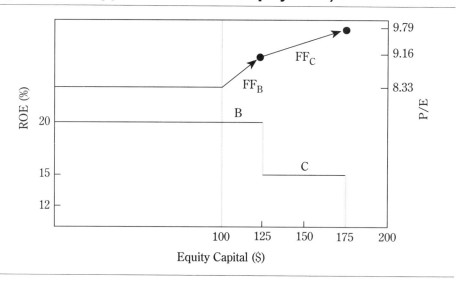

price, and the P/E is pushed up by 0.83 units to 9.16.

Business B's ROE is the same as the 20 percent ROE on the current book, so the firm's overall ROE will remain at 20 percent as earnings from Business B are realized. Anticipated expansion into Business C will, again, raise the P/E, because Business C provides a 3 percent return advantage over the cost of equity capital. As earnings from Business C are realized, however, its 15 percent ROE will reduce the average return on total equity capital to 18.6 percent. Nevertheless, this expected future ROE reduction should not deter the bank from moving into Business C, because by doing so, the bank achieves its optimal size in terms of shareholder value. In general, a new business added to the bank's book that has an ROE greater than 12 percent will have a positive franchise factor and will enhance the P/E value of the bank; an ROE that is positive but below 12 percent will be viewed negatively by shareholders.

The Impact of Changes in Investment Duration and Leverage

To this point, certain simplifying assumptions have been made—that the net spread for each business unit could be sustained in perpetuity and that a leverage ratio of 20 is always attainable. This section discusses how a relaxation of these assumptions influences the franchise factor and, consequently, the P/E.

Figure 4.10 illustrates the relationship between the franchise factor and the net spread when the spread is constant for five years and then changes.[7] For comparative purposes, Figure 4.10 also includes the FF line for perpetuities (see Figure 4.6). For spreads above 35 basis points, the line for perpetuals appears above the five-year line. This dominance is expected, because the bank surely prefers good spreads forever to good spreads for only five years. At spreads below 35 basis points, however, the ROEs are below 12 percent and the FFs are negative. Hence, the five-year period would be "preferred," at least on a relative basis.

Figure 4.10. The Franchise Factor versus the Net Spread when the Net Spread Changes after Five Years

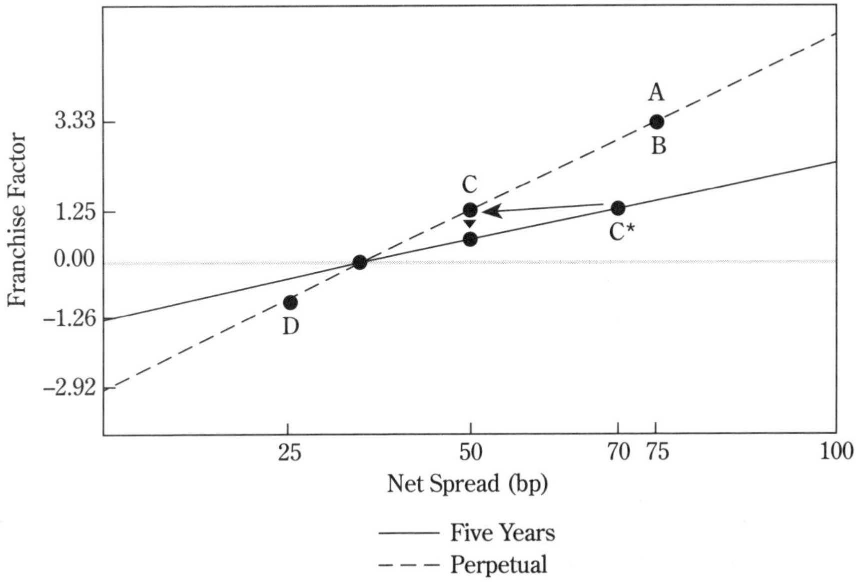

As an example of the relationship between the franchise factor and the magnitude and duration of net spread, consider an investment, Business C^*, that offers a 70-basis-point net spread for five years. Although Business C^*

---

[7]To compute FF when the net spread varies over time, find a perpetual-equivalent net spread by equating the present value of the varying spread pattern to the present value of the perpetual-equivalent net spread. In the examples of this section, for which spreads are sustained for five years, equity capital is assumed to earn the 12 percent market rate beyond the initial five-year period. For details of the computation of perpetual-equivalent returns, see Chapter 3.

initially has a 20-basis-point higher net spread than Business C, the franchise factors for C* and C are equal. Consequently, equal investments in C* and C have the same P/E impact, because the net spreads for C* and C have the same present value. In effect, the higher net spread of C* during the first five years is just enough to counterbalance its lower net spread in later years.

Figure 4.10 also clarifies the impact of a change in *expectations* regarding a given net spread. Suppose that, as a result of increased competition in spread banking, Business C's net spread of 50 basis points is expected to last only five more years. The revised franchise factor can be found in Figure 4.10 by moving vertically from Point C to the five-year spread line, where FF is only 0.54. This 57 percent decrease in the franchise factor (from 1.25) means that the P/E gain from a $50 investment in Business C is 57 percent lower than expected.

Changes in the leverage ratio can also affect the P/E dramatically. For any positive net spread, the ROE decreases as the leverage multiple falls. Consequently, lowering the leverage results in a lower franchise factor and a decrease in the P/E impact of a new investment opportunity, as shown in Figure 4.11. The upper line in Figure 4.11, as in Figure 4.6, represents the relationship between the franchise factor and the net spread when the leverage multiple is at the assumed level of 20. The lower line represents the franchise factor when the leverage is lowered to 10. As indicated earlier, Business C provides a franchise factor of 1.25 when the leverage is 20 but provides a negative franchise factor when the leverage is 10. Thus, the investment in Business C should not be made if the leverage is 10.

Figure 4.12 illustrates how leverage and the net spread produce a given ROE. As the leverage multiple decreases, achieving good returns through spread banking becomes extremely difficult, because an ever-increasing net spread is necessary to achieve a desired ROE. A leverage multiple of 10, for example, at a net spread of 150 basis points is required to match the 20 percent ROE on the existing book of business.

By the same token, if the net spread becomes too tight, an unacceptably high leverage multiple may be necessary to achieve a target ROE. For example, if the net spread is 50 basis points, a leverage multiple of 30 is required to achieve a 20 percent ROE.

Restructuring the Existing Book of Business

The concept of a base P/E derives from the implicit assumption that earnings on the current book of business (that is, the current ROE, r) can be

Figure 4.11. The Franchise Factor versus the Net Spread with Varying Leverage

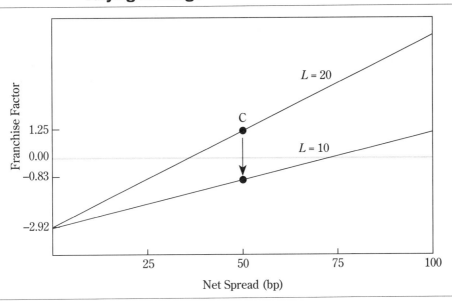

sustained in perpetuity.[8] If the current book can be restructured, however, and a higher ROE obtained, current shareholders should benefit.

The analysis begins with the observation that the base P/E can be expressed in a formula that is similar to the overall P/E formula.[9] In the earlier formula for P/E, incremental P/E value was shown to depend on the franchise factors of *future* investments. For the base P/E, a similar type of incremental P/E value can be ascribed to the franchise factors of the subunits of the *current* book of business.

In the bank example, a leverage multiple of 20 was applied to the current book, and the corresponding average net spread on leveraged assets was 75 basis points. These assumptions resulted in a 20 percent average ROE. Now the assumption is added that the current book of business comprises three subunits—B_1, B_2, and B_3—each of which represents $33.33 in equity capital. The net spreads for these subunits are 133 basis points, 75 basis points, and 17 basis points, respectively. Table 4.1 summarizes the characteristics of the

---

[8]Although earnings will obviously fluctuate with changing market conditions and changes in the firm structure, remember that in the context of this model, E and r should be interpreted as long-term sustainable values.

[9]See Appendix C for development of this FF formulation for the base P/E.

Figure 4.12. Leverage Required to Achieve a Given Return on Equity versus Net Spread

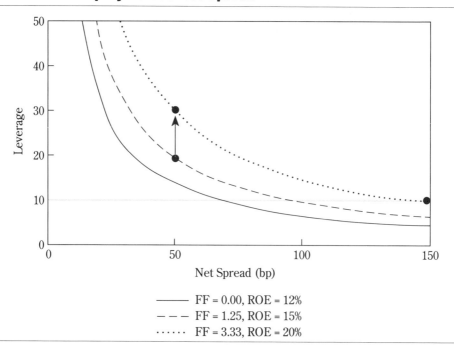

FF = 0.00, ROE = 12%
FF = 1.25, ROE = 15%
FF = 3.33, ROE = 20%

Table 4.1. The P/E Value of Subunits of the Current Book Equity

Business Subunit	Dollar Value	Net Spread (basis points)	Return on Equity	Franchise Factor	Incremental P/E Value
B_1	$33.33	133	31.6%	8.17	2.72
B_2	33.33	75	20.0	3.33	1.11
B_3	33.33	17	8.4	-1.50	-0.50
Overall	$100.00	75	20.0	3.33	3.33

subunits. The incremental P/E attributable to each subunit is computed by multiplying the unit's franchise factor by its size ($33\frac{1}{3}$ percent of the total $100 in current book equity). The total incremental P/E provided by the subunits is equal to an overall current-book franchise factor of 3.33.

To arrive at the base P/E of 8.33, the incremental P/E value of 3.33 is added to $1/r$ (that is, 1.0/0.2, or 5.0).[10] This result is illustrated by the vector diagram

---

[10]In the formula for the full P/E, the incremental P/E is added to $1/k$. Appendix C demonstrates that, when computing the base P/E, the incremental P/E must be added to the book equity capital-to-earnings ratio ($1/r$).

in Figure 4.13. Observe that the first vector emanates from the 5 point on the P/E axis. The slope of this vector, 8.17, is the franchise factor for Subunit B_1. The vector extends over the first $33.33 of equity capital, thereby boosting the P/E by 2.72 units, to 7.72. Similarly, the second vector extends over the next $33.33 in equity capital and raises the P/E by an additional 1.11 units, to 8.83. The final vector corresponds to a negative franchise factor and thus slopes downward. The P/E is reduced by 0.50 units, which brings it down to the 8.33 base level.

Figure 4.13. Vector Diagram of the P/E Value for the Current Book of Business

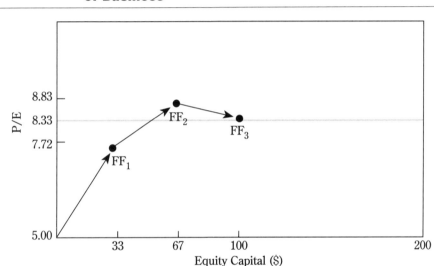

Clearly, Subunit B_3 reduces value. Shareholders would be better off if this last business could be unwound and the book equity released for more effective deployment. For example, if the full $33.33 book value of Subunit B_3 could be redirected to earn the 12 percent market rate, FF_3 would increase from −1.50 to zero, reflecting a 6 percent increase in earnings, from $20.00 to $21.20 (see FF_3^* in Figure 4.14).[11] As an interim step, FF_3^* could be viewed as increasing the base P/E to 8.83. The new level of earnings would be quickly

---

[11]The new weighted-average return on book equity is computed as follows $(0.33 \times 31.6$ percent$) + (0.33 \times 20.0$ percent$) + (0.33 \times 12.0$ percent$) = 21.2$ percent. Note that the 6 percent earnings increase (and the 6 percent price increase) could also be computed by dividing the instantaneous 0.50-unit P/E change by the base P/E of 8.33.

Figure 4.14. Restructuring the Current Book of Business

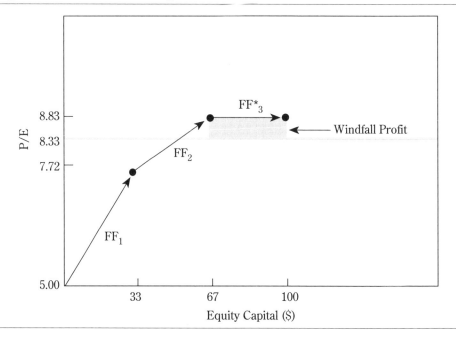

capitalized into a 6 percent increase in the market price, however, as the process of market equilibrium drove the P/E back to 8.33. The net effect would be to provide an immediate windfall profit (the height of the shaded area in Figure 4.14) to current investors.

Summary

Spread banking is particularly well suited to FF analysis for several reasons. In spread banking, the return on equity capital for a given book of business is determined by the spread between borrowing and lending rates and the degree of leverage. For many spread-banking activities, the allowable leverage (or, equivalently, the equity capital requirement) is specified through regulation of one form or another. This specification results in well-defined values for the return on equity; thus, the franchise factor can be readily computed. In addition, the financial nature of spread banking generally leads to a relatively simple time pattern of returns, in contrast to the complex investment and payback flows generated by a typical manufacturing project. Moreover, spread-banking lines of business tend to be more homogeneous and better delineated in scope than manufacturing businesses. At the conceptual level, at least, the relative simplicity of spread banking makes the franchise factors for a spread-banking firm easier to characterize than those for a general industrial concern.

Any anticipated opportunity with a positive franchise factor raises the price/earnings ratio; a new investment with a negative franchise factor lowers the P/E. By accepting all P/E-enhancing business and rejecting all non-P/E-enhancing business, a spread-banking firm can set a long-term target that will maximize its P/E.

By the same token, if a subunit of the existing business has a negative franchise factor, removing that subunit will benefit the shareholders. If a merger or restructuring achieves cost efficiencies that result in an increase of net spread, the franchise factor will increase. Finally, any action that raises a subunit's franchise factor will benefit existing shareholders by providing them with an immediate windfall profit.

5. The Franchise Factor for Leveraged Firms

One striking result discussed in Chapters 3 and 4 is the high level of future franchise investment required for even moderately high price/earnings ratios. For example, a P/E of 15 implies that new franchise investments must have a magnitude of 2.5 to 5.0 times the current book value of equity, even when the available return on the new investments is fairly high—in the range of 15 to 18 percent. This chapter addresses the question of whether debt financing might moderate these unusual findings and lead to reasonable levels for the required franchise investment.

The general topic of the effect of leverage on P/E has received little attention in either academic or practitioner literature. Because leveraging the current book shrinks both shareholder equity and firm earnings, intuition regarding the net impact of leverage on the price/earnings ratio is unreliable. Does leverage lead to increasing, decreasing, or perhaps stable P/Es?

The Impact of Leverage on Current Earnings

The value of a firm derives from two fundamental sources: the tangible value of the current book of business, and the franchise value based on future opportunities that enable the firm to experience productive growth. The total market value is simply the sum of these two terms, or

Market value = Tangible value + Franchise value.

The focus of this section is primarily tangible value (TV), defined as the total of two quantities: (1) the *book value* of assets and (2) the additional *premium over book value* for firms that are able to generate above-market returns on existing book assets. Thus,

Tangible value = Book value + Premium over book.

Note that this definition of "tangible" is *not* the usual accounting definition.

As an illustration, consider a tax-free firm that has no franchise opportunities and the following characteristics:

Characteristics		Per-Share Values	
Book value (*B*)	$100 million	Book value	$100
Return on equity (*r*)	15 percent		
Earnings (*E*)	$ 15 million	Premium over book for current earnings	25
Total market value	$125 million	Share price	125

This firm is unleveraged and has 1 million shares outstanding. Although the $15 million in earnings (15 percent of $100 million) generated by today's book will fluctuate from year to year, a simplified deterministic model is assumed in which the firm generates a perpetual earnings stream of $15 million annually.[1] The market capitalization rate for the unleveraged firm is assumed to be 12 percent, and the cost of debt 8 percent, regardless of the extent of leverage or the likelihood of bankruptcy. For this example of a firm without productive growth prospects, the tangible value (and the firm's total market value) is $125 million. This theoretical value results from capitalizing the prospective $15 million in earnings at the 12 percent market rate. The $25 million premium over book value is a direct consequence of the fact that the return on equity is 3 percent greater than the market capitalization rate.

The P/E for this firm is 8.33, determined by dividing the market value of $125 million by the total earnings of $15 million. Now, consider the impact of leverage. Assume an equilibrium model in which debt is used to repurchase shares so that the firm's total value remains unchanged. Thus, leverage alters the financial structure of the existing firm, but it does not expand the capital base. This equilibrium model assumes that the firm is fairly priced and that all transfers take place at fair market value. No windfalls come to any shareholders—be they the original shareholders who sold out during the repurchase process or the remaining shareholders in the leveraged firm.[2]

If the firm is free of debt, all its earnings belong to the equityholders. The use of debt to repurchase shares has two immediate effects: The earnings

---

[1]The more general case of risky cash flows can be accommodated by replacing the constant return values with expected values. Note that in addition to ignoring risk, this chapter considers only firms in which *operating* earnings are unaffected by leverage.

[2]Even in this equilibrium world in which the firm's total value remains constant, different financial structures will lead to different P/Es.

available to shareholders are reduced by interest payments, and the aggregate shareholder claim to the firm's (unchanged) total value is reduced by the total value of the debt. For example, as shown in Figure 5.1, if the firm is leveraged 50 percent, its debt will be 50 percent of its book value ($50 million), its annual interest payments at 8 percent will be $4 million, and its earnings will then be $15 million – $4 million (or $11 million).[3]

If the firm is leveraged to 100 percent of book value, the interest payments will be $8 million, and the earnings will drop to $7 million. Note that the assumption of a constant 8 percent debt rate ignores the fact that both agency costs and the probability of bankruptcy increase with leverage.

Figure 5.1. Total Earnings under Varying Degrees of Leverage
(dollars in millions)

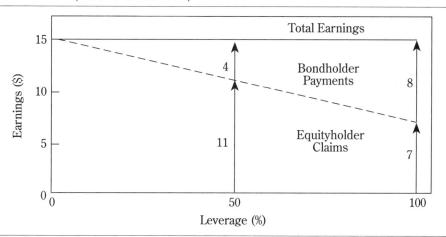

Leverage and the Tangible-Value Firm

In addition to the effect of leverage on the distribution of earnings claims between bondholders and equityholders, leverage also reduces shareholder equity. For the example firm, if its unleveraged market value of $125 million is assumed to be constant under increasing leverage, $50 million in loan

[3]The degree of leverage can be characterized in many different ways. In general, academic studies reflect the debt load as a percentage of the total market value of all the firm's securities (both debt and equity). Among equity market participants and credit analysts, however, the common practice is to express the leverage percentage relative to the total capitalization, that is, as a percentage of the firm's initial book value prior to any leveraging. We follow this latter convention because it is more intuitive. The general methodology of this study is not affected by this choice of leverage *numeraire*.

proceeds is used to repurchase shares, and the price per share does not change, the total value of the firm will remain at $125 million but the equity value will drop to $75 million. At a leverage ratio of 100 percent of book (an impractical but theoretically illuminating level), $25 million in residual shareholder value still remains, because leverage is defined here relative to book value rather than to market value.

The findings on earnings and shareholder equity can now be combined to determine how leverage affects the P/E. For the firm with 50 percent leverage, a P/E of 6.82 is obtained by dividing the revised $75 million equity value by the $11 million in earnings. At 100 percent leverage, the P/E drops to 3.57. The full range of leverage ratios produces a declining P/E curve.[4]

The preceding examples demonstrate that leverage leads to a declining P/E for any firm that derives all of its value from its current book of business. As long as the debt cost is less than the market rate, the P/E will start at 8.33 and follow a pattern of decline similar to the pattern of the no-franchise-value firm in Figure 5.2.

Growth Opportunities and the Franchise-Value Firm

The firm in the preceding sections generated $15 million in earnings a year but had no prospects for productive growth. Turn now to the more representative situation in which a firm has opportunities for future growth through investment at above-market returns. As in previous chapters, assume that firms are able to take advantage of all franchise investment opportunities because the market should always be willing to supply sufficient funds for such purposes.

The opportunity to invest in productive new businesses represents, in itself, a franchise value to this firm, even though the opportunity does not contribute to current book value. Assume that this franchise amounts to $80 million of net present value above and beyond the cost of financing the requisite future investments. The addition of this $80 million franchise value brings the total market value of the firm to $205 million:

$$\text{Market value} = \text{Tangible value} + \text{Franchise value}$$

$$= \$125,000,000 + \$80,000,000$$

$$= \$205,000,000.$$

---

[4]These same price/earnings ratios could have been obtained by examining the earnings per share resulting from leverage-induced declines in both total earnings and in the number of shares outstanding.

Figure 5.2. P/E versus Leverage for Three Firms

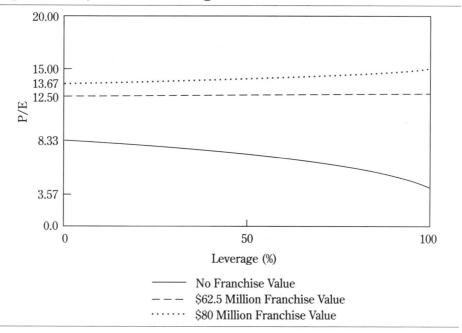

Without leverage, the P/E of this firm is 13.67 ($205 million divided by $15 million in current earnings), which is 5.33 units higher than the 8.33-unit base P/E of the unleveraged tangible-value firm illustrated in Figure 5.2.

Now look at the effect of leverage on the equity value and the P/E multiple of the franchise-value firm. At 50 percent leverage, the equity value falls by $50 million, from $205 million to $155 million, and the earnings drop to $11 million. Consequently, the P/E increases to 14.09 ($155 million/$11 million). At 100 percent leverage, the equity value drops by $100 million, leaving only $105 million. Because earnings decline to $7 million, the P/E grows to 15. Intermediate values for the P/E of the $80 million franchise-value firm are plotted in Figure 5.2, in which the P/E curve can be seen to rise with increasing leverage.

In general, any firm with a positive franchise value will have an initial (unleveraged) P/E that is greater than the 8.33-unit base P/E. If the unleveraged P/E is greater than a certain "threshold" value, the P/E will follow a pattern of increase with higher leverage ratios.

To see how such a threshold P/E responds to leverage, consider a firm with $15.0 million in current earnings and a franchise value of $62.5 million. Its total market value will be $187.5 million, and its initial P/E will be 12.5. The P/E is also 12.5 at 50 percent leverage. In fact, when the franchise value is $62.5 million, the P/E remains unchanged at 12.5 for *all* leverage ratios.

Combining the results from these three examples, Figure 5.2 graphically illustrates a finding that might surprise many market participants. The directional effect of leverage on P/E depends on the "value structure" of the existing firm. For a no-growth firm for which the equity value is derived solely from current earnings, the P/E always starts at 8.33 if the capitalization rate is 12 percent, and higher debt ratios lead to lower P/Es. The same declining P/E pattern is observed for all firms with P/Es below a threshold value (12.5 in this example). In contrast, for firms with future franchise opportunities that place their initial P/Es above the threshold level, leverage results in higher P/Es.

Figure 5.2 could have been obtained without reference to either the base P/E or the franchise value; the results of this analysis are totally general because they require only the basic assumptions of a fixed debt cost and a constant firm value. The critical determinant of the direction of the leverage effect is the initial P/E. The base P/E and the franchise value simply provide a convenient way to explain the mechanisms that lead to different leverage effects.

Leverage and the Franchise Factor Model

The basic FF model can be applied to leveraged firms by extending the definitions given in earlier chapters. First, the base P/E is revised by reducing the tangible value of the unleveraged firm by the size of the debt incurred. This adjusted tangible value corresponds to the capitalized value of the current earnings stream under the new debt load. The leveraged base P/E is now calculated by dividing the adjusted tangible value by the annual earnings, net of interest payments:

$$\text{Base P/E (leveraged)} = \frac{\text{Tangible value} - \text{Debt value}}{\text{Net earnings}},$$

where net earnings are annual earnings minus annual interest payments.

For example, if the tangible value is $125 million and the firm is 50 percent leveraged against a $100 million book value, then the debt value is $50 million and the adjusted tangible value is $75 million. The graph of the resulting base P/E (versus leverage) is exactly the same as the "no franchise value" curve in Figure 5.2, for any firm that has a 15 percent return on unleveraged equity.

Because the debt-induced decrement to shareholder value is embedded in the adjusted tangible value, the franchise value can be viewed as remaining constant in the face of leverage. This invariance can be interpreted in the following way: (1) The current shareholders are entitled to the full value of the franchise; (2) the franchise value reflects the excess of the return on new investment *above* the cost of future capital; and (3) the weighted-average cost of future capital will theoretically be equal to the market capitalization rate, regardless of the extent of leverage used in future financings.

The Leveraged Franchise Factor

In the case of leverage, the P/E increment from franchise value can be found by dividing that value by the net earnings. Because the net earnings *decrease* as leverage increases, the P/E increment from a given franchise will always be greater than in the unleveraged case. In the FF model, the P/E increment from franchise value is captured in the product of the franchise factor and the growth equivalent. To assume that G will not be affected by leverage is logical. Therefore, because G does not change, the entire impact of leverage is, in effect, "loaded" into a raised FF (see Appendix D for details):

$$\text{FF (leveraged)} = \frac{R-k}{(r-ih)k},$$

where
i = interest rate on debt, and
h = leverage as a percentage of book value.
As an example, assume R = 18 percent and r = 15 percent. With k = 12 percent, FF is 3.33 for the unleveraged firm (that is, for h = 0).

At first, the franchise factor grows slowly with leverage, reaching 4.55 at 50 percent leverage (see Figure 5.3):

$$\text{FF (50 percent leveraged)} = \frac{0.18 - 0.12}{[0.15 - (0.08 \times 0.50)] \times 0.12}$$

$$= 4.55.$$

At higher leverage percentages, FF increases more rapidly, reaching 7.14 for the 100 percent leveraged firm. The increasing franchise factor suggests that the P/E gain from a given franchise situation increases when a firm takes on a higher proportion of debt funding.

Figure 5.3. Franchise Factor versus Leverage

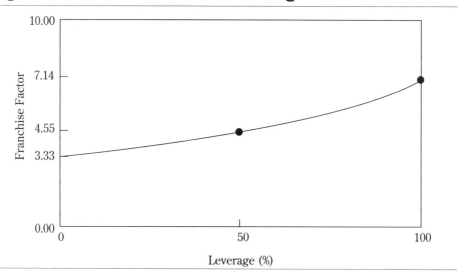

The Total P/E

The two P/E components are plotted in Figure 5.4 to show their responses to leverage. The base P/E reflects the firm's tangible value, which always declines with added debt. In contrast, the incremental P/E from the franchise value exhibits an ascending pattern. The sum of these two terms is the firm's P/E.

If G is 160 percent and the unleveraged FF is 3.33 (corresponding to $R = 18$ percent and $r = 15$ percent), the incremental P/E is 5.33 (3.33 × 1.6) and the total P/E is 13.67 (8.33 + 5.33).[5] With this G value, the P/E increases with leverage. Lowering the G value results in a lower P/E increment from the franchise value and, consequently, an overall P/E that rises more slowly. At a G of 125 percent, the incremental franchise P/E will just offset the declining base P/E.[6] The net result will be an overall P/E that is constant in the face of leverage.

The combined effects of the level of franchise opportunities and the degree of leverage are shown in Figure 5.5. At zero leverage, the P/E starts at an unleveraged base value of 8.33 and rises by 3.33 units (the unleveraged FF)

---

[5] The incremental franchise P/E is FF × G, and the corresponding franchise value is E × FF × G. With G = 160 percent, FF = 3.33, and E = $15 million, the implied franchise value is $80 million, as in the earlier example.

[6] If G = 125 percent and FF and E are as before, the implied franchise value is $62.5 million. This value leads to the threshold P/E of 12.5.

Figure 5.4. P/E versus Leverage
(growth equivalent = 160 percent)

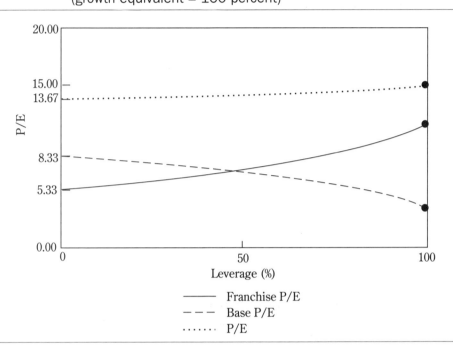

for each unit increase in *G*. At 50 percent leverage, the base P/E drops to 6.82 but the P/E grows faster because of the greater FF slope of 4.55 (see Figure 5.3). For 100 percent leverage, the base P/E drops farther, to 3.57, but the P/E line has an even greater slope than with lower leverage, a slope that corresponds to the leveraged FF value of 7.14.

In Figure 5.5, all the lines cross at a *G* of 125 percent, thereby giving a common P/E of 12.5. For firms with this P/E multiple, the earnings yield (that is, the reciprocal of the P/E) is equal to the 8 percent debt rate. Consequently, the addition of debt blends in with the original structure and leaves the earnings yield unchanged. From another vantage point, one can see that substantial franchise investments—125 percent of current book value—are needed just to sustain this relatively modest P/E of 12.5. When the growth equivalent is less than 125 percent, the decline in the base P/E with leverage overpowers any gain from franchise value; thus, at low *G* values, the P/E is greatest when the firm is unleveraged. If the growth equivalent is greater than 125 percent, the P/E response to leverage is positive, which means that, with leverage, a somewhat lower *G* value is needed to sustain a given P/E. The

Figure 5.5. P/E versus the Growth Equivalent at Varying Degrees of Leverage

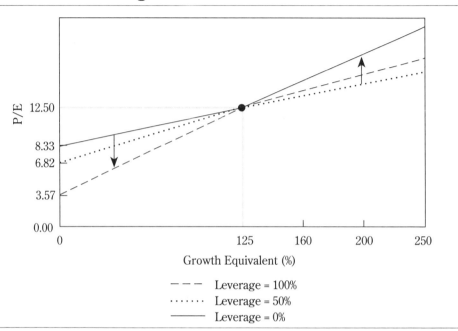

reduction in *G* is not sufficiently dramatic, however, to alter the earlier finding that substantial investments are required to sustain even moderately high P/Es. Thus, regardless of financial structure, the key to high P/Es remains access to franchise opportunities.

Sensitivity Analysis

Previous sections of this chapter demonstrated that the P/E may rise or fall with leverage, and both the direction and magnitude of the P/E change depend on the extent of the firm's franchise opportunities. This section looks at the *magnitude* of P/E variation for "reasonable" levels of leverage and initial P/E.

Figure 5.6 shows the variation of P/E with leverage for initial P/Es ranging from 8.33 to 16.67. Regardless of the initial P/E, the leverage effect on P/E is modest for firms that are as much as 40 percent leveraged. The muted leverage effect stems from the counterbalancing behavior of the base P/E and the franchise P/E. Another factor is the *numeraire* chosen to measure the degree of leverage. Expressing the debt as a percentage of book value rather than market value, in effect, understates the theoretical extent to which a firm can leverage. For firms with high P/Es, the book value may be only a small

Figure 5.6. P/E versus Leverage at Varying Initial P/Es

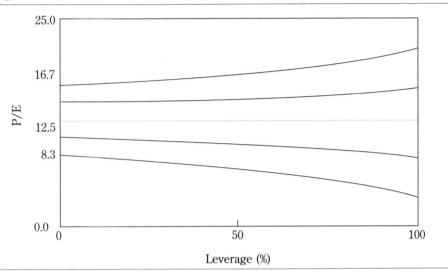

percentage of market value. Consequently, a high leverage ratio relative to book value may actually be a modest ratio relative to market value. Figure 5.7 shows how the leverage as a percentage of market value compares with the same amount of debt expressed as a percentage of book value.

The Impact of Taxes

To this point, the analysis has proceeded under a no-tax assumption. In the real world, the differential taxation of debt and equity creates several problems and opportunities. In terms of adjustments to the FF model, two tax effects are relevant: Earnings are reduced by the after-tax (rather than pretax) interest payments, and the total value of the firm is augmented by the introduction of debt.[7] The value enhancement can be modeled by assuming that the additional value is just the magnitude of the "tax wedge" (that is, the tax rate times the debt amount).

The two tax effects can be incorporated into the base and franchise components of the P/E by replacing the nominal leverage with the "after-tax" leverage (see Appendix D for a derivation of this result). For example, if the firm's marginal tax rate is 30 percent, one can determine the P/E at 50 percent leverage by using the base P/E and the franchise factor for a nontaxable firm

---

[7]The discussion here assumes a taxable corporation and tax-exempt investors; the effects of investor tax rates are thus not considered.

Figure 5.7. Market Percentage of Debt versus Book Percentage of Debt

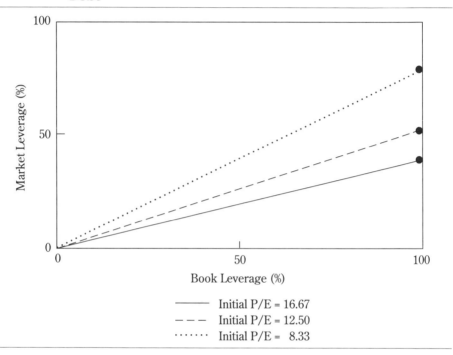

with a leverage of 35 percent (that is, 70 percent of 50 percent).

Figure 5.8 illustrates how the P/E impact of leverage is moderated for taxable firms. The P/E lines still intersect when G is 125 percent, but at all other values of G, the P/E line for 50 percent leverage (and a 30 percent tax rate) is closer to the P/E line for the unleveraged firm than it was in the tax-free environment of Figure 5.5.[8]

Summary

For firms with high franchise values and high P/Es, the theoretical market response to leverage—no matter what the taxation environment—is to place an even higher P/E on the existing earnings. Low-P/E stocks should experience the opposite effect—a decline in P/E with a rise in leverage.

Over a realistic range of leverage ratios (0–40 percent), however, the P/E

---

[8]Figure 5.8 presents a comparison between a taxable and a tax-exempt entity and assumes that, in the absence of leverage, both firms provide the same return on equity on an after-tax basis.

Figure 5.8. The P/E Effect of Taxes

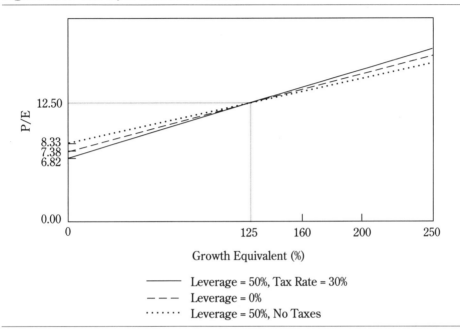

Growth Equivalent (%)

—————— Leverage = 50%, Tax Rate = 30%
— — — Leverage = 0%
········ Leverage = 50%, No Taxes

changes are relatively modest. Thus, even with an expanded FF model that incorporates taxes and leverage, the key finding of all the studies reported so far in this monograph remains intact: Regardless of the firm's financial structure, the fundamental basis for high P/Es is access to substantial franchise investments. For typical rates of return, these new investments must reach levels that can be measured in multiples of the firm's current book value.

6. Franchise Value and the Growth Process

The preceding chapters focused on the current value of a firm's price/earnings ratio. This chapter moves forward from that instantaneous snapshot to explore how the P/E evolves over time. For this purpose, the concepts of tangible value (the capitalized value of a firm's current earnings stream) and franchise value (the capitalized value of the potential payoff from all future franchise investments) are particularly useful as explanatory tools.

Because franchises are both perishable and finite, it is usually advantageous for a firm to fund these opportunities as soon as they become available. As projects are funded, the investment process converts franchise value to tangible value, with the result that the relative proportion of franchise value typically declines as franchise prospects are realized. The purpose of this chapter is to show that this franchise realization leads to a P/E that eventually declines until it reaches the base P/E value.

As an example of the franchise conversion process, imagine a retailer with a unique concept who projects that, over time, a substantial number of stores can be built that will provide earnings at a rate above the cost of capital. Such projected earnings enhance the price of the firm's equity because current equityholders have a stake in these future flows. As new stores are built, the number of prospective stores declines and a portion of the total franchise potential is funded—and, therefore, "consumed"—which lowers the franchise value. At the same time, the value of the new stores adds to the firm's current book value. Potential earnings are translated into actual earnings, and the firm's earnings base increases, thereby raising the tangible value. This transformation of franchise value into tangible value reduces the P/E because the franchise component of the P/E is diminished.

Price/earnings ratios obviously rise as well as fall, however, and situations exist in which P/Es appear to be stable. One situation that can lead to a rising P/E is a delay in franchise consumption. The very nature of certain franchise situations may entail a period of waiting before productive investments can be made. In such instances, franchise consumption will not begin immediately and the present value of the franchise will grow just through the passage of time. Under these conditions, the P/E will rise until the consumption phase begins.

The P/E will also increase when a business makes a major innovation or discovery that provides a new and unanticipated boost in franchise possibilities. Such "unexpected" franchise value provides an immediate windfall profit to existing shareholders and leads to a sudden jump in P/E. Thereafter, the cycle of franchise consumption resumes, and the P/E again ultimately declines to the base P/E.

This framework leads to the following generalizations regarding the behavior of a firm according to the franchise factor model:

- Franchise consumption will lead to abnormal earnings growth.
- Abnormal earnings growth will come to an abrupt end as soon as all franchise opportunities have been fully exploited.
- The P/E will erode toward the base P/E, even while the earnings growth remains high.
- During the franchise period, price appreciation will be lower than earnings growth, with the gap being roughly equivalent to the rate of P/E decline.
- After the franchise is fully consumed, earnings, dividends, and price will all grow at a single rate that will be determined by the firm's retention policy.

These results raise questions about equity valuations based solely on projections of recent earnings growth over a prespecified horizon period. By itself, the earnings growth rate is not a sufficient statistic. Even with the same franchise structure, different investment policies can lead to vastly different levels of earnings growth over various time periods, all of which add the same value to the firm and lead to the same P/E.

According to the FF model, the challenge is to peer beyond the recent earnings experience to discern the nature, dimensions, and duration of a firm's franchise opportunities. These investment opportunities create the franchise value that is the ultimate source of high P/Es.

Conversion of Franchise Value to Tangible Value

The market value of a firm, as discussed in Chapter 5, can be expressed as the sum of the firm's tangible value and franchise value:

$$\text{Market value} = \text{Tangible value} + \text{Franchise value.}$$

In essence, the tangible value is a sort of "economic book value," computed by discounting projected earnings from current businesses. The franchise value represents the value to current shareholders of all future flows that arise from new businesses that the firm will develop over time. This value is simply the total net present value of the returns from all future franchise investments. Together, the P/E, franchise value, and tangible value provide a snapshot of the current firm and its future potential. This snapshot reveals little, however, about how the firm will change in time.

The flow chart in Figure 6.1 shows how franchise value is converted to tangible value. Because both of these quantities are present values of future cash flows discounted at the market rate, with the passage of time, the tangible value and franchise value each generate "interest" at the market rate. For the tangible value, this annual interest takes the form of the firm's earnings. In theory, the allocation of earnings is quite visible: Dividends are distributed; retained earnings are reinvested within the firm, thereby furthering growth in tangible value.

The interest associated with the franchise value is less visible than that associated with the tangible value. These FV pseudo-earnings are similar to the accretion on a discount bond. On the one hand, without franchise consumption, the franchise value increases in magnitude from simple accretion over time. On the other hand, when a franchise investment actually is funded, the total present value of the residual franchise investments drops by the amount of the outflow. Thus, the franchise value will be eroded by the realization of franchise opportunities. These realizations are tantamount to payments out of the franchise value and into the firm's tangible value.

When a franchise opportunity becomes available for immediate investment, whether funded through retained earnings or external financing, the actual franchise investment will produce an incremental earnings stream that, when capitalized, adds to the firm's tangible value. Because the potential value of this earnings stream was already embedded in the firm's franchise value, the act of funding a franchise opportunity simply transforms a potential value into (quite literally) a tangible value. Thus, franchise investment consumes franchise value as future potential becomes current reality. The firm's theoretical total market value will be increased by the value of any retained earnings and/or external funding. Apart from this added investment, however, the firm's market value is not altered by the franchise consumption process.

Franchise Consumption

Consider a tax-free, unleveraged firm, Firm A, with a book value of $100

Figure 6.1. Schematic Diagram of Franchise Consumption

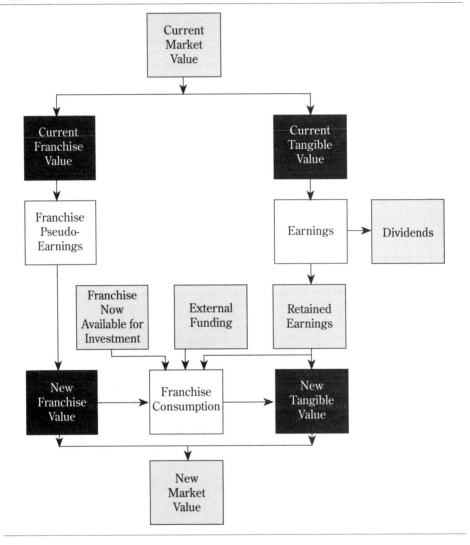

million and a return on equity of 15 percent. The earnings of $15 million a year (15 percent of $100 million) are assumed to continue year after year, and the firm's tangible value of $125 million is computed by capitalizing the perpetual earnings stream at an assumed 12 percent market rate. Firm A's market value is assumed to be $225 million, based on the tangible value of $125 million and additional franchise value of $100 million. The firm's P/E is 15 (that is, $225 million/$15 million).

The $100 million in franchise value is based on the firm's ability to make new franchise investments that provide a 20 percent return on equity in perpetuity. Each $1 million of such investments will generate an earnings stream of $200,000 a year. Capitalizing this earnings stream at the assumed market rate of 12 percent produces additional tangible value of $1.67 million (that is, $200,000/0.12).

The *net* value added for the firm's shareholders will be $0.67 million, because an incremental $1 million investment is required to realize the $1.67 million value. Thus, a franchise value of $100 million is derived from the opportunity to make a series of franchise investments with a total present value of $150 million ($100 million = $150 million × 0.67).

Because the total of all franchise investments is defined in present-value terms, the franchise value is the same whether the $150 million in investments is made immediately or spread out over time. Figure 6.2 illustrates a specific time pattern of franchise investments. This schedule is assumed to reflect the points at which investment opportunities first become available; the schedule cannot be further accelerated, and the firm will pursue these opportunities as expeditiously as possible, either through retained earnings or through external financing.

Figure 6.2. The Franchise Consumption Process
(dollars in millions)

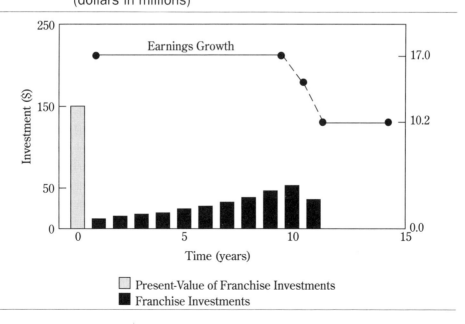

85

In this example, Firm A's franchise opportunities can be fully exploited through earnings retained at a rate of 85 percent. During the first year, the firm earns $15 million, invests $12.75 million (85 percent of $15 million) in a franchise business, and pays out the remaining $2.25 million in dividends to shareholders. During the second year, the $15 million in earnings is augmented by $2.55 million in earnings from the new enterprise (20 percent of $12.75 million). This increase represents earnings growth of 17 percent, which provides more capital for investment at the end of the second year.

This pattern of increasing investment continues through the 10th year. At this point, almost all of the franchise value has been consumed. The consumption process is completed in the 11th year, and additional retained earnings can be invested only at the 12 percent market rate. With the onset of such market-rate investments, the rate of earnings growth drops to 10.2 percent (85 percent of 12 percent).[1]

Figure 6.3 shows how the book value of Firm A grows over time while the present-value magnitude of the remaining franchise opportunities shrinks. Initially, the present value of all future franchise investments, the growth equivalent, is 150 percent of the book value. At the end of the first year, the book value grows as the first $12.75 million in franchise investment becomes part of the firm's book of business. The present value of future franchise investments also experiences a slight increase, because the increase in present value one time period forward is greater than the $12.75 million investment. When the incremental franchise investments begin to exceed the pseudo-earnings, however, the present value of future franchise investments decreases.

In the 11th year, the retained earnings will exceed the remaining franchise potential; thus, the excess retention must be invested at the market rate. From Year 12 on, the book-value increases are solely the result of market-rate investments. By this point, the P/E will have declined to the base P/E value of 8.33. During this same 11-year period, as also depicted in Figure 6.3, a corresponding decline occurs in the available franchise investment when expressed as a percentage of book value (the growth-equivalent value).

Role of the Franchise Factor

The franchise factor for Firm A can now be computed according to the

---

[1]The key assumption here, unlike in the dividend discount model, is that the totality of a firm's franchise investment opportunities will be fully consumed within a company's specific time frame. Thereafter, the growth rate is determined *solely* by the market rate and the firm's dividend payout policy.

Figure 6.3. Book-Value Growth during Franchise Consumption
(dollars in millions)

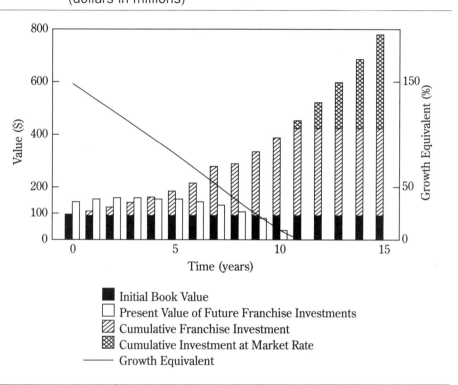

formula used in previous chapters, ˌ

$$FF = \frac{R-k}{rk}$$

$$= \frac{0.20 - 0.12}{0.15 \times 0.12}$$

$$= 4.44.$$

At the outset, Firm A has a (present-value) franchise investment potential of $150 million and a growth equivalent of 150 percent. Thus, the price/earnings ratio is initially,

$$P/E = \text{Base } P/E + (FF \times G)$$

$$= \frac{1}{k} + (FF \times G)$$

$$= 8.33 + (4.44 \times 1.50)$$

$$= 15.$$

In time, as the franchise value is consumed in accordance with the prospective schedule of investment opportunities, the book value grows. This process leads to a decline in the value of the growth equivalent until it reaches zero after the franchise is fully consumed in the 11th year. This pattern of G decay was exhibited in Figure 6.3 and is shown again in Figure 6.4, which also illustrates how both the franchise factor and the P/E change over time. The

Figure 6.4. The Changing P/E

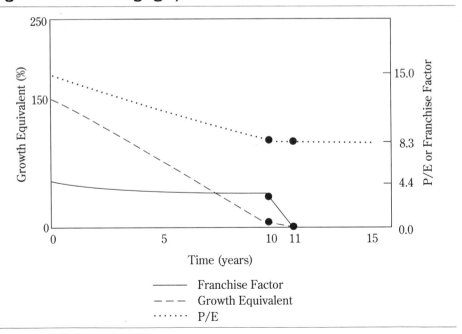

franchise factor is fairly stable as it decreases slowly over the 11-year franchise period.[2]

The incremental P/E (that is, the value beyond the base P/E of 8.33) is simply the product of FF and G. As time passes, the P/E will, therefore, reflect the rapid decay in G and the more modest decline in FF. By the 11th year, the P/E increment is totally eroded and the P/E assumes the base value of 8.33.

The Franchise Value over Time

The path of the P/E over time can be better understood by observing how the franchise value declines during the franchise consumption process. Figure 6.3 illustrated how the present value of future franchise investments changes during the 11-year consumption period. The franchise value itself follows this same pattern of change. Figure 6.5 shows the path of the firm's overall market value and its franchise- and tangible-value components.

The relationship between the remaining present value of franchise investments and the changing proportions of franchise and tangible value can be viewed from a slightly different perspective by expressing franchise value and tangible value as percentages of market value (see Figure 6.6). The proportion of franchise value declines steadily even during the early years, when some growth occurs in the present value of franchise investments. Note that the P/E declines along with the proportion of franchise value.[3]

The relationship between the P/E and the relative proportions of franchise value and tangible value can be made explicit by expressing the P/E in terms of the ratio of franchise value to tangible value:[4]

$$P/E = (\text{Base } P/E) \times (1 + f\text{-ratio}),$$

where the f-ratio = FV/TV.

---

[2]The decrease in franchise factor is explained by the fact that the return on book equity (which appears in the denominator of FF) changes over time whenever the return on new investment and the return on existing book are different. The return on equity actually is a weighted average of the old and new returns. Because in this example the new return (20 percent) is higher than the current return (15 percent), the blended rate rises slowly over time, which leads to a correspondingly modest decrease in franchise factor.

[3]When the franchise is fully consumed by a constant growth in earnings from the outset, the P/E will fall continually until it reaches the base P/E. This result does not hold, however, for arbitrary franchise structures.

[4]Because Market value = TV + FV = (TV)(1 + FV/TV), P/E = Market value/E = (TV/E)(1 + FV/TV) = (1/k)(1 + f-ratio).

Figure 6.5. Components of Firm Value
(dollars in millions)

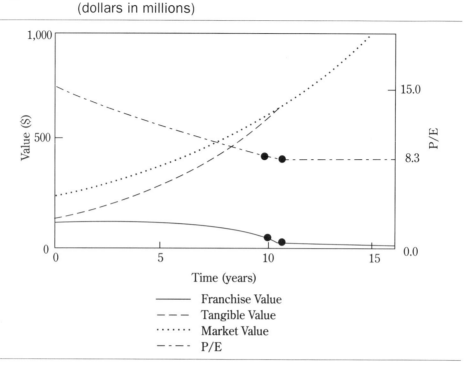

This formula shows that the *f*-ratio includes *all* of the information needed to compute the P/E. Another interpretation of this formula is that the *f*-ratio is the percentage by which the actual P/E exceeds the base P/E. Figure 6.7 illustrates how, over time, the *f*-ratio determines the P/E.

Growth from Market-Rate Investments

To this point, all investment has been treated as part of the franchise realization process, but a variety of situations may cause the firm to make investments that provide only market-rate returns. For example, although a franchise has been fully consumed, management may continue to retain a certain portion of the firm's earnings, which can then earn only the market rate. Such investments will produce growth in book value and tangible value, so total firm value will grow, but those investments do not boost the P/E above the base P/E (see Figure 6.8). If Firm A maintains its 85 percent retention rate even after the franchise is consumed, the postfranchise retention will result in a 10.2 percent earnings growth because such retained earnings can earn only the 12 percent market rate. A retention rate of 50 percent during the

Figure 6.6. Changing Proportions of Franchise Value and Tangible Value

(dollars in millions)

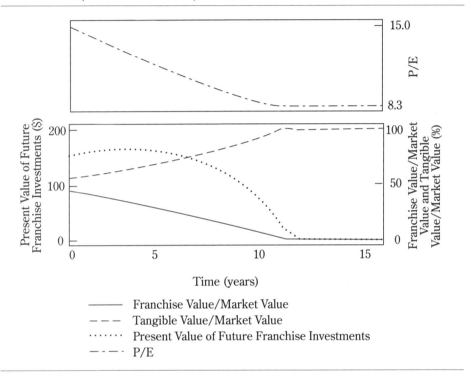

postfranchise period, on the other hand, will result in a 6 percent (0.50×12 percent) earnings growth. In any case, in this postfranchise period, the choice of retention rate will have no effect on the P/E, which must remain at the base level of 8.33.

The Myth of Homogeneous Growth

The intuitive appeal of uniform growth is powerful. In an ideal world, the interests of management, shareholders, analysts, and accountants would be well served by such a simple growth process. Given such an intersection of powerful interests, one should not be surprised that the uniform-growth concept pervades much of our intuition about how equity value "should" develop over time. The appeal of simple, uniform growth can create a self-ful-filling prophecy—at least temporarily. How convenient it would be if all expansion took the form of a single growth rate that applied homogeneously

91

Figure 6.7. The P/E and the *f*-Ratio

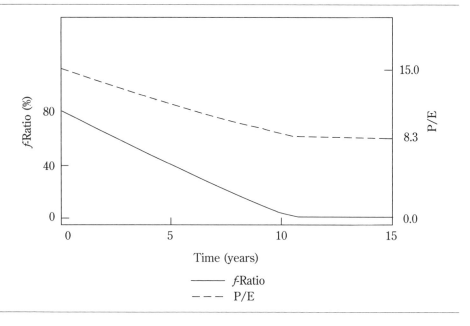

Figure 6.8. The P/E Effect of Terminal Growth

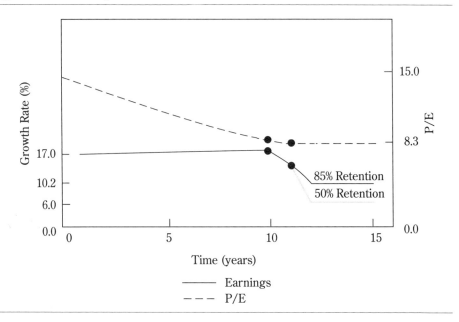

to all of the firm's variables—price, book value, earnings, and dividends. In the real world, however, growth is erratic; it exhibits neither uniformity over time nor homogeneity in its impact on each of the firm's characteristics.

Consider the growth rates of price and of earnings for Firm A with the uniform 85 percent retention rate shown in Figure 6.9. During the franchise consumption phase, the earnings growth rate is fixed at 17 percent. In contrast, the price appreciation is only 11 percent at the outset and declines slightly over the franchise consumption period, which results in a widening gap between the price and earnings growth rates. When franchise consumption is complete, however, all retained earnings are invested at the market rate, and both price and earnings grow uniformly at the same 10.2 percent rate.

Figure 6.9 also illustrates the case in which Firm A adopts a 50 percent retention rate in the postfranchise period, which leads to 6 percent earnings growth. With either retention rate, after franchise consumption, price appreciation coincides with the earnings growth rate.

The Myth of the Stable P/E

If a firm could count on homogeneous growth, its price/earnings ratio would remain stable over time, but in the context of the franchise model, the only stable P/E is the base P/E that characterizes pre- and postfranchise periods.[5] The FF model considers P/Es to be in continual flux—rising as future franchise opportunities approach and then declining as available franchise investments are funded and consumed. If the firm's franchise is consumed over some finite period of time, the P/E will ultimately decline at the end of that time to the base P/E. Consequently, high P/Es are intrinsically unsustainable.

In fact, in the franchise model, if high earnings growth is derived from franchise consumption: (1) the high earnings can be expected to come to an abrupt, not a gradual, end; (2) the P/E ratio will tend to erode, even during the period of high earnings growth; and (3) the price growth will likely be quite different from the earnings growth. The discrepancy between earnings growth and price growth has already been illustrated in Figure 6.9.

---

[5]For example, the standard infinite-horizon dividend discount model implies a stable P/E (and constant *f*-ratio) over time. In franchise model terms, the infinite DDM requires that franchise investments be available to accommodate precisely the retentions from a growing earnings stream. It is hard to believe that many franchises would come in such neat packages. An alternative interpretation might be an outsized franchise whose consumption is constrained by the availability of retained earnings. In today's financial markets, however, external financing sources could be applied to exploit such above-market opportunities expeditiously.

Figure 6.9. Price and Earnings Growth

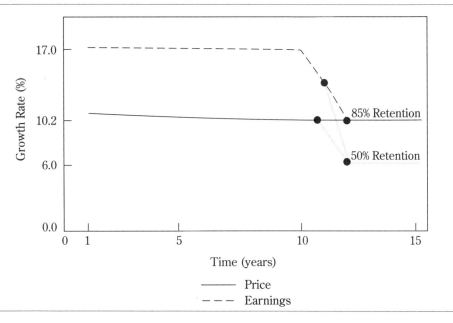

The gap between price appreciation and earnings growth over time that is illustrated in Figure 6.9 can be understood by examining the percentage change in the P/E. A general relationship holds among the earnings, price, and P/E growth rates:

$$g_P \cong g_E + g_{P/E} \, .$$

This approximation does not depend on the franchise model.[6]

In Figure 6.10, the three growth rates are plotted for the franchise and the postfranchise periods for Firm A with an 85 percent postfranchise retention rate and with a 50 percent postfranchise retention rate. These examples illustrate how the changing P/E affects price growth. As discussed earlier, the growth in earnings remains constant at 17 percent until it comes to a halt and declines to 10.2 percent or 6 percent, depending on the postfranchise retention rate. At the outset, the P/E growth rate is a negative 5.13 percent. When that rate is combined with the 17 percent earnings growth rate, the

---

[6]Because $(1 + g_p)$ = New price/Old price and $P = E(\text{P/E})$, it follows that $(1 + g_p) = (1 + g_E)(1 + g_{P/E})$. Thus, $g_p = g_E + g_{P/E} + (g_E)(g_{P/E})$. Dropping the last term, which is fairly small, results in the given approximation formula.

Figure 6.10. The P/E Growth Rate

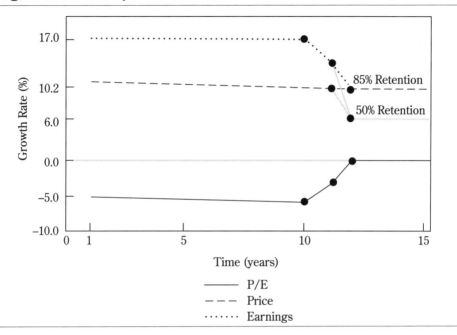

result is approximately equal to the 11 percent price growth. As time progresses, the growth rates in price and P/E fall moderately. When the P/E stabilizes during the postfranchise period, $g_{P/E}$ is zero, and the earnings and price growth rates then coincide.

Alternative Franchise Structures

To this point, the illustrations have focused on a simple pattern of franchise investment that gave rise to a 17 percent earnings growth rate over 11 years. This section will show that the same principle of growth operates when the FF model is applied to different franchise consumption patterns.

Figure 6.11 presents a comparison of Firm A with a firm, Firm B, that has a longer opportunity period. Firm B's franchise opportunities can be funded by a 70 percent retention rate with corresponding earnings growth of 14 percent. At the outset, both firms have the same franchise value, tangible value, and P/E, but Firm B's P/E follows a slower path of decline and reaches the base P/E of 8.33 at the end of its 15-year franchise period.

Now consider Firm C, which has the same initial franchise value as Firms A and B, but its franchise opportunity cannot begin to be realized for five years. Firm C also maintains the 85 percent retention rate before, during, and after

95

Figure 6.11. P/Es for Firms with Different Rates of Franchise Consumption

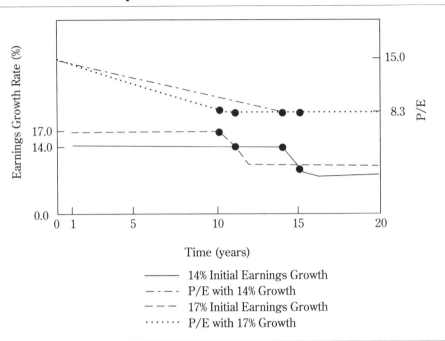

Time (years)

——— 14% Initial Earnings Growth
— · — · P/E with 14% Growth
— — — 17% Initial Earnings Growth
· · · · · · · P/E with 17% Growth

the franchise is consumed. During Firm C's five-year prefranchise period, the retained earnings are invested at the 12 percent market rate, resulting in a 10.2 percent earnings growth rate. When franchise consumption begins, the earnings growth rate jumps to the 17 percent level; in the postfranchise period, it drops back to 10.2 percent.

Figure 6.12 compares the P/Es and earnings growth rates of Firms B and C. Note how the P/E for the delayed-franchise Firm C rises slightly during the five-year prefranchise period. It then peaks and declines to reach the base P/E level at the end of the seventeenth year.

The explanation for the rising P/E can be found in the franchise-value buildup shown in Figure 6.13. Recall that both the franchise value and tangible value develop pseudo-interest at the market rate. Without franchise consumption, however, the franchise value's pseudo-earnings are added to create the new franchise value. The tangible value grows at a somewhat slower rate because a portion of its earnings is being distributed in the form of dividends. Thus, during the prefranchise period, franchise value grows faster than tangible value, the ratio of these two quantities (that is, the *f*-ratio) increases, and

Figure 6.12. P/Es for Firms with (Firm C) and without (Firm B) Delayed Franchise Consumption

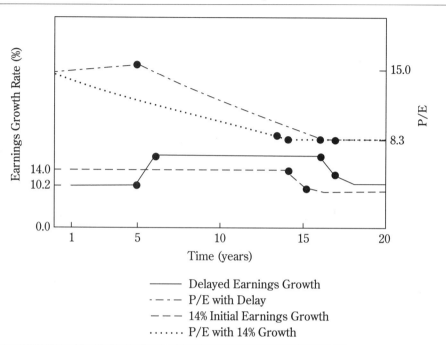

the P/E rises (see Figure 6.14). In the fifth year, the onset of franchise consumption leads to slower franchise-value growth and more rapid increase in the tangible value. This consumption leads to a declining *f*-ratio. Consequently, the P/E peaks, erodes throughout the balance of the franchise investment period, and then settles at 8.33 when the franchise is depleted.

The Franchise Model and Surprise Events

The analysis thus far has been based on a franchise value that incorporates *anticipated* opportunities for investment at above-market rates. In practice, one cannot foresee all situations in which a firm's size, distribution channels, capital, proprietary technology, patents, and strategic alliances will lead to above-market returns. Prospects will range from those that are immediate and clearly visible to those that are distant and only possible. Theoretically, this entire range of scenarios is incorporated in the firm's franchise value, but surprises—both positive and negative—are frequent.

The *f*-ratio and P/E of a firm that encounters an unexpected positive jump

Figure 6.13. Components of Firm Value for the Delayed-Franchise Firm (Firm C)

(dollars in millions)

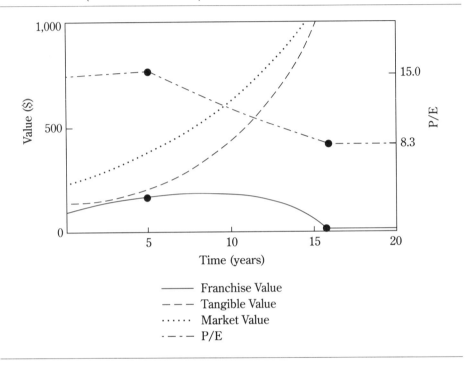

in franchise value, Firm D, are shown in Figure 6.15. For the first five years, these quantities follow the same paths as they did for Firm A (see Figure 6.7). In the fifth year, however, Firm D makes a sudden discovery that creates an immediate increase in the firm's prospects for that year. The firm now has the opportunity to invest an additional $150 million (in present-value terms) in projects that provide a 20 percent return on equity in perpetuity. Thus, the new discovery adds another $100 million in franchise value to the firm (0.67 × $150 million), and the jump in franchise value is transmitted directly to the firm's market value.[7]

The discovery does not affect the tangible value, because the surprise relates only to *future* earnings. Thus, the composition of total firm value—the relative magnitude of franchise value and tangible value—changes, and the

---

[7]If an unexpected event were to result in a loss of franchise value, the market value and the P/E would suddenly drop by an appropriate amount.

Figure 6.14. The f-Ratio and P/E for the Delayed-Franchise Firm (Firm C)

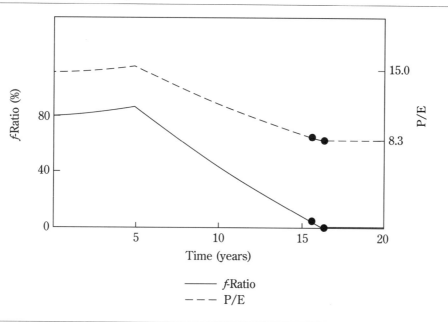

value of the *f*-ratio will change accordingly. Figure 6.15 illustrates how the change in the *f*-ratio creates a sudden upward thrust in P/E. Once the surprise has occurred and been incorporated in the pricing structure of the firm, the consumption of franchise value and the decline in the P/E proceed in much the same manner as in the earlier examples. Figure 6.15 thus reinforces the central role of the *f*-ratio in determining both the magnitude and the underlying dynamics of changes in the P/E ratio.

Summary

In an idealized world without surprises, a firm's prospective franchise investments would be well defined and the franchise value associated with the franchise investments would completely determine the firm's price/earnings ratio. This theoretical P/E would be subject to "gravitational" forces pulling it down to the base P/E as the franchise was depleted. Just as nature abhors a vacuum, so economics abhors a franchise.

In the real world, of course, P/E multiples rise and P/E multiples fall. New information about companies and markets continually flows toward investors

Figure 6.15. P/E Impact of an Unexpected Increase in Franchise Prospects (Firm D)

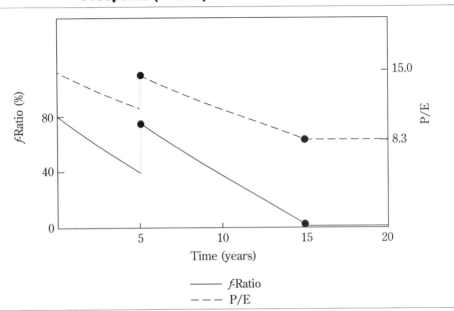

as fresh scenarios are uncovered, old scenarios are discarded, and probabilities are redefined. The combination of the revaluation of prior franchises and the discovery of new prospects is embedded in changing P/Es. Even when dealing with the real world in all of its complexity, however, the (admittedly idealized) framework of the franchise factor model can help in analyzing the various factors that shape the P/E behavior of different firms.

7. The Growth Illusion: The P/E "Cost" of Earnings Growth

This chapter shifts the focus from the prospective earnings used to compute a theoretical price/earnings ratio to the realized earnings that evolve over time. Once the P/E is set, high realized earnings growth represents a rapid depletion of the opportunities that composed the firm's prospects at the outset. This depletion leads to the surprising implication that an *inverse* relationship exists between *realized* earnings growth and the *realized* P/E over time. This relationship contrasts with the *positive* link between higher *prospective* earnings growth and the *prospective* P/E.

Historical earnings growth is commonly used as a baseline for estimating future earnings growth. Price appreciation is then assumed to follow the projected earnings growth. By tacitly assuming that the P/E will remain stable, investors elevate earnings growth to the central determinant of investment value.

A problem exists, however, with the stable-P/E assumption, which can be simply illustrated. Consider a corn farmer who owns two plots, each comprising 100 acres of prime land. The first plot is producing corn at its highest possible efficiency. The second plot is currently fallow while being nurtured and developed for maximum productivity next year. In placing a value on the farm, the farmer or the farmer's banker will surely take into account not only the current earnings from the productive plot but also the future earnings from the currently fallow second plot. Thus, today's price is based on a projection of tomorrow's earnings. If the price/earnings ratio is based on the earnings from the currently producing plot, the farm will carry a high P/E multiple.

By the end of the next year, if the second plot has reached its full potential, the total realized earnings will show tremendous growth—essentially double the farm's visible earnings in the first year. This earnings growth provides no new information, however, because it simply reflects the realization into current earnings of the previously known prospective earnings. Consequently, the total value of the farm will have changed relatively little.

The net P/E change, however, will be dramatic: The P/E will drop by virtually half. Thus, the second-year earnings, although much higher than the first year's, are accompanied by a large P/E decline. The lowered P/E indicates that, even though putting the second plot into production may represent quite a significant achievement, the farmer's efforts were really only *value preserving.* No fundamental enhancement of the farm's initial value occurred.

This chapter will show that the price/earnings ratio plays a dynamic role in the evolution of firm value over time. The P/E is not merely a passive prop on a stage dominated by earnings growth. This finding raises questions about the common practice of assessing value by discounting a growing stream of dividends and then applying a stable P/E to the earnings rate achieved at the horizon.

The real world is, of course, more complicated than any closed theoretical system. As unforeseen (and unforeseeable) prospects and dangers ebb and flow and as uncertain potential becomes confirmed reality, the earnings signal and the P/E ratio interact in a more intricate fashion than can be captured in any analytical model. Nevertheless, in terms of a fundamental baseline for analysis, the central message still holds: Earnings growth alone cannot provide a valid gauge for assessing investment value.

The Substitution Effect in Tangible-Value Firms

To understand how firms create value requires a benchmark against which incremental gains (and losses) can be measured. To this end, consider the firm as a cash machine: At the end of each year, after paying all its bills, the firm will have some net amount of cash available for payment to investors or for reinvestment. If all such cash flows could be accurately predicted, the value (price) of the firm could be calculated by discounting the net cash flows at some "market" rate.

For simplicity, place this firm in an environment of no taxes and no debt. As in previous chapters, the market rate (k) is a stable 12 percent, and that rate is assumed to be a fair compensation for the riskiness of equity. In addition, assume that investors have ample opportunity to invest in other firms that offer the same return and bear the same risk. Given the value of cash flows from all current and future businesses and the corresponding price per share, this analysis will show that there is a natural year-to-year evolution of price, earnings, and the P/E. The projected path of these variables can be used as the baseline against which actual changes can be measured.

As a first example, consider a tangible-value firm with a basic business producing earnings of $100 annually. The firm has no opportunity to expand by investing in new businesses that provide returns greater than 12 percent. Therefore, although the firm may have an excellent business, it cannot create additional value for shareholders beyond that value represented by its "tangible" earnings stream (assuming that investors have the ability to achieve 12 percent returns on their own). The price of this TV firm is $833, found by discounting the perpetual $100 earnings stream at the 12 percent market rate.[1]

This firm does not have the potential to add incremental value, but it may have a retention policy that leads to growing earnings. For example, suppose that of the $100 in first-year earnings, the firm pays out $35 in dividends at year end and retains $65 to reinvest at the 12 percent market rate. In the second year, the firm will earn an additional $7.80 (12 percent of $65) beyond the initial $100 earnings. In exchange for giving up $65 in dividends, investors will see total earnings grow by 7.80 percent. This realized growth in earnings (and the associated price increase) is simply a "substitution" that exactly compensates investors for the dividend payments they have forgone. That is, if the $65 had been paid directly to investors, they also could have invested that amount at 12 percent and earned this same $7.80. For the P/E at the outset, the initial $833 price is simply divided by the $100 earnings to obtain a P/E of 8.33 times earnings.

This example illustrates a well-known rule for calculating earnings growth: With b as the retention rate and with R as the return on retained earnings,

$$g_E = \text{Earnings growth}$$

$$= \text{Retention rate} \times \text{Return on retained earnings}$$

$$= bR.$$

In this example, with a 65 percent retention rate and a 12 percent return, earnings growth equals 7.80 percent (that is, 0.65×12).

Because price appreciation for a TV firm arises solely from earnings increases, the price growth rate must equal the 7.80 percent earnings growth rate. As Figure 7.1 shows, this equality of price growth and earnings growth holds for all retention rates. Moreover, because price and earnings grow at the same rate, their ratio (the P/E) does not change; it remains at 8.33.

In a stable 12 percent market, equity investors should earn 12 percent through a combination of price growth and dividend yield. Thus, one can view

---

[1]Based on Chapter 3, all earnings streams are assumed to be in the form of "normalized" perpetuities.

Figure 7.1. Price Growth, Earnings Growth, and P/E Growth for a Tangible-Value Firm

(with initial P/E of 8.33 and investment at 12 percent)

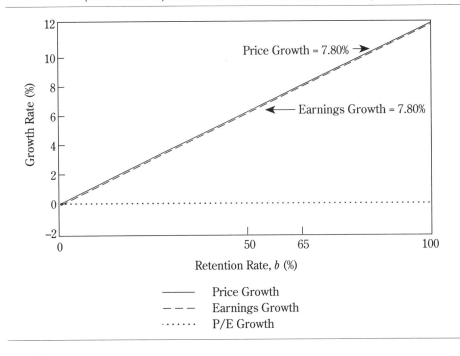

the price growth (i.e., the capital appreciation) as determined by the market rate and the dividend yield. With $65 in earnings retained and the remaining $35 paid as dividends ($d$), the dividend yield is 4.20 percent:

$$\text{Dividend yield} = \frac{d}{P}$$

$$= \frac{(1-b)E}{P}$$

$$= (1-0.65) \times \frac{\$100}{\$833}$$

$$= 0.35 \times \frac{\$100}{\$833}$$

$$= 4.20 \text{ percent.}$$

That the investor's total return is 12 percent can now be verified by adding the dividend yield and the price growth:

$$\text{Total return} = \text{Dividend yield} + \text{Price growth}$$

$$= \frac{d}{P} + g_P$$

$$= 4.20 \text{ percent} + 7.80 \text{ percent}$$

$$= 12 \text{ percent}.$$

Because the total return is k, the general price-growth formula can be written as

$$g_P = k - \frac{d}{P}$$

$$= k - \frac{(1-b)E}{P}$$

$$= k - \frac{1-b}{\text{P/E}}.$$

This formula shows that the dividend yield for a given year is determined by the initial P/E and the expected earnings retention rate. Because the price growth rate is simply the difference between the market rate (k) and the dividend yield, it follows that the retention rate (b) and the initial P/E establish the price growth. In the absence of surprises about the nature of a firm's business prospects, the price of any firm's common shares should, theoretically, rise at this predetermined rate.[2]

The Substitution Effect in Franchise-Value Firms

Consider now the relationships among growth in price, growth in earnings, and growth in P/E for firms with initial P/Es that are greater than the 8.33 base level. Such firms have both tangible value and franchise value, which

---

[2]In the special case of a TV firm with P/E = $1/k$, the formula for g_P reduces to bk. This result confirms the earlier observation that, for TV firms, $g_P = g_E = bk$. For a general discussion of the factors that influence share price, see Keane (1990).

combine to produce the total value.

In the TV firm, FV was zero and all retained earnings were invested at 12 percent. Because any realized earnings growth is always capitalized into a higher TV, growth in earnings for the TV firm equaled price growth. In contrast, a firm for which the franchise value is greater than zero has an additional value term with a growth pattern that is likely to be quite different from g_E. Because price growth now results from a combination of TV growth and FV growth, price growth cannot be determined from g_E alone.

In this first franchise-firm example, suppose that a firm with $100 in earnings from current businesses is trading at a P/E of 15. Assume also, as before, that at the end of the first year, 65 percent of earnings is retained and reinvested at the 12 percent market rate. (In other words, the assumption is that this firm is not prepared to take advantage of the higher return franchise investment that will become available at some point in its future.) In this case, as Figure 7.2 illustrates, the realized g_E is 7.80 percent, just as it was for the TV firm However, the dividend yield and g_P for the FV firm will both differ from what they were for the TV firm. According to the formula, for the FV firm,

$$g_P = k - \frac{1-b}{P/E}$$

$$= 0.12 - \frac{1.00 - 0.65}{15.00}$$

$$= 9.67 \text{ percent}.$$

This increased price growth compensates for the lower dividend yield of the FV firm; the lower dividend yield is the result of the higher price (that is, the higher P/E):

$$\frac{d}{P} = \frac{\$35}{\$1,500}$$

$$= 2.33 \text{ percent}.$$

At higher retention rates, the amount available for dividends decreases and, therefore, the dividend yield declines. In the limiting case of 100 percent retention, the dividend yield is zero; g_P is the only source of return, and its value must equal the required 12 percent return. At this 100 percent retention point, $g_P = g_E = k$ regardless of the P/E.

Figure 7.2. Price Growth for a Franchise-Value Firm and a Tangible-Value Firm

(with initial P/E of 15 and investment at 12 percent)

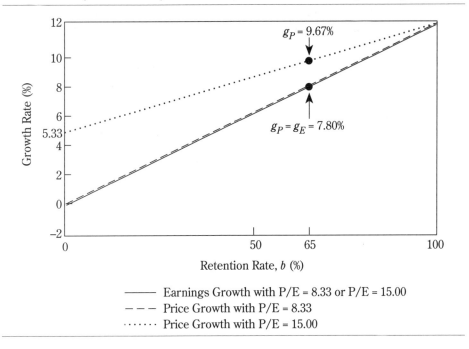

- —— Earnings Growth with P/E = 8.33 or P/E = 15.00
- – – – Price Growth with P/E = 8.33
- ⋯⋯ Price Growth with P/E = 15.00

For all retention rates below 100 percent, the price growth for the firm with an initial P/E of 15 will always exceed the price growth for the firm with the lower P/E of 8.33 (see Figure 7.2). This result stems from the FV that gave rise to the higher P/E. In the example, the firm starts out with a P/E of 15 but invests its retained earnings at only 12 percent, thereby failing to use any of its franchise potential. Assuming that the franchise is not perishable (that is, that the opportunity to invest will continue to exist if available franchise investments are not made immediately), the franchise value will grow with time (at the 12 percent rate), and as discussed in Chapter 6, this FV growth will be reflected in price growth.

This example shows that the 9.67 percent price growth for the FV firm can be interpreted as an average of the 12 percent "returns" on 100 percent of the franchise value and the 12 percent returns on the 65 percent of earnings that are retained. Specifically, g_P can be expressed as the weighted average of the TV growth rate—that is, g_E—and the FV growth rate, where the weights are

107

the proportions of TV and FV:[3]

$$g_P = \left(\frac{TV}{P} g_{TV}\right) + \left(\frac{FV}{P} g_{FV}\right)$$

$$= \left(\frac{TV}{P} g_E\right) + \left(\frac{FV}{P} g_{FV}\right).$$

Applying the formula to the example firm results in

$$g_P = \left(\frac{\$833}{\$1,500} \times 7.8 \text{ percent}\right) + \left(\frac{\$667}{\$1,500} \times 12 \text{ percent}\right)$$

$$= 4.33 \text{ percent} + 5.33 \text{ percent}$$

$$= 9.67 \text{ percent}.$$

With price and earnings growing at different rates, the stability of the price/earnings ratio is lost. The new P/E can always be found, however, by taking the ratio of the increased price to the increased earnings:

$$\text{New P/E} = \frac{P(1 + g_P)}{E(1 + g_E)}$$

$$= \text{Old P/E} \left(\frac{1 + g_P}{1 + g_E}\right).$$

This general formula provides the P/E growth figure:

$$g_{P/E} = \text{P/E growth rate}$$

$$= \frac{\text{New P/E}}{\text{Old P/E}} - 1$$

$$= \frac{1 + g_P}{1 + g_E} - 1.$$

---

[3]This same value could, of course, be obtained from the expression $g_P = k - (d/P) = 12.00$ percent $- 2.33$ percent $= 9.67$ percent. The preceding analysis was designed, however, to provide insight into the respective roles of TV and FV in the firm's overall price growth.

Figure 7.3. Price, Earnings, and P/E Growth versus Retention Rate
(with initial P/E of 15 and investment at 12 percent)

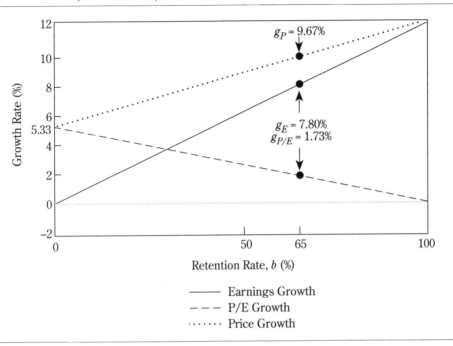

Substituting the example values of g_P and g_E results in

$$g_{P/E} = \frac{1 + 0.0967}{1 + 0.0780} - 1$$

$$= 1.73 \text{ percent.}$$

Figure 7.3 illustrates this result for the example retention rate of 65 percent and also shows the effect at other retention rates. With zero retention, all earnings are paid out as dividends, g_E is zero, and g_P is entirely attributable to the growth of FV through the passage of time. As the retention rate increases, the realized g_E increases and the gap between price and earnings growth shrinks, with the result that $g_{P/E}$ declines, finally reaching zero at 100 percent retention.

The relationship among the three growth rates discussed here is quite general; it holds for any value for the return on new investments (refer to Chapter 6). Moreover, an approximate $g_{P/E}$ can be obtained by taking the difference between g_P and g_E:

$$g_{P/E} \approx g_P - g_E .$$

Applying this approximation to the preceding example results in

$$g_{P/E} \approx 9.67 \text{ percent} - 7.80 \text{ percent} = 1.87 \text{ percent},$$

rather than the precise 1.73 percent. The difference between these two values is to be expected from Figure 7.3, where careful scrutiny reveals a slight curvature in the representation of $g_{P/E}$.

The nature of price growth is clarified by rewriting the approximation formula:

$$g_P \approx g_E + g_{P/E}.$$

Because g_P is determined by the firm's initial P/E and the retention policy, the left side of the approximation can be regarded as fixed for any single period. Therefore, a direct trade-off always exists between realized $g_{P/E}$ and realized g_E.

The Conversion Effect: Franchise Investment

This section focuses on the growth effects of realized franchise investments with returns in excess of 12 percent. Each such investment represents a *conversion* of a portion of the firm's franchise potential into incremental earnings and, hence, a higher tangible value.

When the firm makes franchise investments, earnings tend to grow rapidly, but when growth in earnings is greater than growth in share price, the result is a decline in the firm's P/E. At the outset, the firm's price implicitly reflects a fixed level of future franchise investments. Unless new opportunities are discovered, all of this franchise potential will ultimately be "used up," and the P/E will decline toward its base level.[4]

To illustrate this franchise conversion process, consider again the franchise firm with the initial P/E of 15. The price-growth line for this firm was illustrated in Figure 7.3: If the firm maintains a 65 percent earnings retention

---

[4]An exception to this P/E decline occurs in a franchise-value structure in which all measures continue to grow at a given uniform rate—that is, under the special conditions that are implicit in the standard dividend discount model (see Appendix E).

policy and invests only at the 12 percent market rate, g_P will be 9.67 percent.

Suppose now that the firm is able to use its franchise potential and invest retained earnings in projects that return 15 percent. (Because the franchise firm's prospective P/E reflects a potential for above-market-rate investments, the availability of such 15 percent projects is no surprise.) As always, the value of g_P is determined by the market rate, the retention rate, and the P/E. Hence, with the same 65 percent retention rate and the (higher) 15 percent return on investment, g_P remains at 9.67 percent. In fact, the g_P line in Figure 7.3 applies regardless of the rate the firm can obtain on new investments. The 15 percent return does, however, alter the line that depicts *realized* earnings growth.

Figure 7.4 illustrates the realized growth in earnings over the full range of retention rates. For all retention rates, the 15 percent return results in a greater g_E than for the 12 percent return situation depicted in Figure 7.3. These enhanced earnings come at the expense, however, of growth in franchise value: When investments are made at 12 percent, no FV is used, so FV simply grows at 12 percent, but when franchise investments are made at 15 percent,

Figure 7.4. Earnings Growth Rates with Retained Earnings (R) Invested at 12 Percent and 15 Percent
(with initial P/E of 15)

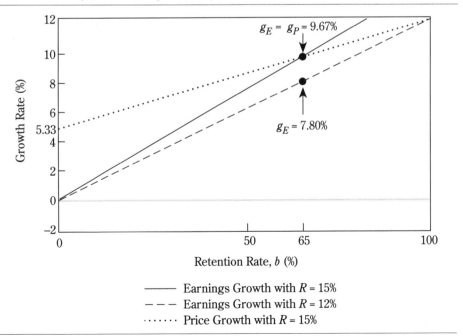

a corresponding reduction in the FV results. At the same time, the "new business" provides an addition to earnings and becomes part of the firm's tangible value. This pattern is the essence of the franchise conversion process.

As illustrated in Figure 7.4, at a retention rate of 65 percent, g_P and g_E both happen to take on the same value of 9.67 percent. Consequently, the P/E will remain unchanged for this particular combination of parameters. For any other retention rate, however, g_P and g_E take different values, and the P/E stability is lost. The result is shown in Figure 7.5.

At all retention values other than 65 percent, $g_{P/E}$ is either greater than or less than zero and the P/E will change accordingly over the one-year period. With retention rates in excess of 65 percent, g_E is greater than g_P and the growth

Figure 7.5. P/E Growth with Retained Earnings Invested at 15 Percent
(with initial P/E of 15)

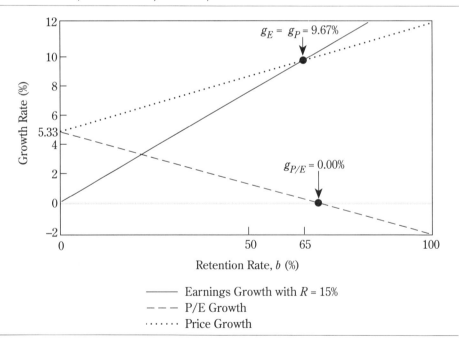

rate of P/E becomes negative, so the P/E begins to decrease. If this growth imbalance is sustained year after year, the P/E will continue to decline toward the base P/E of 8.33. In summary, when the balance between return and retention rate is altered in virtually any way, the stability of the price/earnings ratio is lost.

The Value-Preservation Line

So far, the discussion has generated two different combinations of realized growth in earnings and growth in P/E that can lead to the same growth in price. In both cases, the initial P/E is 15 and the retention rate is 65 percent. In turn, this combination establishes the dividend yield to be 2.33 (which is $[1-0.65/15]$) and an equivalent price growth of 9.67 percent (that is, $12-2.33$). In Figure 7.3, with a 12 percent return on investment, the g_P of 9.67 percent is associated with a g_E of 7.80 percent and a $g_{P/E}$ of 1.73 percent. In Figure 7.5, with a 15 percent return on investment, the same g_P of 9.67 percent is obtained with g_E equal to 9.67 percent and a zero $g_{P/E}$. In fact, a continuum of combinations of P/E growth and earnings growth exists that can lead to the same 9.67 percent price growth.

The explanation lies in the general P/E growth formula developed previously:

$$g_{P/E} = \frac{1+g_P}{1+g_E} - 1$$

$$= \frac{1.0967}{1+g_E} - 1.$$

Figure 7.6 presents a "value-preservation line" (VPL) that illustrates the many combinations of g_E and $g_{P/E}$ that theoretically could provide the required first year's g_P of 9.67 percent. Point A represents realized earnings growth with investment at 12 percent (corresponding to the example in Figure 7.3).[5] As the investment rate increases, so does the realized value of g_E. The "cost" of this growth is a reduction in $g_{P/E}$. Point B represents the 15 percent investment at which $g_{P/E}$ reduces to zero (as in the example in Figure 7.5).

To understand the utility of the VPL, suppose now that at year end, the firm invests $65 in retained earnings in a franchise project returning 20 percent in subsequent years. This return brings additional earnings in the second and following years, and the realized growth in earnings increases from 9.67 percent to 13 percent (20 percent of $65).

---

[5]At the end of the first year, the realized g_E and $g_{P/E}$ at Point A bring the firm to a new P/E multiple of 15.3 (that is, 1.0173×15). With a different P/E at the start of the second year, that year will also have a new VPL.

113

Figure 7.6. The Value-Preservation Line

(with initial P/E of 15 and *b* = 65 percent)

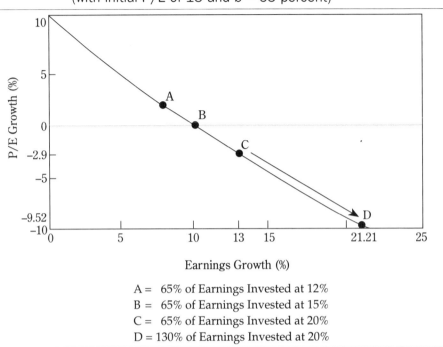

A = 65% of Earnings Invested at 12%
B = 65% of Earnings Invested at 15%
C = 65% of Earnings Invested at 20%
D = 130% of Earnings Invested at 20%

Figure 7.6 illustrates the movement down the VPL that this enhanced growth represents. Point C shows that the price/earnings ratio declines because $g_{P/E}$ falls to –2.9 percent:

$$g_{P/E} = \frac{1.0967}{1 + g_E} - 1$$

$$= \frac{1.0967}{1.13} - 1$$

$$= -2.9 \text{ percent}.$$

At the end of one year, the P/E will have decreased from 15 to 14.6 (= 15 – 2.9 percent of 15). The decline in P/E with increasing franchise investment follows naturally from the fact that more franchise value is being used up when higher yielding projects are undertaken.

The VPL is always determined by the forward P/E (the price at the beginning of the year divided by the year's anticipated earnings) and the retention rate (or dividend payout rate) that applies to those earnings. Investment (and financing) decisions taken at year end will determine the earnings for the subsequent year and will set the forward P/E that applies at the beginning of the subsequent year. Thereafter, the next year's VPL will be determined by the new price/earnings ratio and the new retention rate.

Accelerated Growth through External Funding

When a firm issues new shares, it receives cash in return for a proportional claim on the existing tangible and franchise value. If the new cash is used in investments that return more than 12 percent, some conversion of FV into earnings (that is, into TV) will occur. This conversion alters the distribution of FV and TV, which lowers the P/E. The outcome of these alterations, combined with the "dilution" of the original earnings, is a complex transformation of the firm's ownership and value structure. Fitting such external financing into the VPL framework is at first puzzling, but the surprising finding is that equity sales simply push the accelerated earnings growth farther down the same value-preservation line.

Suppose the firm can invest $130 (that is, $65 in addition to the $65 in retained earnings) at 20 percent. With only $65 in retained earnings, the firm must issue new shares to raise the additional $65. A straightforward computation shows that, when the additional $65 is invested at 20 percent, growth in earnings per share accelerates to 21.2 percent.[6]

Point D in Figure 7.6 illustrates this new growth level. At this point, the FV is being taken down more quickly than the natural 12 percent rate at which it grows. The result is a 9.5 percent decline from the original P/E of 15 to a P/E of 13.6.

Growth Signals

The value-preservation line is useful for distinguishing value-generating growth from value-depleting growth. Recall that the line itself represents an expected level of price appreciation based on an estimated market capitalization rate of 12 percent, an earnings retention rate of 65 percent, and an initial theoretical P/E of 15. Each point on the line (such as A, B, C, and D in the

---

[6]Issuing new shares dilutes the growth in earnings per share relative to what it would have been if no new shares had been issued. If no external financing were needed, earnings would grow at 26 percent (that is, 0.20×130 percent). The 21.2 percent represents a 4.8 percent drop-off—compared with the hypothetical 26 percent—that is attributable to dilution in both earnings and franchise value. For more details, see Appendix E.

previous examples) represents a combination of realized earnings and growth in price/earnings that is consistent with the required price growth (9.67 percent in the example).[7] No matter what the firm does—invests at 12 percent, 15 percent, or 20 percent; sells shares; buys back shares—the realized g_E and $g_{P/E}$ will counterbalance in such a way that the price grows at 9.67 percent.[8] In this sense, all actions that leave the firm on the VPL can be viewed as merely value preserving; such actions only exploit the legacy of franchise opportunities that the marketplace has already anticipated. To bring about true *value enhancement*, management must create improvements in the firm's prospects that go beyond the embedded expectations.

This observation leads to the realization that the value-preservation line and the zero-P/E-growth line can be viewed as separating all possible pairings of year-to-year earnings growth and P/E growth into the four regions depicted in Figure 7.7:

- Region I lies above the VPL and above the zero-P/E-growth line. The properties of this region are consistent with intuition regarding the positive nature of growth. Each point represents both unexpected value-enhancing earnings growth and P/E growth.
- In Region II also, earnings and P/E growth are positive, but the P/E growth is insufficient to ensure that investors will receive a market-level return. Consequently, an unexpected value depletion occurs.
- In Region III, the P/E is declining and earnings growth is not sufficient to maintain value.
- Region IV shows that value enhancement can accompany a declining P/E. In this region, strong earnings growth places the firm above the VPL.

To investigate these regions, consider two examples:

■ *Point B_1.* Suppose a firm's realized earnings growth is 15 percent but its $g_{P/E}$ is –1 percent. With a realized g_E of 15 percent, the P/E should decline by about 5 percent to remain on the VPL. The firm's more modest P/E decline indicates that the firm has discovered unanticipated opportunities for future investment that will serve to replenish FV. Such new findings will result in a

---

[7]The single-period model used for this chapter can be extended dynamically by repeatedly applying the model to year-end values.

[8]In these examples, only actions that retain the risk pattern of the firm are being considered. If the firm changes its risk class dramatically—for example, through disproportionate debt financing—the appropriate discount rate (k) will change and the firm will migrate to a new VPL. As long as all the firm's initiatives for the year—funding, acquisitions, distributions, or investments—take place at the implicit 12 percent discount rate, the firm will remain on the same VPL during the one-year period.

Figure 7.7 The VPL as a Baseline for Interpreting Growth Signals

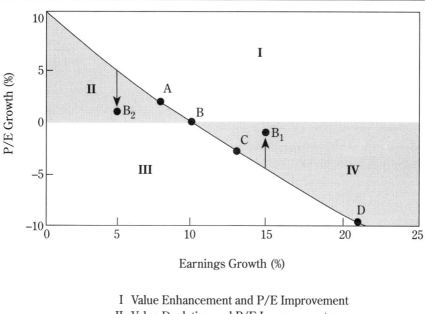

I   Value Enhancement and P/E Improvement
II Value Depletion and P/E Improvement
III Value Depletion and P/E Decline
IV Value Enhancement and P/E Decline

price growth in excess of 9.67 percent, that is, a windfall profit to current shareholders. (After the share price has adjusted to the new level of expectations, the P/E will change and a new VPL will result for the subsequent year.)

■ *Point B_2*. Suppose that the realized g_E for a firm is 5 percent and the $g_{P/E}$ is 1 percent. For the firm to be on the VPL, the (low) 5 percent earnings growth should be coupled with a P/E growth in excess of 4 percent. The observed P/E growth of only 1 percent may indicate an unexpected loss in FV. It could have come about by, for example, failing to take advantage of available, but perishable, opportunities, in which case, the firm may have lost the opportunities forever. Alternatively, the firm may be using cash flows from "good" businesses to subsidize the growth of marginal businesses. Such "covert reinvestment" can lead to earnings growth, but at a cost in terms of overall firm value. In either case, g_P will fall below 9.67 percent. Consequently, investors will fail to achieve the full 12 percent market return, even when dividends are considered.

As the preceding examples demonstrate, even positive levels of growth in both earnings and P/E do not always assure the price appreciation required for a fair return. Interpreting the significance of earnings growth is difficult in the absence of a base level of P/E growth.

In practice, the problem is, of course, considerably more complicated than in the examples. Year-to-year earnings growth may be visible in an accounting sense, but discovering true economic earnings growth is challenging. In a market of constantly changing interest rates and risk premiums, absolute and relative price/earnings ratios will also always be on the move. In this environment, it is not easy to determine how much of a realized P/E change is the result of new market conditions rather than changes in the firm's underlying franchise value. Without an analytical framework for identifying the baseline correspondence between earnings growth and P/E changes, one cannot even begin to follow meaningfully the path of a firm's P/E over time.

Summary

Equity analysts and investors must look to a variety of measures to gain insight into the prospects for current and future businesses. Intuitively, the temptation is to view firms with especially high earnings growth as offering special value. This intuition is supported by the standard DDM, which appears to equate price growth with earnings growth. Prospective growth must, however, be differentiated from realized growth.

Firms can show substantial earnings growth without creating a single dollar of extra value for shareholders. One path to this result is to increase earnings retention and reinvest at the market rate. To assess the significance of realized earnings growth properly, one must first consider the associated baseline level of P/E growth (or decline) that is consistent with the firm's initial prospects and valuation. Then, one must probe the limits of the firm's franchise to determine the source of any extraordinary realized earnings. The key is to ascertain whether such excess growth is a positive new signal or simply a drawdown of the franchise value that was already implicitly incorporated in the firm's price/earnings ratio.

These findings demonstrate that a corporate manager should not view high earnings growth as compelling evidence of a total job well done. High earnings derived from an embedded franchise may only indicate good performance in exploiting preexisting opportunities. Such growth is value preserving (and, accordingly, may represent a significant managerial achievement), but strictly speaking, it is not value enhancing. To add incremental value, managers must have the vision (and/or the good fortune) to extend the corporate reach to opportunities beyond those already embedded in the firm's valuation.

8. The Effects of Inflation

Even in today's low-inflation environment, pension fund sponsors, managers of endowment funds, and other long-term investors are under continual pressure to achieve positive real returns while avoiding excessive exposure to risk. Investors are compelled to take on some risk, however, because real returns on risk-free Treasury bills, which at all times tend to be small, are often negative. In fact, during the past 65 years, inflation has averaged about 3.2 percent annually, and real riskless annual returns on Treasury bills have been negative almost as often as they have been positive.[1] Inflation-adjusted intermediate- and long-term government bond returns have averaged about 2.0 percent, while inflation-adjusted returns on stocks have averaged 8.8 percent. The cost of these substantial real returns on equity, however, has been volatility on the order of 21 percent a year.

Because all companies do not perform equally well in the face of persistent inflation, investors must try to separate inflation effects from real growth. This task is not easy, however, because some inflation effects are almost always embedded in a firm's earnings statements and financial ratios. This chapter discusses how the franchise factor model can be used to ferret out the effects of expected inflation on the price/earnings ratios of unleveraged firms.

In general, companies that can increase earnings to keep pace with inflation tend to be more valuable than comparable firms without this flow-through capacity.[2] The underlying assumption is that the degree of flow-through capacity is known. At one extreme, a company actually may benefit from inflation if it can raise prices arbitrarily as costs increase. At the other extreme, companies that lack pricing flexibility may find that profits erode steadily as inflation persists. (The chapter does not consider the more realistic but complicated case of unexpected inflation changes.)

---

[1]See Ibbotson Associates (1991).

[2]For a discussion of the effects of inflation on equity returns, see Buffet (1977). A theoretical analysis of the effects of inflation on corporate value is provided in Modigliani and Cohn (1979). A recent empirical study shows that high-flow-through industries tend to have higher share prices than low-flow-through ones (see Asikoglu and Ercan 1992).

Earnings and Inflation

To begin the analysis of the impact of inflation on a firm's earnings and P/E, consider three firms that have the same $100 million book values but the following different earnings patterns (depicted in Figure 8.1):[3]

- Firm A has stable earnings of $15.00 million a year from existing businesses.
- Firm B has stable earnings of $9.62 million a year.
- Firm C has earnings growing with inflation, starting from a base of $9.62 million.

Assume a constant inflation rate (I) of 4 percent and a uniform discount rate, which is the equity capitalization rate of 12 percent (k). The current focus is each firm's existing business, not the earnings impact of new investment.

Figure 8.1. Time Path of Earnings for Firms A, B, and C
(dollars in millions)

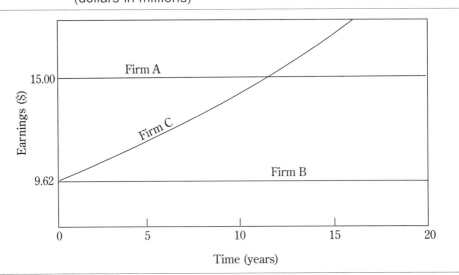

Firm A's current business is clearly more valuable than that of Firm B, because the former's earnings are 56 percent higher. We can compute the present value (PV) of the perpetual earnings streams of Firms A and B by dividing annual earnings by the discount rate. Thus, the PV of Firm A is $125.0

---

[3]At this point, "earnings" are *economic* earnings—the firm's real cash flow that could be paid to shareholders (see Bodie, Kane, and Marcus 1989). In Chapter 10, a distinction is made between economic and accounting earnings.

120

million and the PV of Firm B is $80.1 million.

Because Firm C's earnings are growing with inflation, its earnings will be $10.00 million ($1.04 \times$ $9.62 million) after one year and $10.40 million ($1.04 \times$ $10.00 million) after two years. After slightly more than 11 years, Firm C's earnings actually will exceed the unchanging $15.00 million Firm A earns. Firm C is a *full-flow-through* firm, because its earnings fully reflect year-to-year inflation increases.[4]

Comparing Firms C and B shows clearly that PV_C is greater than PV_B, because the earnings of both firms start at $9.62 million, but Firm C's earnings grow and Firm B's do not. The contrast between Firms C and A is less obvious. The computation of PV_C uses the following formula for the discounted present value of an earnings stream that grows at annual rate I:

$$PV_C = \text{(Initial earnings)} \left(\frac{1+I}{k-I} \right).$$

With I = 4 percent and k = 12 percent, this formula shows that PV_C is $125 million, the same as PV_A.

Because the $45.9 million difference between PV_B and PV_C is entirely attributable to Firm C's flow-through capacity, this 56 percent increase can be considered to be the value of full flow-through. By the same token, when I is 4 percent, the constant earnings of Firm A can be viewed as "inflation equivalent" to Firm C's growing earnings. This equivalence concept is developed more fully in a later section.

The P/E attributable to earnings from the current businesses of the three firms is computed by dividing the price (or present value) by the base earnings. As in earlier chapters, this portion of the firm's price/earnings ratio is the base P/E, which is 8.33 for Firms A and B, and 13 for Firm C.

Note that Firms A and B have the same base P/E, despite the difference in the level of these firms' earnings. The reason, as demonstrated in earlier chapters, is that the share price for any firm with constant earnings adjusts upward in direct proportion to the level of earnings. Because Firms A and B have level earnings, their only sources of growth are new investments, the basic fuel of high P/Es. In contrast, Firm C's current earnings do not reflect the full value of even its current business. Firm C has the valuable ability to "grow" its earnings with inflation, and this special growth capacity brings the base P/E up from 8.33 to 13.

---

[4]For a discussion of the effects of flow-through on investment values, see Leibowitz, Sorenson, Arnott, and Hanson (1987) and Estep and Hanson (1980).

Inflation-Equivalent Returns

Because the earnings generated by Firms A and C have the same present value under a 4 percent inflation rate, those earnings can be termed inflation equivalent according to the following definition:

■   *Inflation-equivalent earnings (E^*)*. If a firm's earnings grow at a rate that is proportional to the anticipated inflation rate, some stream of level earnings (E^*) will have the same present value as the growing stream.

The same type of definition can be applied to a firm's return on equity. Because Firms A, B, and C all have a $100 million book value, the initial value of their earnings immediately translates into a percentage return. Thus, Firm A's 15 percent ROE can be viewed as inflation equivalent to the combination of Firm C's initial 9.62 percent return and the growth of its earnings at a 4 percent annual rate. This example suggests the following definition:

■   *Inflation-equivalent ROE (r^*)*. If a firm's earnings grow with inflation, the ROE associated with the inflation-equivalent level earnings (E^*) can be regarded as a standardized inflation-equivalent ROE (r^*) for the growing earnings stream.

Therefore, although Firm C has an initial ROE of 9.62 percent, its earnings growth pattern leads to an inflation-equivalent ROE equal to Firm A's 15 percent.

As a second example of inflation equivalence, consider Firm D, which has the same book value and inflation flow-through capacity as Firm C but initial earnings that start from a base level of $10.58 million (that is, 10 percent higher than C's $9.62 million). Applying the formula used to compute PV_C shows that PV_D is $137.5 million.

The inflation-equivalent firm (Firm D^*) is found by requiring that D^* have constant earnings (E_D^*) and that PV_D be $137.5 million. The inflation-equivalent earnings are calculated by setting the present value of the constant earnings (E_D^*/k) equal to PV_D and multiplying by the nominal rate (k). That is,

$$E_D^* = kPV_D$$

$$= k \times \$137,500,000.$$

With $k = 12$ percent,

$$E_D^* = 0.12 \times \$137,500,000$$

$$= \$16,500,000$$

and

$$r_D^* = \frac{\$16,500,000}{\$100,000,000}$$

$$= 16.50 \text{ percent.}$$

Note that in this particular example, the computations could have been avoided by observing that r_D^* should be 10 percent higher than Firm A's 15 percent ROE. For comparative purposes, Figure 8.2 adds the time path of earnings for Firms D and D* to the other firms' earnings graphs in Figure 8.1.

Consider now the base P/Es of Firms D and D*. When their common present values of $137.5 million are divided by their respective initial earnings, the P/Es are 13 for D and 8.33 for D*. Thus, the base P/E rises to 13 for Firms C and D, each of which has earnings that grow at the inflation rate. As these examples indicate, all full-flow-through firms will have the same base P/E.

The computation of the base P/E for Firms C and D discounted their growing streams of *nominal* earnings at the *nominal* discount rates, and that present value was then divided by the starting earnings. It can also be shown that another approach to finding the base P/E for all full-flow-through firms is to take the reciprocal of the real rate of return on equity capital.[5] An intuitive explanation of this result is that, because the inflation rate is incorporated into the 12 percent discount rate, any inflation-related increase in the value of earnings (as reflected in the P/E numerator) should be offset precisely by the inflation component of the 12 percent discount rate (reflected in the denominator). This offset reduces the effective discount rate to the real rate. For Firms C and D, the real rate of 7.69 percent results in a base P/E of 13 (that is, $1/0.0769$). In contrast, because Firm D* is a constant-earnings firm, it should have the same 8.33 base P/E as constant-earnings Firms A and B.

The Inflation Adjustment Factor for Full-Flow-Through Firms

This section introduces an inflation adjustment factor (γ) that can be used to determine the inflation-equivalent ROE (r^*) from the initial ROE (r) of a firm whose earnings grow at the inflation rate. The formula for the inflation

---

[5]With a 4 percent inflation rate and a 12 percent nominal rate, the real rate (k_r) is computed from $(1 + k_r)(1.04) = 1.12$. Thus, $k_r = (1.12/1.04) - 1.00 = 7.69$ percent.

Figure 8.2. Time Paths of Earnings for the Five Firms

(dollars in millions)

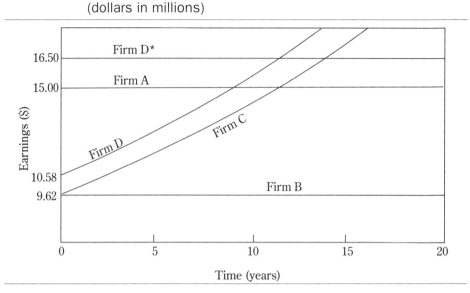

adjustment factor can be shown to be[6]

$$\gamma = \frac{k(1+I)}{(k-I)}.$$

When this formula is applied to Firms D and D* with I = 4 percent and k = 12 percent, γ equals 1.56. With this value of γ and r_D at 10.58 percent, r_D^* is computed as follows:

$$r_D^* = \gamma r_D$$

$$= 1.56 \times 10.58 \text{ percent}$$

$$= 16.50 \text{ percent.}$$

This value is the same as in the earlier computations. This result means that

---

[6]In the earlier example, for a firm with initial earnings that grow with inflation (E_D), the level-earnings equivalent is $E_D^* = k \times PV_D = kE_D(1+I) / (k-I)$. Assuming that both the original firm and its inflation equivalent have book value B, the inflation-equivalent $ROE(r_D^*)$ is defined to be E_D^*/B. That is, $r_D^* = E_D^*/B = [k(1+I)/(k-I)](E_D/B)$. Because the second expression is r_D, γ is defined to be $[k(1+I)/(k-I)]$.

an initial ROE of 10.58 percent and earnings that grow fully with inflation are equivalent (in present-value terms) to a standardized level ROE of 16.50 percent. Such is the power of inflation flow-through.

The relationship between r^* and r can be plotted in general as a straight line emanating from the origin and having slope γ (see Figure 8.3). Note that although this section deals only with firms without debt, leverage will significantly enhance the positive benefits of inflation flow-through.

Figure 8.3. Inflation-Equivalent ROE versus Initial ROE with Full Inflation Flow-Through
(inflation rate = 4 percent)

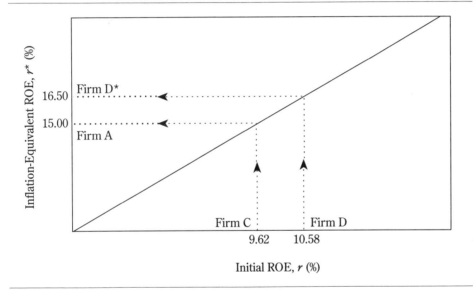

The P/E Effect of Partial Inflation Flow-Through

To this point, only two extremes of inflation flow-through have been considered—zero and 100 percent.[7] This section develops the inflation-equivalence concept by studying the effects of partial inflation flow-through. Consider Firm F, which has the same $100 million initial book value as the other example firms but a 50 percent inflation flow-through. Firm F's earnings start from the

---

[7]In actuality, both of these "extremes" can be exceeded. If expenses rise more rapidly than revenues, net earnings will decrease with inflation, resulting in negative flow-through. Similarly, if costs can be contained, a flow-through of greater than 100 percent may be possible. In fact, one can argue that, in order for equity to act as a counterbalance against inflation, it *must* achieve a flow-through rate exceeding 100 percent.

same $9.62 million base as those of Firms C and D, and with a 4 percent inflation rate, its earnings grow at a 2 percent annual rate (50 percent of 4 percent, see Figure 8.4).

Figure 8.4. Time Paths of Earnings: Firm F with 50 Percent Inflation Flow-Through Compared with Firms A, B, and C

(dollars in millions)

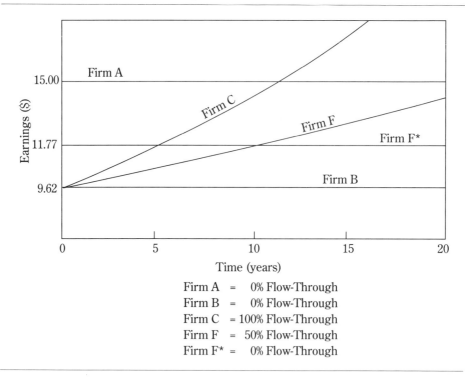

Firm A = 0% Flow-Through
Firm B = 0% Flow-Through
Firm C = 100% Flow-Through
Firm F = 50% Flow-Through
Firm F* = 0% Flow-Through

Because Firm F's earnings grow at a slower rate than Firm C's earnings, Firm F's inflation-equivalent ROE would be expected to fall somewhere below 15 percent. The inflation adjustment factor (γ) can be used to adjust for partial flow-through if I is replaced by λI. Thus,

$$\gamma = \frac{k(1 + \lambda I)}{k - \lambda I},$$

where λ is the inflation-flow-through rate and I is the inflation rate. Applying this formula to Firm F's earnings reveals that, with a 50 percent flow-through rate, γ falls to 1.224 and r_F^* is 11.77 percent (note the inflation-equivalent Firm F^* in Figure 8.4):

$$E_F^* = \$9,620,000 \ \gamma$$

$$= \$9,620,000 \times 0.12 \times \left[\frac{1 + (0.50 \times 0.04)}{0.12 - (0.50 \times 0.04)} \right]$$

$$= \$9,620,000 \times 1.224$$

$$= \$11,774,880.$$

Figure 8.5 illustrates how γ varies with the flow-through rate. With zero flow-through, no inflation adjustment is necessary and $\gamma = 1$. As the flow-through rate increases, so does γ, with the most rapid rise occurring as full flow-through nears.

As indicated in Figure 8.3, γ can be interpreted as the slope of the line that represents the relationship between an initial ROE and its inflation equivalent. Thus, the greater the flow-through rate, the greater the value-multiplication effect. Figure 8.6 shows this effect with inflation-equivalence lines correspond-

Figure 8.5. Variation of Inflation Adjustment Factor with Flow-Through Rate
(inflation rate = 4 percent; nominal rate = 12 percent)

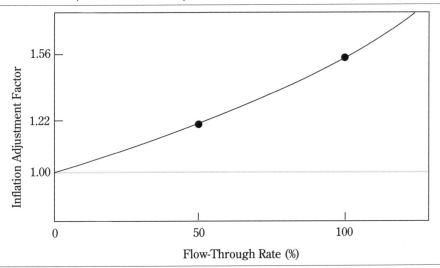

Figure 8.6. Inflation-Equivalent ROEs with Zero, 50 Percent, and 100 Percent Flow-Through Rates

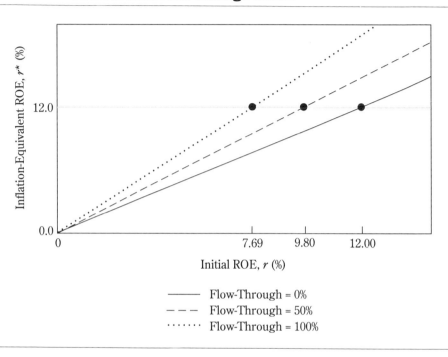

ing to zero, 50 percent, and 100 percent flow-through. Note that a return that appears to be below the assumed 12 percent nominal rate actually can represent an above-market ROE on an inflation-equivalent basis. For example, with full flow-through, a base ROE of only 7.69 percent is sufficient to provide a return equal to the 12 percent market rate. With 50 percent flow-through, that required base-level ROE rises to 9.80 percent.

The Base-P/E Inflation Adjustment. The inflation adjustment factor can be used to express the dependence of the base P/E on the inflation-flow-through rate. Because all level-earnings firms have a base P/E of $1/k$, the following relationship exists (see Figure 8.6):[8]

---

[8]If E° is the level-earnings equivalent of an earnings stream that starts at the value E and grows with inflation, then $E^\circ/E = \gamma$ and $P/E^\circ = 1/k$, so $P/E = (P/E^\circ)(E^\circ/E) = (\gamma)(P/E^\circ) = \gamma(1/k)$.

128

Base P/E (inflation-flow-through firm) = $\gamma\left(\dfrac{1}{k}\right)$.

For example, in the case of Firm F, γ was 1.224, so with k = 12 percent, the base P/E for Firm F is 10.2 (or, 1.224 × 8.33).

Figure 8.7 shows how the base P/Es of all the example firms are related to the inflation-flow-through rate. Because Firms A, B, D^*, and F^* are constant-earnings firms, they all have 8.33 as their base P/Es. As the flow-through rate increases, γ and the base P/E rise at an ever-increasing rate. At 100 percent flow-through, γ rises to 1.56 and the base P/E reaches 13.

Figure 8.7. Base P/E versus Inflation-Flow-Through Rate

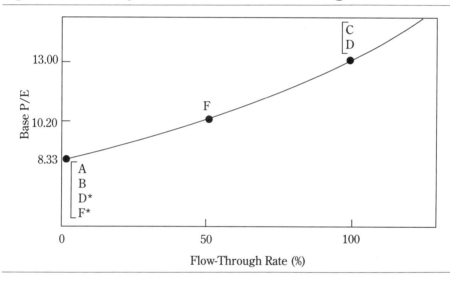

Inflation and the Earnings Horizon

The convenient and simplified concept of a perpetual earnings stream does not result in any loss of generality, because one can always find a perpetual stream with the same present value as a projected pattern of changing earnings. When exploring the effects of inflation flow-through, however, the required inflation adjustments have a definite sensitivity to the length of the earnings stream. Obviously, a 100 percent flow-through capacity will have a much more dramatic impact on the value of a 20-year constant earnings stream than it will on a 5-year stream.

Table 8.1 illustrates the magnitude of the inflation adjustment factor (γ) for

Table 8.1. Inflation Adjustment Factor for Different Earnings Horizons

(earnings horizon in years)

Flow-Through Rate	∞	20	15	10	5
0%	1.00	1.00	1.00	1.00	1.00
50	1.22	1.16	1.13	1.10	1.06
100	1.56	1.35	1.28	1.20	1.12
150	2.12	1.58	1.46	1.32	1.18

Note: Assumed inflation rate is 4 percent.

level earnings streams that persist for specified horizon periods.[9] For example, a 20-year earnings stream that starts from a base level of $10.00 million and grows at the inflation rate (100 percent flow-through) can be shown to have a present value of $100.50 million. This $100.50 million is also the present value of 20 years of level annual earnings of $13.45 million. The inflation adjustment factor of 1.345 is the ratio of the $13.45 million in constant earnings to the initial $10.00 million of the growing earnings stream. As might have been anticipated, this value of γ for the 20-year earnings horizon is lower than the 1.56 value for the perpetual stream. As the horizon period shortens, so does the adjustment factor. For example, with 100 percent flow-through and only five years of earnings, the adjustment factor drops to 1.12.

Because the base P/E for perpetual-earnings firms is $\gamma(1/k)$, the perpetual base P/E rises, as shown in Table 8.2, from 8.33 (that is, $1 \times [1/0.12]$) when the flow-through is zero to 17.67 when the flow-through is 150 percent (2.12 × 8.33). As the horizon period shortens, the present value of the earnings stream decreases (for any flow-through rate); consequently, the base P/E declines. With only a finite number of years of earnings, the effect of flow-

---

[9]When the earnings horizon is finite, $\gamma = [k(1 + \lambda I)/(k - \lambda I)] \times (1 - [(1 + \lambda I)/(1 + k)]^N)/(1 - [1/(1 + k)]^N)$. The first term in brackets is the adjustment factor when the earnings stream is a perpetuity. The second factor represents a finite time adjustment.

Table 8.2 Inflation-Adjusted Base P/E for Different Earnings Horizons

(earnings horizon in years)

Flow-Through Rate	∞	20	15	10	5
0%	8.33	7.47	6.81	5.65	3.60
50	10.20	8.63	7.69	6.20	3.81
100	13.00	10.05	8.72	6.80	4.03
150	17.67	11.79	9.93	7.48	4.25

through is muted. For example, Table 8.2 shows that, with a 20-year horizon, the base P/E ranges from only 7.47 to 11.79 for flow-through rates of zero to 150 percent. This relatively narrow range of base P/Es reflects the smaller adjustment factors that apply in the 20-year case.

New Investment and Inflation Flow-Through

To complete the characterization of the firm under the FF model, the value of the franchise P/E must now be added to the base P/E. Recall that the franchise P/E is derived from the firm's franchise value—the total net present value attributable to all prospective investments. The NPV is determined from the spread of each investment's return over the cost of capital and the magnitude of investments that can earn this positive spread.

For simplicity, assume that all new investments have a return (R) that has an inflation-equivalent perpetual return (R^*). If γ_{NEW} is the value of the inflation adjustment factor for new investments, then

$$R^* = \gamma_{NEW}R.$$

Using the market discount rate (k) defined as a level annual rate, the following expression can be written:

Return spread on new investment $= R^* - k$.

The total extent of new investment is measured by the growth equivalent (G)—the sum of the present values of future investments expressed as a percentage of the current book value (B_0). Assume that all forecast capital expenditures are measured in today's dollars. Finally, assume also that, at the time actual outlays occur, costs will have risen at the same rate as inflation.

Under these assumptions, the present value of new investments (that is, the value of G) will be unaffected by inflation. Consequently, all inflationary effects will be embedded in the return spread. Because the return spread is perpetual by assumption, the FV is computed as follows:[10]

---

[10] In the full-flow-through case, the ratio of the return spread to the nominal rate can also be expressed as the difference between a real return and a real discount rate, divided by the real rate. Applying the inflation adjustment factor to this "real spread ratio" results in the perpetual-equivalent nominal spread ratio ($[R^* - k]/k$).

$$FV = \frac{(R^* - k)GB_0}{k}$$

$$= \left(\frac{R^* - k}{k}\right)GB_0 .$$

The franchise P/E is found by dividing this expression for FV by the initial earnings (rB_0):

$$\text{Franchise P/E} = \frac{FV}{rB_0}$$

$$= \left(\frac{R^* - k}{rk}\right)G.$$

The first term on the right side ($[R^* - k]/rk$) is the franchise factor (FF*); it measures the P/E gain that results from each unit of prospective investment.[11] Using the terminology of the FF model,

$$\text{Franchise P/E} = \text{FF}^* \times G,$$

where

$$\text{FF}^* = \frac{R^* - k}{rk}$$

$$= \frac{\gamma_{NEW}R - k}{rk}.$$

This definition of FF* is the same as for the FF developed earlier in this monograph except that here the future return is R^*.

The General P/E Formula with a Steady Inflation Rate

The inflation adjustments made to the base-P/E and franchise-P/E formulas can now be combined to obtain the following general P/E formula:

---

[11]Recall that because G is measured relative to B_0, a one-unit change in G is equal to 100 percent of the firm's current book value.

$$P/E = \gamma_{CUR}\left(\frac{1}{k}\right) + (FF^* \times G),$$

where γ_{CUR} is the inflation adjustment factor for current business.

As a first example of a franchise firm, return to Firm C and assume that, in addition to maintaining its current business, it can invest in new businesses for which earnings grow with inflation. If the initial return on the new investment (R) is 12 percent and new investments have 100 percent flow-through, then

$$\gamma_{NEW} = \gamma_{CUR}$$

$$= 1.56$$

and

$$R^* = \gamma_{NEW}R$$

$$= 1.56 \times 12 \text{ percent}$$

$$= 18.72 \text{ percent}.$$

By using this value of R^* and an initial ROE of 9.62 percent, FF^*_C can be computed as follows:

$$FF^*_C = \frac{R^* - k}{rk}$$

$$= \frac{0.1872 - 0.12}{0.0962 \times 0.12}$$

$$= 5.82.$$

This result allows specification of the relationship between the P/E and the magnitude of new investment opportunities, as measured by G:

$$P/E_C = \gamma_{CUR}\left(\frac{1}{k}\right) + (FF_C^* \times G)$$

$$= 1.56 \times \left(\frac{1}{0.12}\right) + 5.82G$$

$$= 13.00 + 5.82G.$$

The graph of this relationship is a straight line emanating from the inflation-adjusted base P/E of 13. Figure 8.8 shows that a G value of only 86 percent is sufficient to bring the P/E to a level of 18.

The value of FF^* (and, consequently, the P/E) is highly sensitive to the extent of flow-through on new investments. To clarify the relationship between FF^* and the flow-through rates, consider two additional firms, C' and C'', which are identical to Firm C in all respects except that their flow-through rates for new investments are 50 percent and zero, respectively. The values of γ_{NEW}, R^*, and FF^* for Firms C' and C'' are shown in Table 8.3. Note that FF^* (for Firm C') is zero, because $R^* = k = 12$ percent. Without inflation flow-through, future investments with a 12 percent base return do not provide incremental P/E value.

Figure 8.9 generalizes the preceding results by showing how the value of R affects FF^* for each of the three flow-through rates. Because Firm C'' does not

Figure 8.8. P/E versus Growth Equivalent for Firm C

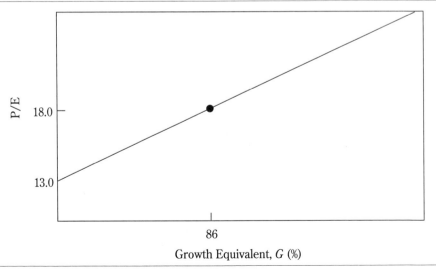

Table 8.3. Summary of Current and Future Returns for Firms C, C′, and C″

Firm	Initial ROE (r)	Inflation-Equivalent ROE (r^*)	Base Return on New Investment (R)	Inflation Flow-Through Rate on New Investment (λ_{NEW})	Inflation Adjustment Factor (γ_{NEW})	Inflation-Equivalent Return (R^*)	FF^*
C	9.62%	15.00%	12.00%	100.00%	1.56	18.72%	5.82
C′	9.62	15.00	12.00	50.00	1.22	14.69	2.32
C″	9.62	15.00	12.00	0.00	1.00	12.00	0.00

have any flow-through capacity, it must achieve an R greater than the 12 percent market rate to ensure a positive FF. Firm C, however, can achieve an R^* of 12 percent with an R of only 7.69 percent, because it provides 100 percent inflation flow-through ($\gamma \times 7.69$ percent = 1.56×7.69 percent = 12.00 percent).

Figure 8.9. Franchise Factor versus Initial Return on New Investment for Firms with Different Degrees of Inflation Flow-Through

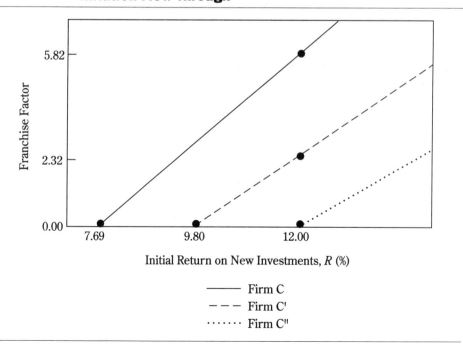

For firms with inflation flow-through, a below-market initial return on new investments can still lead to a positive franchise value. The increasing steepness of the FF* lines with higher flow-through rates reflects the growing inflation-adjusted spread on new investments. The higher the value of the FF*, the less investment is required to raise the P/E by one unit. Thus, firms with inflation flow-through for both current and future businesses have higher base P/Es and an enhanced responsiveness to new investment.

Figure 8.10 plots P/E against the growth equivalent for Firms C, C', and C''. Observe that all the P/E lines emanate from the same inflation-adjusted base P/E of 13 (that is, 1.56 × 8.33) but the lines have different slopes reflecting the different values of FF*. For C'', the P/E line is horizontal because, without inflation flow-through, new investments with a 12 percent return cannot raise the P/E above the base level of 13. In contrast, Firm C' can achieve a P/E of 18 by making new investments with a *G* value of 216 percent. Finally, as already noted, Firm C with 100 percent flow-through achieves a P/E multiple of 18 with a far smaller growth equivalent (86 percent) than Firm C'.

In general, the inflation-flow-through character of a firm's current business is assumed to be a given. In contrast, the selection of future investment

Figure 8.10. P/E versus Growth Equivalent for Firms C, C', and C''

Growth Equivalent, *G* (%)

——— Firm C
– – – Firm C'
······· Firm C''

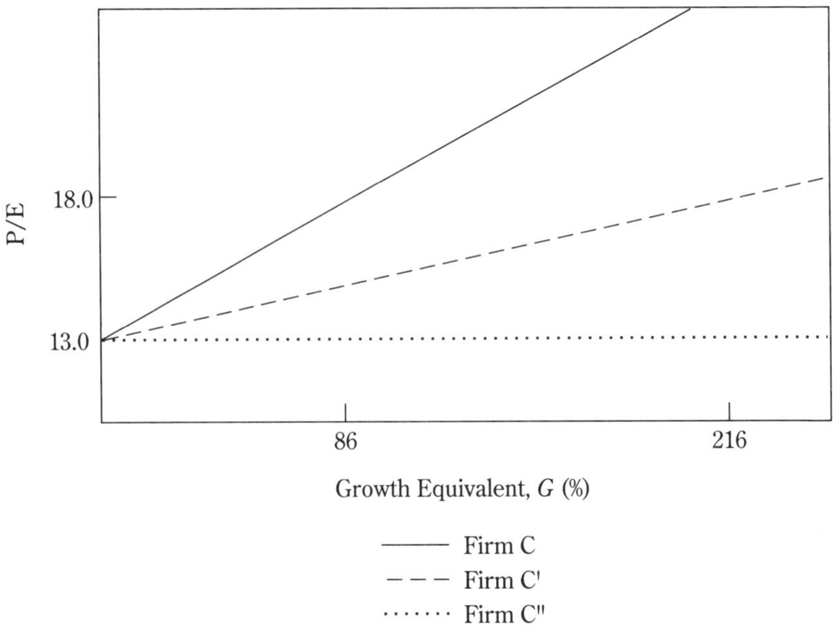

opportunities may be strongly influenced by the potential of new businesses to generate earnings that grow with inflation.[12]

Summary

The franchise factor model allows separation of a firm's price/earnings ratio into two components: a base P/E that is attributable to a firm's current businesses and a franchise P/E that is derived from the firm's future investment opportunities. Earlier chapters demonstrated how the FF model can be modified to incorporate tax and leverage effects; this chapter added inflation adjustments that must be applied to the simplified theoretical P/E when inflation is steady and predictable. The inflation adjustment factor can be used to modify both ROEs and the base P/E in accordance with a firm's inflation–flow-through capacity. With these modifications, the theoretical P/E model shows that, even in a low-inflation environment, a firm's ability to increase earnings with inflation is valuable, because it materially enhances both the base P/E and the franchise P/E.

---

[12]Although the analysis in this chapter assumes that the economic and accounting values of earnings, book value, and returns coincide, this assumption is rarely valid in practice. For example, manufacturing firms that use depreciated book-value accounting may understate their earnings under certain circumstances. The FF model given in Chapter 10 adjusts for accounting differences. That theoretical model can be used to restate the inflation-flow-through model as follows: $P_T/E_A = q_E \gamma(1/k) + q_r \mathrm{FF}_T^* G_A$, where $\mathrm{FF}_T^* = (R_T^* - k)/r_0 k$, r_0 is the ratio of initial economic earnings to initial economic book value, q_E is the ratio of economic earnings to accounting earnings, and q_r is the ratio of the economic return to the accounting return.

9. Resolving the Equity Duration Paradox

Estimates of equity duration are particularly important when investment managers or pension plan sponsors allocate assets and seek to control the overall interest rate risk of their portfolios.[1] When the theoretical stock price is based on a standard dividend discount model, the result is a duration of 20–50 years, with the longer duration being associated with high-growth firms. Such long DDM durations are, however, grossly inconsistent with the observed market behavior of equities.[2] Empirical studies show that equities generally have low durations—on the order of 2–6 years (see Figure 9.1). Thus arises the "equity duration paradox." The analysis in this chapter shows how the separation of value into a tangible and a franchise component can help resolve this paradox.

The chapter begins by demonstrating that the DDM price can be decomposed into an implicit tangible value and franchise value. Because the standard DDM is based on perpetual growth at a constant rate, the implicit FV reflects the value of a continuing stream of investments from retained earnings. In this context, the FV, similar to a deep-discount bond, tends to have a very long duration. In addition, the magnitude and duration of the FV increase dramatically as the assumed perpetual growth rate rises. When combined with the more moderate duration of the DDM's implicit TV, the super-long FV duration leads to the high overall duration associated with the standard DDM. Moreover, higher growth rates result in even longer durations.

The inflation-adjusted form of the franchise factor model (the FF* model) is then used to explain the lower observed market duration of equity. This model shows that the TV and FV respond differently to changes in the expected

---

[1]For an early discussion of the relationship between inflation and changes in stock prices, see Williams (1938). For recent analyses, see Leibowitz (1986); Leibowitz, Bader, and Kogelman (1992); and Leibowitz, Sorensen, Arnott, and Hanson (1987). A detailed comparison of the total return on a stock and the total return on a bond is provided in Leibowitz (1978).

[2]For comparative purposes, note that the modified duration of coupon bonds rarely exceeds 10 years and that the effective duration of the Salomon Brothers Broad Investment-Grade Bond Index is approximately 5 years.

Figure 9.1. Equity Duration, January 1983 to February 1992

(using rolling 36-month correlations)

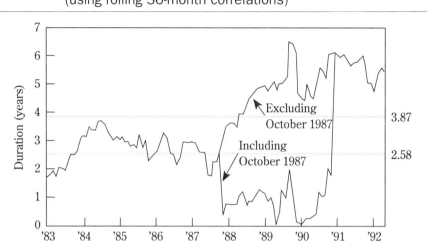

inflation rate. On the one hand, the firm's TV is based on an earnings stream that is relatively predictable, because these earnings are generated by existing businesses. This cash flow certainly gives the TV "bondlike" characteristics and results in a TV duration that is comparable to that of long-maturity bonds. On the other hand, because the FV is based on future investment, its very nature suggests that it should be relatively *insensitive* to future inflation effects. For discount rate changes driven by inflation, the general FF° model argues for a low FV duration—comparable to a short-duration floating-rate note—just the opposite of the long duration implied by the DDM. Thus, the inflation-adjusted FF° model naturally leads to low duration values that *are* consistent with the observed behavior of equity markets.

Decomposing the Dividend Discount Model

The DDM assumes that the theoretical value of a company's stock (P) can be obtained by summing the present values of all future dividend payments.[3] The standard DDM price formula is $P = d/(k - g)$ (see Table 9.1 for symbol definitions).

In the absence of growth (that is, with g equal to zero), the fixed annual earnings are paid out as dividends. Price P is simply the value of a perpetual annuity discounted at a nominal market rate (k). More generally, when g is

---

[3]For a review of the standard DDM, see Bodie, Kane, and Marcus (1989).

Table 9.1. DDM Assumptions
(dollars in millions)

Variable Name	Symbol or Formula	Example Value
Initial book value	B	$100
Return on book equity	r	16%
Initial earnings	$E = rB$	$16
Earnings retention ratio	b	0.50
Dividend payout ratio	$1 - b$	0.50
Initial dividend	$d = (1 - b)E$	$8
Dividend growth rate	$g = rb$	8%
Nominal discount rate	k	12%
Stock price	$P = d/(k - g)$	$200

greater than zero, the investor's return will be derived from a growing stream of dividends (d) and the associated appreciation in share price.[4]

For example, when k = 12 percent, g = 8 percent, and d = $8 million, the stock price is $200 million and the dividend yield is 4 percent. Thus, over a one-year period, the 12 percent return comprises a 4 percent dividend yield and an 8 percent growth rate.

To see the sensitivity of P to rate changes, assume that earnings and dividends do not change. Now, consider the effect of a decline of 1 basis point in the value of k, from 12 percent to 11.99 percent. Then,

$$P = \frac{\$8,000,000}{0.1199 - 0.0800}$$

$$= \$200,501,253.$$

The $0.50 million price change represents a 0.25 percent increase to the base price level of $200 million. This computation shows that the duration of the stock price (D_P, the ratio of the percentage change in price to the change in rates) is 25 (the 0.25 percent increase derived from the 0.01 percent rate

---

[4]The separation of dividend payments from price appreciation becomes clearer when the DDM price equation is solved for k: $k = (d/P) + g$. The first term on the right side of the equation is the dividend yield.

move).[5] This straightforward computation is the cornerstone for the belief that equity duration is very long, but that belief is not supported by the observed statistical duration of equity, which tends to be between 2 and 6 years.

Figure 9.2 plots the DDM price (left scale) and duration (right scale) for a wide range of nominal rates under the assumptions given in Table 9.1. The sensitivity of P to nominal rate changes is reflected in the steepness of the price curve. This steepness (sensitivity) increases at low rate levels and decreases at higher rate levels. Note that the duration curve follows a path similar to that of the price curve.

Figure 9.2. Price and Duration in the DDM
(dollars in millions)

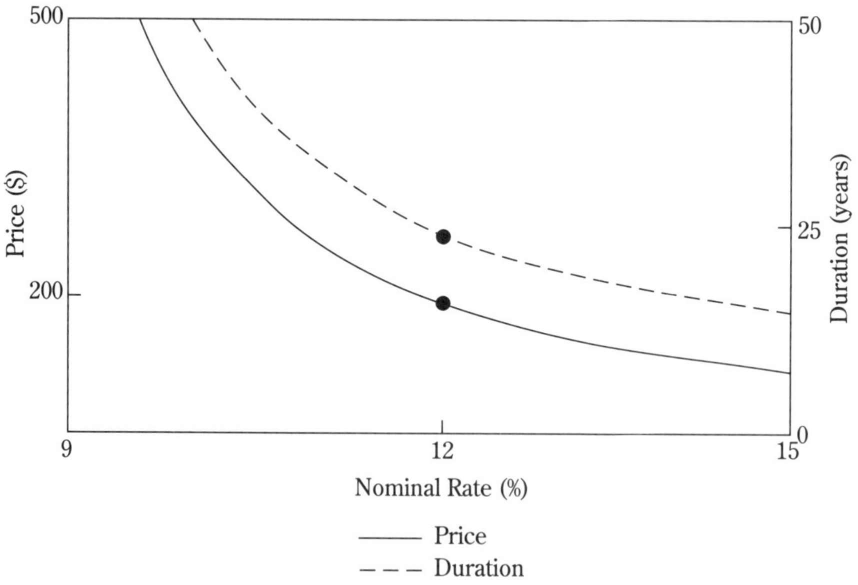

Nominal Rate (%)

——— Price
– – – Duration

The Standard DDM as a Special Case of the Franchise Factor Model

Because equity flows are by their nature uncertain, any attempt to analyze equity value via a strictly bondlike model will probably produce some unreal-

---

[5]The standard DDM duration can also be computed by taking the derivative of the price function. Specifically, DDM duration $= (-1/P)(dP/dk) = (1/P)[d/(k-g)^2] = 1/(k-g)$. When k = 12 percent and g = 8 percent, this formula leads to $1/(k-g) = 1/(0.12 - 0.08) = 1/0.04 = 25$.

istic results. In fact, a key finding of this study is that the disparity between the DDM duration and market results reflects primarily the implicit DDM assumption that earnings streams are completely fixed under all circumstances. The FF model can be used to reconcile the disparity between duration and market results by first recasting the standard DDM into FF-model terms.

Recall that the DDM implicitly assumes that new and current businesses provide the same return on equity. Next, consider the DDM constant-growth assumption as a special case for the time path of all new investments. As demonstrated in Appendix A, these assumptions lead to the growth-equivalent formula $(G = g/[k - g])$.

To verify that the FF model gives the same value of P as the DDM, the values from Table 9.1 are used in the formulas for TV and FV:

$$TV = \frac{E}{k}$$

$$= \frac{\$16,000,000}{0.12}$$

$$= \$133,333,333;$$

$$FV = FF \times G \times E$$

$$= \left(\frac{r - k}{rk}\right)\left(\frac{g}{k - g}\right)E$$

$$= \left(\frac{0.16 - 0.12}{0.16 \times 0.12}\right) \times \left(\frac{0.08}{0.12 - 0.08}\right) \times \$16,000,000$$

$$= 2.08 \times 2.00 \times \$16,000,000$$

$$= \$66,666,667;$$

and

$$P = TV + FV$$

$$= \$133,333,333 + \$66,666,667$$

$$= \$200,000,000.$$

The calculations show that TV accounts for 66.7 percent of the price when $k =$ 12 percent and the ratio of FV to TV is 0.50.

The relative proportion of tangible value to franchise value is extremely sensitive to the level of nominal rates (see Figure 9.3). For example, if k is 13 percent, TV falls only slightly, but FV drops by almost 50 percent, and the ratio of FV to TV falls to 0.30. Similarly, when k is 11 percent, FV rises by much more than TV in both absolute and relative terms. A further decline in k to 10 percent leads to a franchise value that is substantially greater than the tangible value. The extreme rate sensitivity of FV and the modest sensitivity of TV imply that FV duration (D_{FV}) is significantly greater than TV duration (D_{TV}).[6] (The reasons for these duration differences are the subject of the next section.)

Figure 9.3. Tangible Value and Franchise Value for the DDM under Changing Nominal Discount Rates
(dollars in millions)

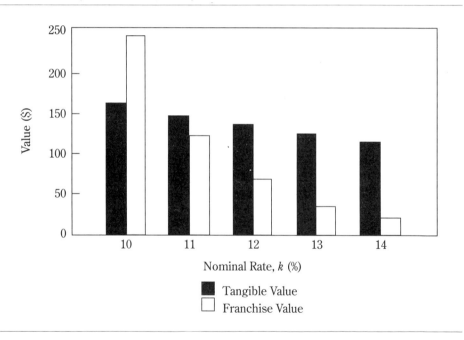

Next, the overall equity duration is calculated by taking the weighted average of the two durations, using as weights the relative proportions of

---

[6]For the DDM, the durations can be computed from the following formulas:
$D_{TV} = (-1/\text{TV})\,(d\text{TV}/dk) = 1/k$, and $D_{FV} = (-1/\text{FV})\,(d\text{FV}/dk) = r/[k(r-k)] + 1/(k-g)$.

144

tangible value and franchise value. When k is 12 percent, then D_{TV} is 8.33 and D_{FV} is 58.33; so

$$D_P = \ (66.67 \text{ percent of } 8.33) + (33.33 \text{ percent of } 58.33)$$

$$= 5.56 + 19.44$$

$$= 25.$$

Because this special case of the FF model is equivalent to the standard DDM, the duration is the same 25 years computed earlier for the DDM. The decomposition makes visible, however, that most of the rate sensitivity (19.44 years) reflects changes in the franchise value, even though the franchise value is only a third of the price. The tangible value contributes only 5.56 years to the stock price duration.

Figure 9.4 shows how the three durations vary with the nominal market rate.[7] As k rises, D_{FV} becomes increasingly extreme, but the proportion of franchise value declines rapidly. Consequently, at high nominal rates, D_{TV} becomes the primary determinant of D_P. At low nominal rates, D_{FV} is extremely high and FV/TV is very large, which results in ever-greater values of D_P.

Inflation and Tangible Value in the FF Model

Chapter 8 demonstrated how steady inflation affects the components of the general FF* model.[8] This section extends the inflation-adjustment approach to the case of *changes* in expected inflation. The analysis assumes that the flow-through characteristics of a business remain roughly comparable in an environment of either steady inflation or changing expected inflation.

The first step is to show how nominal rate movements driven by changes in expected inflation affect a firm's tangible value. The nominal rate comprises: (1) the real rate of return for riskless bonds, (2) a real risk premium that is characteristic of the equity market (or a particular subsector of that market), and (3) the expected inflation rate. The basic assumptions about these rates are as follows:

---

[7]The trough pattern in the FV duration is derived from that value becoming very large as g or r approaches k (see formula in preceding footnote).

[8]In addition, for a discussion of the effect of inflation flow-through on the value of real estate, see Leibowitz, Hartzell, Shulman, and Langetieg (1987).

Real riskless rate	=	4.19 percent
Equity risk premium	=	3.50 percent
Real equity return (k_r)	=	7.69 percent
Inflation rate (I)	=	4.00 percent
Nominal rate (k)	=	12.00 percent.

Note that the real equity return (k_r) is simply the sum of the riskless rate and the equity risk premium. The nominal rate (k) is derived from the compound effect of inflation and the real return; that is, $k = (1 + k_r)(1 + I) - 1$.

Figure 9.4. Tangible Value, Franchise Value, and DDM Duration versus Changes in Nominal Rates

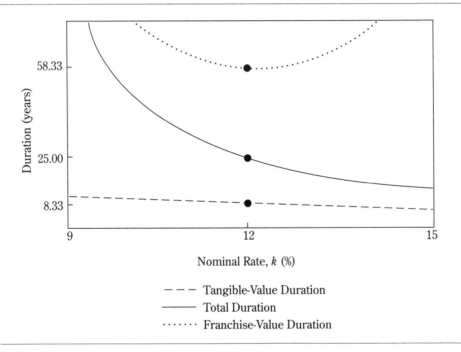

Figure 9.5 illustrates the relationship between the nominal rate and the expected inflation rate (with the real rate held constant) by an upwardly sloping line emanating from the point on the vertical axis that represents the real equity return. The slope of this line is $(1 + k_r)$, or 1.0769, because in this nominal rate model, any change in I is multiplied by $(1 + k_r)$. For example, a 100-basis-point increase in inflation, from 4 percent to 5 percent, raises the nominal rate by 107.69 basis points.

Figure 9.5. Nominal Interest Rate versus Inflation Rate

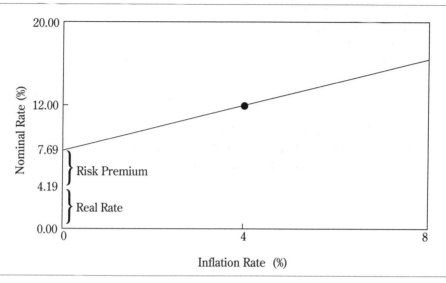

Three Earnings Time Paths. To trace how the tangible value is affected by changes in expected inflation, consider the following three time paths for earnings when the inflation rate is constant at 4 percent (see Figure 9.6):[9]

*   steady earnings of $16 million a year (*no inflation flow-through*),
*   initial earnings of $16 million that grow at the 4 percent inflation rate (*100 percent inflation flow-through*), and
*   initial earnings of $16 million that grow 2 percent a year (*50 percent inflation flow-through*).

■ *Zero inflation flow-through.* In the first example, the firm's earnings are represented by a level, perpetual payment stream unaffected by inflation. In this case, the tangible value is the present value of a perpetuity, which is found by dividing the steady earnings (E) by the nominal rate. As in the DDM example, if k = 12 percent (that is, I = 4 percent), tangible value is $133.33 million (that is, $16 million/0.12).

Because high inflation rates lead to high nominal rates but leave earnings unchanged, TV will decline as I increases (see Figure 9.7). At a 4 percent inflation rate, the TV duration has the same 8.33 value found in the DDM example.

■ *100 percent inflation flow-through.* With 100 percent flow-through, the

---

[9]In this and all other examples, the given flow-through rate is assumed to hold for all time periods.

Figure 9.6. Time Paths of Earnings with Three Inflation-Flow-Through Rates

(inflation rate = 4 percent; dollars in millions)

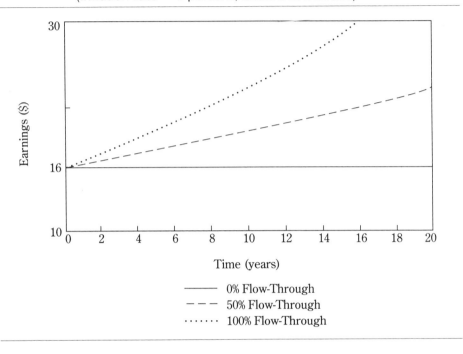

effects of inflation on earnings and the discount rate precisely counterbalance, so the tangible value is the same at all inflation rates and the TV duration is zero. To grasp this counterbalance, consider the contribution of 10th-year earnings to the tangible value. Because earnings grow at the inflation rate, when I = 4 percent,

$$10\text{th-year earnings} = \$16,000,000 \times (1.04)^{10}$$

$$= \$23,683,909.$$

When I is 4 percent, k is 12 percent and

$$\text{Present value of 10th-year earnings} = \frac{\$23,683,909}{(1.12)^{10}}$$

$$= \$7,625,585.$$

Figure 9.7. Tangible Value versus Inflation Rate with Different Degrees of Inflation Flow-Through
(dollars in millions)

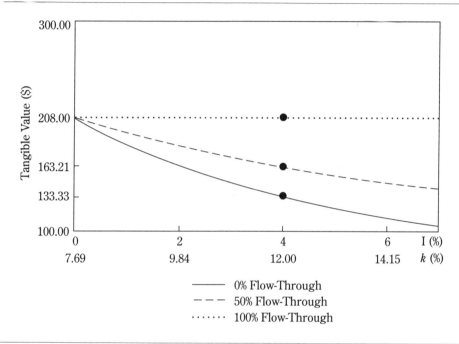

─────── 0% Flow-Through
─ ─ ─ 50% Flow-Through
········ 100% Flow-Through

Note: I is the inflation rate; *k* is the nominal rate.

Summing the present values of each year's earnings reveals that the tangible value is $208 million.

Now suppose that the expected inflation rate increases to 5 percent; each year's earnings rise, as does the corresponding discount rate:

$$\text{10th-year earnings} = \$16{,}000{,}000 \times (1.05)^{10}$$

$$= \$26{,}062{,}314.$$

To find the present value of the earnings, first compute the new nominal rate:

$$k = (1 + k_r)(1 + I) - 1$$

$$= (1.0769) \times (1.05) - 1$$

$$= 13.1 \text{ percent.}$$

With this value of k, 10th-year earnings turn out to have the same present value (PV) as they did when I was 4 percent:[10]

$$\text{PV of 10th-year earnings } = \frac{\$26,062,314}{(1.131)^{10}}$$

$$= \$7,625,585.$$

Because the present value of earnings in each year is the same whether the inflation rate is 4 percent or 5 percent, the tangible value must still be $208 million. Thus, for 100 percent flow-through, the tangible value is independent of the expected inflation rate. At zero inflation, earnings will be constant over time and the nominal and real rates will coincide. Then, the initial earnings (E_0) form a perpetuity that must be discounted at the 7.69 percent *real return* on equity in order to find the tangible value, which is $208 million (that is, $16 million/0.0769).[11]

This result implies that, as noted in the Chapter 8, for 100 percent flow-through, one can obtain the same TV value either by discounting the nominal earnings stream at the nominal rate *or* by discounting the initial earnings at the real rate.

■ *50 percent inflation flow-through.* In the intermediate case of 50 percent inflation flow-through, the tangible value declines with increasing inflation, but not as quickly as in the case of zero flow-through. Thus, the TV duration will be positive, but not as large as it is with zero flow-through. Note also that, when the inflation rate of zero drives the nominal discount rate down to where it coincides with the 7.69 percent real rate, the tangible value will be $208 million for all flow-through rates.

Tangible-Value Duration. Figure 9.8 illustrates that, for a reasonable range of nonzero inflation assumptions, D_{TV} can vary from zero to about ten years, depending on the rate of inflation flow-through. Thus, even on a purely analytical basis, the value of D_{TV} is constrained. One caveat is in order, however: In these examples, D_{TV} is computed under the equivalency assumption of either level annual earnings in perpetuity or earnings that grow steadily

---

[10]To obtain the correct PV, more decimal places are necessary than are displayed in the text.

[11]The reasoning behind discounting at the real return on equity is contained in the observation that, at time n, earnings will be $\$16,000,000 \times (1 + I)^n$ and the denominator (that is, the discount factor) will be $(1 + k)^n = (1 + k_r)^n (1 + I)^n$. In the ratio of these two quantities, the inflation factor "cancels out," leaving only the initial earnings and the real discount factor.

Figure 9.8. Tangible-Value Duration versus Inflation-Flow-Through Rate

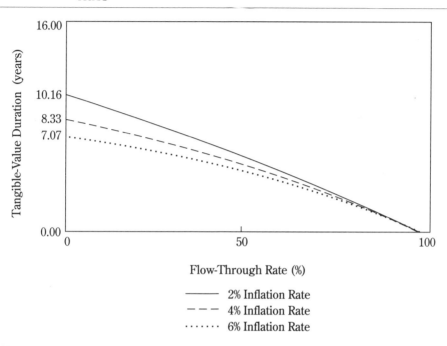

Flow-Through Rate (%)

——— 2% Inflation Rate
– – – 4% Inflation Rate
······· 6% Inflation Rate

with inflation. In actuality, the duration will be related to more complicated underlying physical flows. A later section considers general examples in which existing investments generate substantial earnings growth, but even with such an expansion of potential earnings patterns, D_{TV} is constrained in value, just as in the case of coupon bonds.

The inflation-flow-through examples show that, under general conditions, the value of D_{TV} remains consistent with observed levels of the statistical duration. Thus, D_{FV} must be the source of discrepancy between actual market behavior and the high theoretical durations of 25 to 50 years implied by the standard DDM.

Inflation and Franchise Value

Because the franchise value is computed from the franchise factor and the growth equivalent (*G*), the rate sensitivity of each of these factors is considered separately in this section. First, recall that *G* measures the total dollars that will be expended on new enterprises. These expenditures include investments that reflect the firm's current franchise, expansions into new businesses through acquisitions or direct investment, and all other future capital projects.

Inflation and the Growth Equivalent.   Calculation of G requires the rather heroic assumption that the time path of future investments can be foreseen correctly. All forecast future investments are measured in present-value terms. Furthermore, at the time capital expenditures are made, costs are assumed to have risen at the expected inflation rate.

These assumptions are equivalent to 100 percent inflation flow-through in the value of new investments. Thus, the effects of inflation should cancel out in computing G (as in the case of a TV with 100 percent flow-through). Consequently, if variations in the nominal rate are solely the result of changes in expected inflation, the duration of G should be zero. Thus, G is being treated as a floating-rate note that resets to par at fairly short time intervals.

Inflation and the Franchise Factor.   The effect of the assumptions about G is to load all of the rate sensitivity of franchise value into the franchise factor. If the assumption is maintained that all rate changes are solely the result of changes in expected inflation, the extent of the FF's rate sensitivity will be determined by the flow-through capacity of new businesses.

Recall from Chapter 8 that the relationship between inflation flow-through and the value of FF can be captured in an inflation adjustment factor (γ). In essence, γ converts an initial ROE into an equivalent level return (R^*) that reflects the extent to which earnings grow with inflation. Next, the "inflation-adjusted" R^* is used to calculate an inflation-adjusted franchise factor:

$$\mathrm{FF}^* = \frac{R^* - k}{rk},$$

where $R^* = \gamma R$. The inflation adjustment factor is

$$\gamma = \frac{k(1 + \lambda I)}{k - \lambda I},$$

where λ is the inflation-flow-through rate.

For comparing with the DDM example, assume that $R = r = 16$ percent. Figure 9.9 illustrates the resulting FF^* values for inflation-flow-through rates (λ) of zero, 50 percent, and 100 percent. The similarity between Figures 9.7 and 9.9 underscores the fact that the FF^*–inflation relationship is mathematically similar to the TV–inflation relationship. When new investments have 100 percent flow-through, the FF^* is insensitive to inflation, because the FF^*

Figure 9.9. The Franchise Factor versus the Inflation Rate

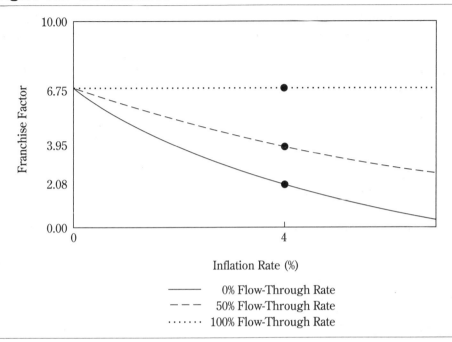

Inflation Rate (%)

—————— 0% Flow-Through Rate
– – – 50% Flow-Through Rate
········ 100% Flow-Through Rate

depends only on the level of real returns (assumed fixed). Hence, for 100 percent flow-through, the FF* duration (D_{FF}) is zero. With zero flow-through, $R^* = r$ and the spread between R^* and k (that is, $R^* - k = r - k$) narrows sharply as inflation increases. This narrowing spread results from the fact that inflation increases are immediately reflected in higher nominal rates without any counterbalancing increase in R^*. Thus, for $\lambda = 0$, FF* declines rapidly with increasing inflation. This rapid decline represents a high sensitivity to rate changes and a correspondingly high D_{FF} value.

Duration of the Franchise Value. Because G has been assumed insensitive to rate changes, the duration of the franchise value is determined solely by the duration of FF*; that is, $D_{FV} = D_{FF}$. This equality leads to an FV duration that depends solely on the flow-through level associated with FF*. Figure 9.10 shows how D_{FV} falls with increasing flow-through rates for FF*.

Because the franchise value deals with future investments, FV presumably reflects more closely than TV the choices that management is free to make at a later date. In general, management will not choose to make new investments having earnings that could be seriously eroded by inflation. Therefore, when

153

Figure 9.10. Franchise-Value Duration versus Flow-Through Rate
(inflation rate = 4 percent)

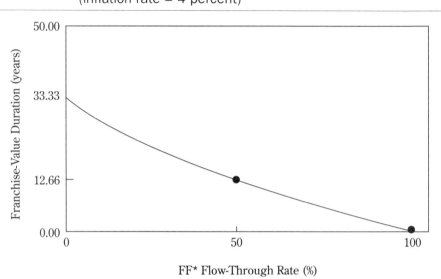

a firm is entering new businesses, inflation-flow-through capability is likely to be an important consideration and the FV based on these investments will have low sensitivity to inflation.[12]

The Spread Effect. The argument in favor of a low duration of franchise value can also be based on the nature of FF^*. On the surface, FF^* appears to be essentially a nominal net investment spread $(R^* - k)$ discounted at a nominal rate and then divided by the fixed value of r. In the full-flow-through case, it can be shown that

$$\frac{R^* - k}{k} = \frac{R - k_r}{k_r},$$

where R is the *initial* return on new investment.[13] The numerator $(R - k_r)$ may be viewed as a net investment spread (NIS) that has a fixed value in *real* terms.

---

[12]In certain cases, truly extraordinary near-term earnings might be sufficient to compensate for the lack of inflation flow-through in later years.

[13]If λ is 100 percent, then $\gamma = [k(1 + I)]/(k - I)$. Because $k = (1 + k_r)(1 + I) - 1$, it follows that $k - I = (1 + k_r)(1 + I) - 1 - I = (1 + I)k_r$. Consequently, $(1 + I)/(k - I) = 1/k_r$, γ is simply k/k_r, and $FF^* = \gamma(R - k_r)/rk = (k/k_r)(R - k_r)/rk = (R - k_r)/rk_r$.

The value of FF* then is proportional to this real NIS discounted by the real rate (k_r). This formulation of FF* is based completely on *fixed* initial return values (r and R) and the real rate (k_r). Hence, for $\lambda = 100$ percent, FF* must be insensitive to changes in expected inflation.

In summary, new investments with inflation flow-through of 100 percent may be viewed in two (mathematically equivalent) ways: (1) They can be seen as providing a real net investment spread that is fixed for all time and across all inflation rates, with the real rate then being the appropriate discounting mechanism, or (2) they can be seen as providing a sequence of net investment earnings that grow with inflation. This growing stream of nominal earnings can then be discounted at the nominal rate, with the result that inflation cancels out (as it did with the tangible value). From either viewpoint, the franchise factor will not be affected by inflation changes, and the FV duration will be zero.

A New Model of Equity Price Duration

This section combines the analysis of TV duration and FV duration to model the overall rate sensitivity, D_P, of a firm's stock. The value of D_P is simply the weighted average of D_{TV} and D_{FV}:

$$D_P = \left(\frac{TV}{P}\right)D_{TV} + \left(\frac{FV}{P}\right)D_{FV}.$$

As an application of this formula, consider the extreme case of a firm for which the tangible value has zero flow-through and the franchise value has 100 percent flow-through. In this case, FV is the same at all levels of expected inflation, but TV will decline as the inflation rate increases. To allow a comparison of the results of the FF* model with those of the DDM example, assume the same initial inputs: r is 16 percent, and the initial book value is $100 million. Thus,

$$E = rB_0$$

$$= \$16,000,000$$

and

$$TV = \frac{E}{k}$$

$$= \frac{\$16,000,000}{k}.$$

When $k = 12$ percent, therefore, TV is $133 million.

Now consider the franchise value. In the DDM example, the growth equivalent was 200 percent of the firm's initial book value (based on a 12 percent nominal rate) and the value of G was highly sensitive to the assumed discount rate. This sensitivity of G contributed greatly to D_{FV} in the DDM example. This chapter argues that the value of G, in sharp contrast to the DDM, should be insensitive to changes in expected inflation. Therefore, assume that the growth equivalent is 200 percent for all inflation rates.

To facilitate a comparison of the DDM and the FF° model, the chosen value of R must lead to the same value of FF° as in the DDM. The previous section showed that, with 100 percent flow-through on new investments, the calculation of FF° can be based on the real net investment spread $(R - k_r)$. If the initial new investment return (R) is 10.256 percent and k_r is 7.690 percent, the real net investment spread is 2.570 percent (10.256 percent – 7.690 percent). This real NIS corresponds to the nominal 4 percent spread used in the DDM example.[14]

Applying the real discount rate to this NIS leads to the same value of the franchise factor as in the DDM example:

$$FF° = \frac{R - k_r}{rk_r}$$

$$= \frac{0.0257}{0.1600 \times 0.0769}$$

$$= 2.08.$$

Thus, the values of FF°, G, and E are identical to those used in the DDM example, as is the resulting franchise value:

---

[14]Because the example assumes 100 percent flow-through, $\gamma = k/k_r = 12$ percent/7.69 percent $= 1.56$, and $R° = 1.56 \times 10.256$ percent $= 16$ percent. Thus, the inflation-adjusted NIS is 4 percent (16 percent – 12 percent). This spread is the same as that in the DDM example.

$$FV = FF^* \times G \times E$$

$$= 2.08 \times 2.00 \times \$16,000,000$$

$$= \$66,666,667.$$

Although these *initial* values for franchise value and tangible value are the same for both the DDM and the FF* model, as inflation expectations change, the values respond in vastly different ways in the two models. Recall that FV exhibited great sensitivity to rate changes in the DDM. In the FF* model, however, with its focus on a real NIS, franchise value is invariant under changing inflation levels. For TV, under the extreme assumption of zero flow-through, the nominal flows are fixed in the FF* model. Hence, tangible-value duration is identical in the two models; D_{TV} is 8.33 at k = 12 percent (see Figure 9.11).

Figure 9.11. Components of Price for a Firm with 100 Percent Flow-Through on New Investments and Zero Flow-Through on Existing Businesses: DDM versus FF* Model

(dollars in millions)

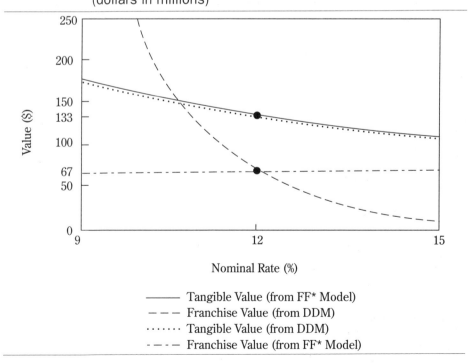

Equity Duration in the FF* Model.   The total price duration for the extreme example of the FF* model can now be determined. Because D_{FV} is zero, the firm derives its rate sensitivity solely from tangible value. The tangible value represents only 66.67 percent of the firm's value, however, so the overall equity duration is much lower than 8.33: $D_P = 0.6667 \times 8.33 = 5.56$.

This finding implies that, if the value of a firm's current business is modest compared with the estimated value of its future investment opportunities, its stock price should have a fairly low duration. In the language of the FF* model, when franchise value is large, the weight of D_{TV} will be small. In contrast, a firm with few investment opportunities and fairly predictable cash flows has a primary weighting on D_{TV}; hence, its equity price duration will be similar to the duration of a long bond.

Figure 9.12 shows how the equity duration, assuming that current earnings persist indefinitely, varies with the ratio of franchise value to tangible value. In essence, D_P is pulled down from a D_{TV} of 8.33 toward a D_{FV} of zero as the proportion of franchise value increases.

Figure 9.12   Equity Duration versus Proportion of Franchise Value
(franchise-value duration = 0)

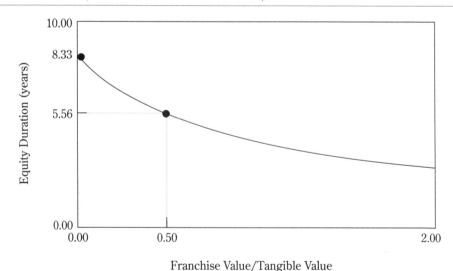

Duration at Varying Growth Rates.   For an example of the effect of changes in the proportion of the franchise value, return to the assumption of a uniform growth rate. Figure 9.13 shows that, while the tangible value remains fixed at $133.33 million, the franchise value increases from zero when

Figure 9.13. Tangible Value and Franchise Value versus Growth Rate

(12 percent nominal rate)

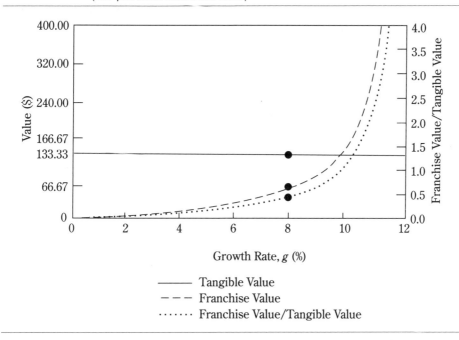

- ——— Tangible Value
- – – – Franchise Value
- ······· Franchise Value/Tangible Value

g is zero, to $66.67 million when g is 8 percent, and to $166.67 million when g is 10 percent. At the same time, the proportion of franchise value to tangible value increases from zero to 1.25.

The FF* model example and DDM example were calibrated to have the same TV, FV, and FV/TV values at the 4 percent inflation rate, but the models' very different responses to changing inflation lead to dramatically different duration values. When g is zero, there is no franchise value, and both the DDM and the FF* model predict an equity duration equal to the TV duration of 8.33. As g increases, the DDM predicts that D_{FV} will also grow. Thus, D_P rises, because both the duration and the weight of franchise value increase. For example, as shown previously, at an 8 percent growth rate, the DDM predicts a D_{FV} of 58.3 and D_P of 25 (see Figure 9.14).

The FF* model takes a completely opposite view to that of the DDM. According to the FF* model, high flow-through should be embedded in the franchise value and D_{FV} should remain low even as g increases. This low value of D_{FV} leads to a total duration (D_P) that decreases as g values increase (see Figure 9.15). Thus, the FF* model resolves the paradox of equity duration:

159

Figure 9.14. DDM Duration versus Growth Rate
(12 percent nominal rate)

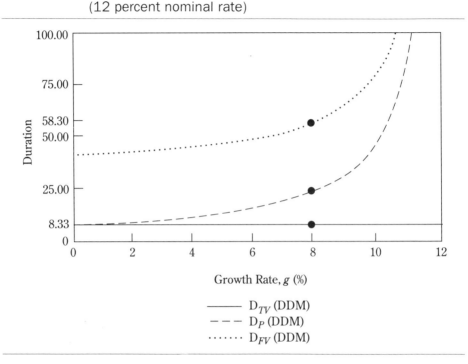

Lower duration values are consistent with overall market behavior.

Earnings Growth and Tangible Value

To this point, the assumption has been that all earnings growth results from incremental earnings from new businesses. Consequently, the value of high-growth firms was dominated by franchise value. In actuality, of course, the existing investments of many companies will experience high earnings growth for some extended period of time. New physical investments often lead to earnings that build slowly at first, then accelerate rapidly before leveling off and, ultimately, declining. Consequently, a future earnings pattern will depend on the stage at which it is viewed. The FF model assumes that all future earnings from *existing* businesses contribute to the tangible value; thus, some firms may be characterized as "growth" companies based on the deferred realization patterns in their tangible-value earnings.

The time path of TV earnings does not affect the base P/E (which remains at $1/k$ when earnings are normalized), but it does change the tangible value's sensitivity to rate changes. For an illustration of this effect, consider several

Figure 9.15. FF* Model Duration versus Growth Rate

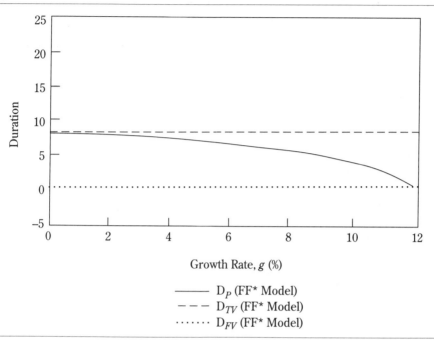

Growth Rate, *g* (%)

——— D_P (FF* Model)
– – – D_{TV} (FF* Model)
······ D_{FV} (FF* Model)

firms with no new investment opportunities (that is, with no franchise value) but with earnings that change over time (as shown in Table 9.2). For comparison with earlier examples, Firm A is defined to have level earnings, zero flow-through, and a tangible-value duration of 8.33. Firms B and C both have earnings that first grow by 10 percent annually (for 5 and 10 years, respectively) and then level off and remain at their terminal values forever. These earnings paths are assumed to reflect all earnings changes fully, regardless of the level of expected inflation (that is, the flow-through rate is zero). Under these conditions, D_{TV} rises from Firm A's 8.33 to 8.90 for Firm B and to 10.20

Table 9.2. Example TV Firms with Changing Earnings

Firm	Years of Growth	Earnings Growth Rate	Subsequent Rate of Earnings Decline	TV Duration
A	0	0%	0%	8.33
B	5	10	0	8.90
C	10	10	0	10.20
D	0	0	10	4.55
E	5	10	10	5.45
F	10	10	10	7.16

161

for Firm C.

Figure 9.16 illustrates the relationship between the earnings growth rate and the TV duration for firms with 5 or 10 years of growth followed by level earnings. If high growth rates (greater than 10 percent) are viewed as sustainable for only 10 or fewer years, durations higher than 12 or 13 years are probably not attainable. Figure 9.16 shows, for example, that a 20 percent growth rate for 10 years leads to D_{TV} of only 11.66. This result indicates that durations of a level predicted by the DDM cannot be achieved even if a firm enjoys high levels of earnings growth from existing investments.

Figure 9.16. Tangible-Value Duration versus Earnings Growth Rates
(0, 10, or 20 years of growth)

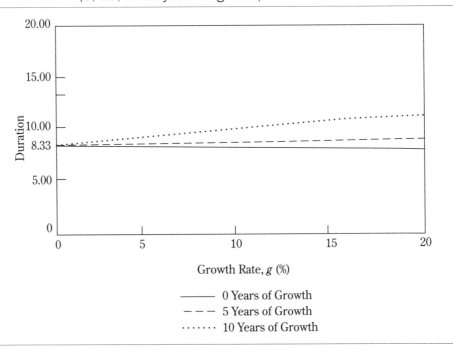

In reality, the earnings generated solely by existing investments are likely to peak and then begin to decline. Firms D, E, and F in Table 9.2 illustrate the TV duration of firms with peaking earnings. Firm D's earnings begin to decline immediately at a 10 percent annual rate, which results in a TV duration of 4.55. Firms E and F fare much better; their earnings first rise by 10 percent annually (for 5 and 10 years, respectively) and then decline at a 10 percent annual rate. Such rising-and-falling earnings paths lead to durations that are substantially

Figure 9.17. Tangible-Value Durations for Firms with Rising-and-Falling Earnings

(0, 5, or 10 years of growth before decline)

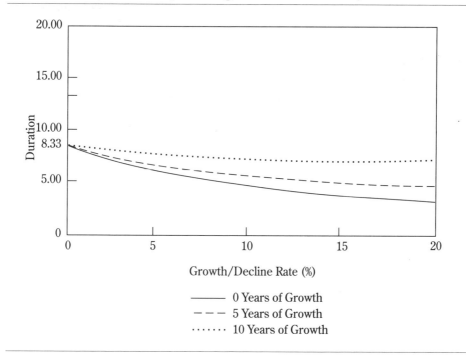

short of the base 8.33. Figure 9.17 illustrates this result for a range of growth rates and subsequent rates of decline.

The preceding duration values were based on the assumption of zero flow-through; that is, the TV-generated earnings stream was completely insensitive to inflation. In practice, if a period of sustained earnings growth is significantly long, some capacity for inflation adjustment would be expected (especially in the later years). Any such flow-through flexibility would lead to a material reduction in the duration values shown in Table 9.2 and Figures 9.16 and 9.17.

The label "growth company" tends to be applied to firms that exhibit earnings growth from a variety of sources, not from current businesses alone. These sources, in various combinations, are the tangible-value growth derived from existing investments, the franchise-value growth associated with new franchise investments, and earnings boosts from new but nonfranchise (and, hence, theoretically unproductive) investments. At the extreme of growth derived primarily from new investments, the high flow-through should result in a low duration. At the other extreme, for firms in which the TV growth of old investments is dominant, the duration will not likely exceed eight or nine years. Thus, the duration of "growth firms" spans a wide spectrum that depends on the sources of the growth.[15] Even in the most extreme case, however, the FF° model duration will be significantly lower than the high levels predicted by the DDM.

The Effect of Changes in Real Rates

To this point, the tacit assumption has been that all nominal rate changes reflect changes in expected inflation. In actuality, of course, real rates and risk-premium spreads will also change. Although a complete analysis of the impact of such rate changes is beyond the scope of this text, the separation of firm value into the tangible value and the franchise value can be used to gain some insights into the nature of this impact.

Because tangible value has bondlike characteristics, its sensitivity to rate changes, regardless of their source, is likely to be comparable to the sensitivity of coupon bonds. In contrast, the sensitivity of franchise value to rate changes is likely to depend on the source of those changes. Although the franchise value may exhibit high flow-through for (hence, low sensitivity to) inflation changes, there is little reason to expect any such protection when nominal rate changes are caused by movements in real rates and/or risk premiums. Thus, fluctuations in real rates or risk premiums may produce FV changes that are comparable to those predicted by the DDM. Then, the overall price sensitivity could reach some of the very high duration levels implied by the DDM. In summary, when evaluating the net impact of interest rate movements on equity prices, one must be careful to distinguish between ordinary inflation effects and the more dramatic impact of changes in real rates and real risk premiums.

Summary

The traditional dividend discount model blends earnings from current and prospective businesses and predicts an extremely high equity duration. The franchise factor model can be used to separate current businesses from future businesses and reveals that inflation changes are likely to have vastly different effects on these two components of firm value. In particular, the franchise value should be rather insensitive to changes in expected inflation. A key

---

[15]For additional perspectives on the rate sensitivity of firms, see Bernstein (1992), Sorensen and Bienstock (1992), and Modigliani and Cohn (1979).

finding, therefore, is that the duration of franchise value should be quite low. The standard DDM does not account for such inflation effects; hence, it implicitly assumes a very long duration for franchise value. As a result, the DDM overstates the duration of all firms, while the FF model leads to equity durations that are consistent with observed statistical durations.

10. Theoretical Price/Earnings Ratios and Accounting Variables

The theoretical price/earnings ratio produced by the franchise factor model, to this point, has been based implicitly on an estimate of the firm's value divided by a normalized value for the current *economic* earnings. The marketplace, however, addresses P/E values by dividing the market price by some measure of *accounting* earnings. This "market P/E" is then subject to daily price volatility and to the nature of accounting charges and conventions.

This chapter begins by clarifying the distinctions between the accounting and the economic values for earnings, book value, and return on equity. A "blended P/E" computed from the theoretical price and the reported accounting earnings is then introduced. This blended P/E should be closer to the market multiple than a purely theoretical P/E.

The blended P/E multiple can be analyzed according to four sources of value:

- accounting book value,
- incremental value attributable to the difference between the market-based and accounting book values,
- incremental going-concern value associated with the existing book of business, and
- future franchise value derived from new investments.

The first two sources are directly related to the value of a firm's assets, and the final two reflect the creation of added value from the firm's franchise. The chapter concludes by discussing what is necessary for a firm to raise its blended P/E.

Economic versus Accounting Variables

The first step in disentangling the components of value is to assess the level of economic earnings associated with the current book of business. For example, consider two standard accounting values that are widely reported:

the book value of equity and the return on book value, the ROE. In the aggregate, for the Standard & Poor's (S&P) Industrials, the ROE has ranged from 9.7 percent to 19.1 percent with an average level of 13.1 percent. The S&P Industrials book value has grown over time in rough correspondence with the ROE levels (see Figure 10.1). The ROE and book value provide only limited insight, however, into the determinants of a firm's P/E ratio at a given point in time. A key ingredient in understanding the P/E is the projection of the firm's *economic* earnings.[1] Unfortunately, the subject of economic earnings entails moving from the "precise" world of accounting principles into the realm of estimation.

One useful route to calculating economic earnings is first to estimate the ratio of the market value of existing assets to the accounting value (q_B). For example, if the accounting value is $100 million and the market value is $200 million, $q_B = 2.0$. This book-value ratio can be used to find the economic earnings if a reasonable assessment of the sustainable economic return (r_T) is made.

Because r_T relates to the market value of assets, it is not a totally free variable. For example, suppose the market value of assets is derived solely from a firm's ability to extract a 12 percent market rate of return. By definition, the firm's r_T would be 12 percent. An r_T of 15 percent suggests that the firm's going-concern value is adding 300 basis points beyond the general market return. An r_T of 7.5 percent would imply that, for whatever reasons, the firm is locked into underperforming assets that could earn an addition 450 basis points if they were redeployed in the general marketplace. These r_T variations make a general statement about the nature and quality of the existing business.

This simple method of analysis has clear-cut implications when the market value of book equity is understated. For example, consider a firm with $13 million in properly reported earnings. If the accounting book value is $100 million, the result is an accounting ROE of 13 percent. This 13 percent ROE—which is generally consistent with historical experience (see Figure 10.1)—may appear to be a satisfactory level of return. If the book value happens to be understated, however, and the true economic book value is $200 million, the true economic ROE slides to the dismal level of 6.5 percent. Thus, when the book value is understated, a proportionately higher accounting ROE is clearly needed for the firm to reach an acceptable level of market return.

The book value will be understated whenever the economic value of assets

---

[1] For example, Stewart (1991) measures economic earnings by NOPAT, "the profits derived from the company's operations after taxes but before financing costs and noncash bookkeeping entries."

168

Figure 10.1. Book Value per Share and Return on Equity for the S&P Industrials

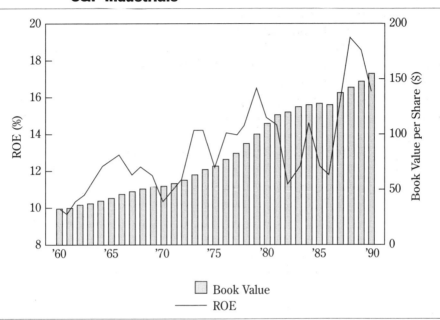

□ Book Value
—— ROE

Source: Standard & Poor's, *Analyst's Handbook* (New York: McGraw-Hill, 1992).

exceeds their accounting costs and/or whenever debt liabilities are overstated. This liability overstatement may occur with some frequency under traditional assumptions because debt with a below-market coupon will remain on the books but high-coupon debt tends to be refinanced.[2] Two companies with the same accounting structure may appear very different in terms of their economic variables. Moreover, this difference may be exacerbated when the comparison is between identical companies domiciled in different countries with disparate accounting conventions.

P/E in Theory and Practice

Two fundamental ingredients are required to produce a P/E—the "P" and the "E." The price can be either a market value (P_M) or a theoretical value (P_T) (see Table 10.1). In the FF model, computation of P_T is basically the same as

[2]This aspect is part of Modigliani and Cohn's (1979) arguments with regard to the effects of inflation on corporate value. Because of this asymmetry in the effect of movements in interest rates, however, the debt-value overstatement actually tends to be chronic, even without the direct effects of inflation.

Table 10.1. Theoretical and Practical Measures of Price and Earnings

Type of Measure	Price	Earnings
Theorical	P_T Discounted present value of projected future economic earnings from current and future investments	E_T Normalized Expected value Sustainable "Discountable" into a price value
Practical	P_M Market value	E_A Visible (reported or accounting values) 12-month trailing earnings Estimated future earnings

in most standard models in which P_T depends on the time path of economic earnings.[3] P_T is usually derived in two steps. The first is to make a set of assumptions regarding future earnings and growth. The second is to calculate the price as the present value of the future flows discounted at a capitalization rate (k) appropriate to the firm's risk class.

The earnings base may be built on either theoretical (E_T) or accounting (E_A) considerations. In previous chapters, the variability of economic earnings was smoothed out by replacing the projected earnings stream with a sustainable, level stream (E_T). By their very nature, economic earnings will differ significantly from any measure of accounting earnings. In fact, equity analysts make a practice of looking beyond reported earnings to make corrections for anomalies such as special charges and reserves.

Various combinations of theoretical, market, and accounting quantities can be used to compute a variety of P/Es. A *theoretical* P/E is found as follows:

$$(P/E)_T = \frac{P_T}{E_T}.$$

The reported or market P/E is

$$(P/E)_M = \frac{P_M}{E_A}.$$

---

[3]See, for example, Williams (1938), Gordon (1962), and Miller and Modigliani (1961).

Because the earnings base is simply a *numeraire* for measuring relative price levels, one can combine theory with market practice by using E_A rather than E_T to compute a blended price/earnings ratio—that is, P_T/E_A (see Figure 10.2). The advantage to denominating P_T in terms of accounting earnings is that P_T/E_A can be viewed as a target level against which the market value (P_M/E_A) can be measured. In time, P_M/E_A might tend toward P_T/E_A, but projected economic earnings are incorporated in the determination of P_T regardless of the earnings used in the P/E denominator.

Theoretical P/Es

The two principal components of the theoretical value of a firm are tangible value and franchise value. Although tangible value is easy to describe, it is difficult to compute because it requires some heroic suppositions regarding today's book value, depreciation, capital expenditures, and a myriad of other factors. To simplify, the analysis here assumes a normalized level of sustainable economic earnings (E_T). The tangible value can then be computed simply as the present value of a perpetuity,

$$TV = \frac{E_T}{k}.$$

FV is, as in previous chapters, derived from prospective earnings associated

Figure 10.2. Blending Theoretical and Practical P/E Measures

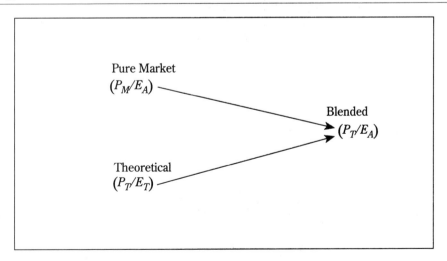

with future franchise investments.

The theoretical price is

$$P_T = \text{TV} + \text{FV}.$$

Dividing P_T by E_T results in

$$\frac{P_T}{E_T} = \frac{\text{TV}}{E_T} + \frac{\text{FV}}{E_T}.$$

Figure 10.3 illustrates schematically the dynamic relationships among TV, FV, earnings, and the theoretical P/E.

In previous chapters, the earnings and price were implicitly assumed to be E_T and P_T. The first term in the formula for P_T/E_T is the base P/E (computed by dividing TV by E_T), or the inverse of the capitalization rate. The second term is the franchise P/E, computed as the product of the franchise factor and the growth equivalent. Recall that FF is a unit profitability measure based on economic returns on book equity (r) and the return on new investment (R) and that G, the growth equivalent, is the present value of all new investments

Figure 10.3. Tangible Value, Franchise Value, and Theoretical P/E

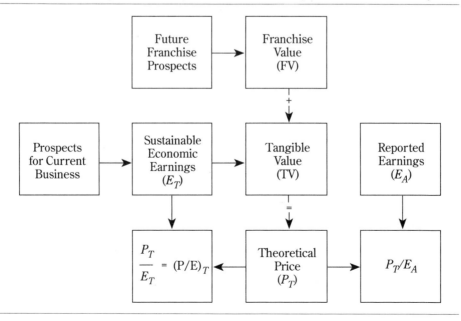

expressed as a percentage of current book value. In summary,

$$\frac{P_T}{E_T} = \frac{1}{k} + (\text{FF} \times G),$$

where

$$\text{FF} = \frac{R - k}{rk}.$$

For an example of the use of this formula, assume the following: k is 12 percent, r is 12 percent, and R is 16 percent. Under these assumptions,

$$\text{Base P/E} = \frac{1}{k}$$

$$= \frac{1}{0.12}$$

$$= 8.33;$$

$$\text{FF} = \frac{R - k}{rk}$$

$$= \frac{0.16 - 0.12}{0.12 \times 0.12}$$

$$= 2.78;$$

$$\text{Franchise P/E} = \text{FF} \times G$$

$$= 2.78G.$$

Using these values in the formula for P_T/E_T results in the following relationship between the P/E and G:

$$\frac{P_T}{E_T} = 8.33 + 2.78G.$$

Thus, a graph of the relationship between P_T/E_T and the growth equivalent is a straight line with a slope of 2.78 emanating from the base P/E value of 8.33. Consequently, each unit increase in growth equivalent, representing a new investment level equivalent to 100 percent of the current book value, results in 2.78 units of additional P/E (see Figure 10.4). For example, if the growth equivalent is 105 percent,

$$\frac{P_T}{E_T} = 8.33 + (2.78 \times 1.05)$$

$$= 11.25.$$

Figure 10.4. Theoretical P/E versus Growth Equivalent

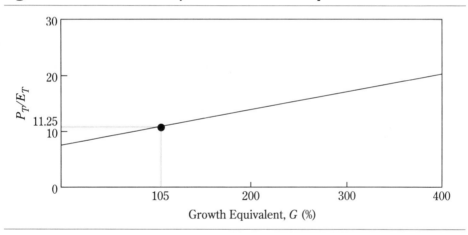

Relative Value of Economic and Accounting Variables

In general, the economic and accounting values of earnings, book value, and returns will exhibit considerable time variability. For example, Figure 10.5 illustrates two firms that have the same economic earnings of $24 million annually. Firm A's accounting earnings, which range from a high of $17.1 million to a low of $13.9 million, consistently understate its economic earnings. Firm B's earnings have a more variable character than Firm A's, and its accounting earnings often dominate its economic earnings.

The relative value of E_T and E_A is given by q_E, which is defined as E_T/E_A. A value of q_E greater than 1 indicates the common situation in which E_A understates E_T. If q_E is less than 1, E_A is overstating E_T. The time paths of q_E for the two example firms are given in Figure 10.6.

Figure 10.5. Firm A (Accounting Earnings Understate Economic Earnings) and Firm B (Variable Pattern of Understated and Overstated Earnings)

(dollars in millions)

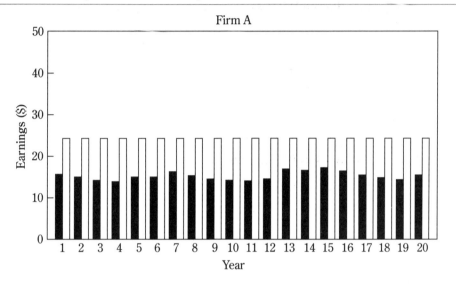

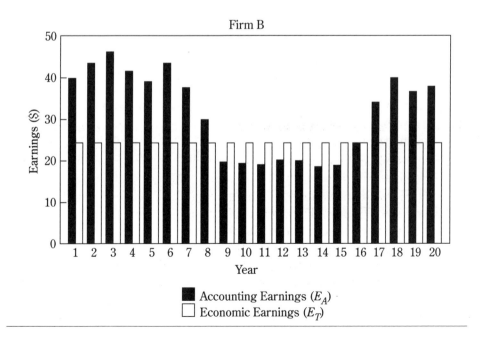

Accounting Earnings (E_A)
Economic Earnings (E_T)

Figure 10.6. The Earnings Ratio (q_E) for Firms A and B

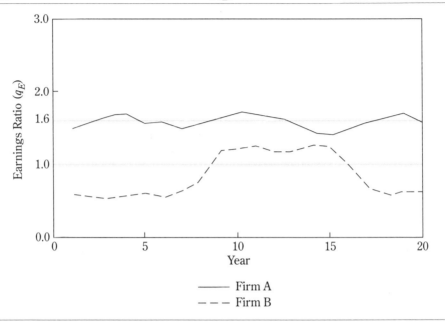

The accounting book value (B_A) is based on the historical value of the firm, accumulated retained earnings, depreciation, and a variety of other factors. The economic book value is defined here to be the true market value of assets (B_T).[4] As in the case of earnings, the relative magnitude of B_T and B_A will change over time. For mature firms with long-term holdings of real estate and substantial physical plants subject to rapid depreciation, the market value of assets may dwarf the book value. Thus, the book-value ratio ($q_B = B_T/B_A$) is likely to be considerably greater than 1.

The economic ROE (r_T) and the accounting ROE (r_A) are found by taking the appropriate ratios of earnings to book values $r_T = E_T/B_T$ and $r_A = E_A/B_A$. The ratio of ROEs is computed as $q_r = r_T/r_A$.

Based on these relationships, $q_E = q_r q_B$. Thus, once q_E has been determined, q_r and q_B are inversely proportional.

---

[4]The assumptions here specify a firm with equity financing only, but as discussed in Chapter 5, the analysis can be readily generalized to firms with a mixture of debt and equity.

Consider Firm C, for which B_A is \$100 million and B_T is \$200 million, so

$$q_B = \frac{B_T}{B_A}$$

$$= 2.$$

In addition, assume that r_A is 300 basis points above the market rate—that is, with k at 12 percent, r_A is 15 percent—and r_T is the 12 percent market rate. Then, E_A is \$15 million ($0.15 \times \$100$ million) and E_T is \$24 million ($0.12 \times \$200$ million). Therefore,

$$q_E = \frac{E_T}{E_A}$$

$$= 1.6$$

and

$$q_r = \frac{r_T}{r_A}$$

$$= 0.8.$$

The example of Firm C shows how accounting earnings can understate economic earnings even if the accounting return is greater than the economic return.[5] The key ingredient is the extent to which economic and accounting book values differ.

Now consider the impact of r_A on q_E by assuming that r_T and q_B are fixed at 12 percent and 2, respectively. Because

$$q_E = \frac{E_T}{E_A}$$

$$= \frac{r_T B_T}{r_A B_A},$$

---

[5]For a thoughtful discussion of the gap between economic and accounting earnings, see Treynor (1972).

it follows that

$$q_E = \frac{r_T q_B}{r_A}$$

$$= \frac{0.12 \times 2.00}{r_A}$$

$$= \frac{0.24}{r_A}.$$

This formula shows that the earnings understatement increases with low accounting ROEs. In the Firm C example, in which r_A was 15 percent, q_E was shown to be equal to 1.6, the point marked with a diamond in Figure 10.7. When r_A is only 10 percent, however, q_E is 2.4. Thus, a significant earnings understatement results when the accounting book value is only half the economic value of assets.

In contrast, when q_B is 1, the degree of earnings understatement at any level of r_A decreases. For example, when r_A is 10 percent, q_E is only 1.2, compared with 2.4 when q_B is 2.

Figure 10.7 assumes that r_T is fixed at 12 percent. Consider now how r_T varies with q_E. From the earlier formulas, it follows that r_T is $(q_E/q_B)r_A$. For example, if q_B remains at 2, and if economic and accounting earnings are both \$15 million, then q_E is 1 and r_T is half of r_A. When r_A is 15 percent, r_T is 7.5 percent and q_r is 0.5.

This little example raises some big questions, because it implies an economic return that can be significantly less than the market rate—for example, when high exit costs trap a firm in an unproductive business or when some of a firm's assets are worth more to a third party than to the firm itself. The basic message is obvious: If the accounting ROE appears satisfactory but the book value greatly understates the market value of a firm's assets, the economic ROE may well be unacceptable.

The Blended P/E

Turn now to the formulation of a blended price/earnings ratio. The basic relationship between the theoretical and blended P/E is simple:

$$\frac{P_T}{E_A} = \frac{E_T}{E_A}\left(\frac{P_T}{E_T}\right)$$

$$= q_E\left(\frac{P_T}{E_T}\right).$$

For Firm C, if the economic return on new investment (R_T) is 16 percent, then as in the earlier generic example, P_T/E_T is 11.25 but

$$\frac{P_T}{E_A} = q_E\left(\frac{P_T}{E_T}\right)$$

$$= 1.60 \times 11.25$$

$$= 18.00.$$

Figure 10.7. Earnings Ratio (q_E) versus Accounting Return (r_A) when the Economic Return (r_T) is the 12 Percent Market Rate

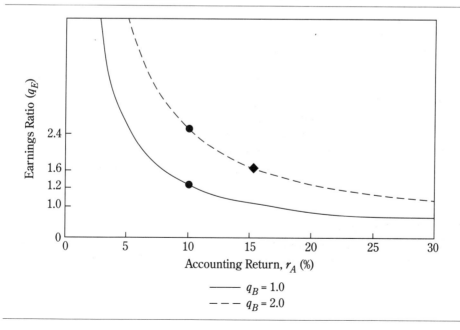

The understated accounting earnings in the denominator lead to a blended P_T/E_A that is greater than the theoretical P_T/E_T.

To gain a better understanding of the factors that influence the blended P/E, it is necessary to delve more deeply into the two factors that capture future growth—the franchise factor and the growth equivalent. The FF is essentially an economic profitability factor for new investments. Hence, it should not be subject to the volatility, conventions, and special charges that are integral to accounting considerations. Based purely on economic values, the theoretical FF could be expressed as

$$\text{FF}_T = \frac{R_T - k}{r_T k}.$$

In contrast to FF, G is always expressed as a percentage of the firm's current book equity (B_A). An accounting growth equivalent (G_A) is chosen rather than a market-value-based growth equivalent (G_T), because B_A is a well-defined number against which growth can be measured.

With these definitions, the blended P/E can be expressed as follows:[6]

$$\frac{P_T}{E_A} = q_E(\text{Base P/E}) + q_r \text{FF}_T G_A.$$

This shows that the influence of the base P/E expands or contracts depending on whether earnings are understated ($q_E > 1$) or overstated ($q_E < 1$).

Measurement of the effect of growth opportunities (G_A, the accounting growth equivalent) is slightly more complicated for the blended P/E than for the theoretical P/E. When computing P_T/E_A, the value of $\text{FF}_T G_A$ must be multiplied by the return ratio (q_r). For a given value of FF_T, this scaling amplifies the P/E impact of new investments when $q_r > 1$ and diminishes that impact when $q_r < 1$. For Firm C, for example, when economic variables are used throughout,

$$\frac{P_T}{E_T} = 8.33 + 2.78G_T.$$

---

[6]The formula for the blended P/E is derived by multiplying P_T/E_T by q_E and observing that $q_E \text{FF}_T G_T = q_E \text{FF}_T G_A / q_B = q_r \text{FF}_T G_A$.

In contrast, the blended P/E for Firm C (with $q_E = 1.6$, $q_B = 2.0$, and $q_r = 1.6/2.0 = 0.8$) is

$$\frac{P_T}{E_A} = 13.33 + 2.22 G_A$$

(see Figure 10.8).

Figure 10.8. P_T/E_A versus Accounting Growth Equivalent
(FF = 2.22; q_E = 1.60; q_B = 2.00)

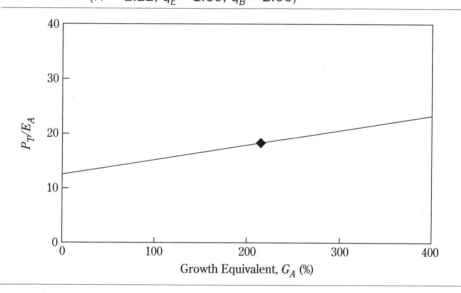

Because q_B is 2.0, G_A is $2.0G_T$, and when G_T is 105 percent, G_A is 210 percent. Hence, for exactly the same firm, the blended P_T/E_A = 18 while the economic P_T/E_T = 13.33.

This example shows how accounting adjustments can change our perception of a firm. The two P/E values are equivalent reflections of the same firm, but they obviously have different connotations, and the blended P_T/E_A, because it is probably the closer to intuition, is likely to be the better basis for evaluation.

Note that even in this context, a P_T/E_A of 18 requires a surprising $210 million (210 percent of the $100 million accounting book value) in new investments with an economic return of 16 percent, 400 basis points above the market rate. Moreover, lower investment returns would require proportionately greater dollar investments to "justify" a multiple of 18. Figure 10.9 shows that, if the return spread falls from 400 basis points to 200 basis points, the present value of new investments must rise from $210 million (Point A) to $420 million (Point B).[7]

Figure 10.9. New Investment versus Return Spread Required for Blended P/E of 18

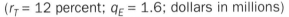

$(r_T = 12$ percent; $q_E = 1.6$; dollars in millions)

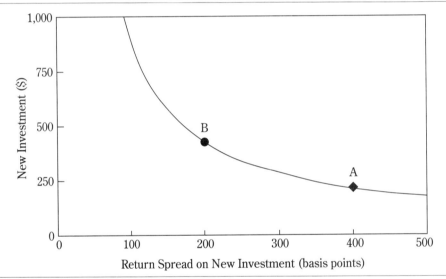

Earnings and Book-Value Effects

As discussed, when accounting earnings understate economic earnings, the effective base P/E rises in proportion to the degree of understatement (as measured by q_E). The rise in P/E means that the proportion of the total P_T/E_A accounted for by the firm's current business is greater than when accounting and economic earnings coincide. The effective base P/E is represented graphically by the level at which the (P_T/E_A)-versus-G_A line emanates from the vertical axis; as Figure 10.10 illustrates, a higher q_E results in a higher starting point for the P_T/E_A line.

The response of P_T/E_A to new investment is reflected in the slope of the P_T/E_A line. As Figure 10.10 also shows, for a given value of q_E, the slope is

---

[7]Recall that the value of FF is proportional to the economic spread on new investment. If the spread is cut in half, the dollar investment must be doubled to maintain the same level of the new investment factor (FF$_T \times G_A$).

182

Figure 10.10. P_T/E_A **versus Growth Equivalent at Various Levels of** q_E **and** q_B
(with $r_T = 12$ percent and $FF_T = 2.78$)

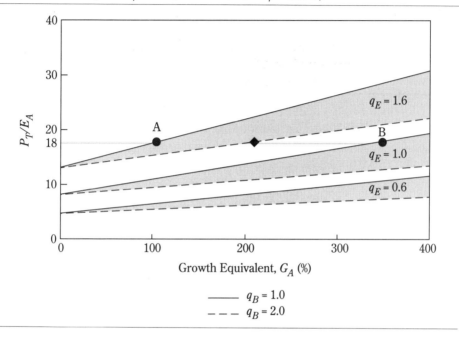

smaller when $q_B = 2.0$ than when $q_B = 1.0$. The smaller slope means that, when the book value is understated, the G_A needed to reach a given P/E is greater than when the economic and accounting book values are the same. This increase in G_A can be explained by the change in the book-value base against which investment is measured; that is, the same dollars of investment loom much larger when measured against a smaller base.

Depending on the levels of q_E and q_B, a strikingly wide spectrum of G_A may be needed to support a P_T/E_A of 18. For example, the values of G_A range from 105 percent for $q_B = 1.0$ and $q_E = 1.6$ (Point A in Figure 10.10) to 210 percent for Firm C (indicated by the diamond). When economic and accounting values coincide (that is, $q_B = 1.0$ and $q_E = 1.0$), G_A rises to 348 percent (Point B). More dramatic still is the case in which $q_B = 2.0$ and $q_E = 0.6$ (not shown on graph). Then, the required G_A rises to 1,560 percent!

Economic Return on Equity and the Blended P/E

In most of the preceding examples, the economic return (r_T) has been fixed at the 12 percent market rate. In this section, q_B is fixed at 2.0 and r_A at 15 percent in order to see how raising or lowering r_T alters the new investment required to justify a P_T/E_A of 18.

Because the contribution of the current book of business to P_T/E_A rises with the current economic return, when the economic return is high, only modest future investments are needed to justify a blended P/E of 18. Figure 10.11 illustrates the relationship between required dollar investment and the return spread on new investment for three different values of r_T. For the base case of R_T = 16 percent (a 400-basis-point spread) and r_T = 12 percent, the required investment of $210 million is indicated by the diamond on the middle curve (which corresponds to the 210 percent G value at the diamond in Figure 10.10). At any given spread, higher economic returns on current assets lead to smaller required future investments.

For each curve in Figure 10.11, q_r and q_E are totally determined by the value of r_T. When r_T = 7.5 percent, no understatement of earnings occurs (q_E = 1.0) and a 14.0 percent return (12.0 percent + 200 basis points) requires $870 million of new investment (Point C) to support the P_T/E_A of 18. At a return on new investment of 16.0 percent (a 400-basis-point spread), the required investment level drops to $435 million (Point D). In contrast, if the current economic return (r_T) is 15.0 percent, accounting earnings understate economic earnings

Figure 10.11. New Investment versus Return Spread with Varying Economic Returns

(blended P/E = 18; r_A = 15 percent; q_B = 2; dollars in millions)

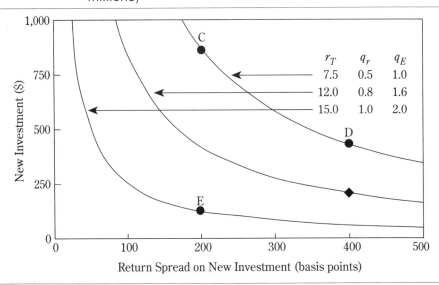

by 50.0 percent, and with a 14.0 percent return on new investment, only $120 million of new investment (Point E) is needed for a P_T/E_A of 18. Thus, the combinations of new return spread and magnitude of new investment that can justify a prescribed P/E multiple are endless.

The Price-to-Book Ratio

Chapter 4 demonstrated that, when accounting and economic variables are indistinguishable, the premium to book value is attributable to two sources: the capitalized value of excess earnings on current book equity, and the net present value of all anticipated future earnings from new investments. In the more realistic case in which accounting and economic values differ, however, the premium of the market value of assets over the accounting value also adds to the price-to-book ratio.

The ratio of the theoretical price to the accounting book value can be expressed as follows:

$$\frac{P_T}{B_A} = 1 + \text{ Market book premium}$$

$$+ \text{ Going-concern return premium}$$

$$+ \text{ Future franchise premium,}$$

or more precisely,[8]

$$\frac{P_T}{B_A} = 1 + (q_B - 1) + \frac{q_B(r_T - k)}{k} + \frac{G_A(R_T - k)}{k}.$$

To clarify how this formula works, it will be applied to some of the examples from the previous section.

Generally, the previous examples assumed that $q_B = 2$; therefore, the second term adds 1 additional unit to P_T/B_A. (This addition simply reflects the ratio of the $200 million market value of assets to the $100 million book value.) The third term in the P_T/B_A formula is zero when the economic return is the same as the market rate. Firms with above-market economic returns offer an additional premium to book value (weighted by the book ratio); firms with

---

[8]The formula for P_T/B_A can be shown to be equivalent to the formula for P_T/E_A multiplied by r_A.

below-market economic returns suffer a penalty. The last term in the P_T/B_A formula reflects the effect of above-market returns on new investments, with the magnitude of those investments expressed relative to the accounting book value.

First, assume Firm D has an r_T of 13 percent, an R_T of 14 percent, a B_A of $100 million, and new investments of $320 million. Then,

$$G_A = \frac{\text{New investment}}{B_A}$$

$$= \frac{\$320,000,000}{\$100,000,000}$$

$$= 3.2$$

and

$$\frac{P_T}{B_A} = 1.00 + 1.00 + 0.17 + 0.53$$

$$= 2.70.$$

This example demonstrates that both the above-market economic return on current book value and the value of new investments add to P_T/B_A.

Figure 10.12 illustrates the separate additions of P_T/B_A from asset-based and franchise-based values. The first two terms in P_T/B_A arise from the $100 million accounting book value and the $100 million incremental value that accrues when assets are marked to market. In addition to this $200 million asset-based value, Firm D has a going-concern value because it earns an above-market economic return on even its properly valued assets. This franchise-based value is obtained by capitalizing the incremental earnings. Therefore,

$$\text{Incremental going-concern value} = \frac{B_T r_T}{k} - B_T$$

$$= B_T \left(\frac{r_T - k}{k} \right)$$

$$= \$200{,}000{,}000 \times \left(\frac{0.13 - 0.12}{0.12}\right)$$

$$= \$16{,}666{,}667.$$

The going-concern value adds 0.17 units to P_T/B_A, because it is 16.7 percent of B_A. (Note the corresponding numbers in the third and fourth columns of Figure 10.12.)

Finally, the franchise value is obtained by capitalizing incremental earnings from new investments:

$$\text{FV} = \text{New investment} \times \left(\frac{R - k}{k}\right)$$

$$= \$320{,}000{,}000 \times \left(\frac{0.14 - 0.12}{0.12}\right)$$

$$= \$53{,}333{,}333.$$

Figure 10.12. Price-to-Book Ratio and Blended P/E in Terms of Asset- and Franchise-Based Firm Value

(dollars in millions)

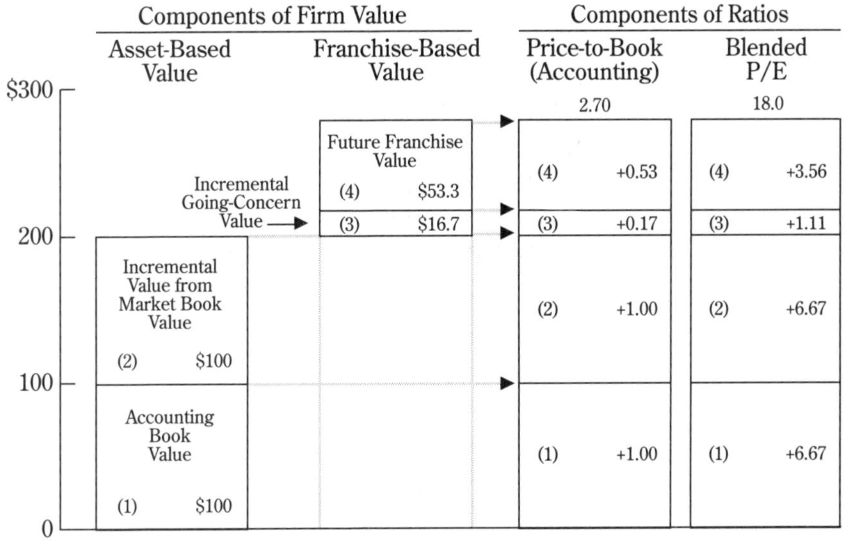

	Components of Firm Value		Components of Ratios	
	Asset-Based Value	Franchise-Based Value	Price-to-Book (Accounting)	Blended P/E
$300			2.70	18.0
		Future Franchise Value (4) $53.3	(4) +0.53	(4) +3.56
200	Incremental Going-Concern Value → (3) $16.7		(3) +0.17	(3) +1.11
	Incremental Value from Market Book Value (2) $100		(2) +1.00	(2) +6.67
100				
	Accounting Book Value (1) $100		(1) +1.00	(1) +6.67
0				

This franchise value adds a final 0.53 units to the P_T/B_A.

The correspondence between the components of value and the components of the P_T/B_A also applies to P_T/E_A. Because P_T/E_A is simply P_T/B_A divided by r_A, when r_A is 15 percent, the four components of firm value shown in Figure 10.12 contribute 6.67 units, 6.67 units, 1.11 units, and 3.56 units, respectively, to the blended P/E of 18.

Note that if r_T had been 7.5 percent and the new investment had been $870 million, with R_T at 16.0 percent, P_T/B_A also would have been 2.7 (that is, 1.00 + 1.00 – 0.75 + 1.45). In this case, the below-market r_T would have reduced firm value, necessitating a substantial new investment to maintain the same price-to-book multiple.

In general, when $r_T < k$, the incremental going-concern value is negative and tends to drag P_T/B_A below q_B. The FV, however, tends to be positive (or, at least, not negative), because the firm probably would not invest intentionally in new projects unless those projects were expected to offer an economic return premium. The extent to which P_T/B_A deviates from q_B reflects the net balance between the current asset-based value and franchise-based value.

The Total Franchise Factor

The separation of P_T/B_A into asset-based value and franchise-based value suggests a new formulation for the blended P_T/E_A. First, rewrite the price-to-book ratio as follows:

$$\frac{P_T}{B_A} = \text{Asset-based value} + \text{Franchise-based value}$$

$$= \quad q_B \quad + \frac{q_B(r_T - k)}{k} + \frac{G_A(R_T - k)}{k}.$$

$$= \quad q_B \quad + \frac{q_B(r_T - k)}{k} + \frac{G_A(R_T - k)}{k}.$$

Then, because $E_A = r_A B_A$, the blended P_T/E_A can be found by dividing P_T/B_A by r_A. Thus,

$$\frac{P_T}{E_A} = \text{Asset-based P/E} + \text{Franchise-based P/E}$$

$$= \frac{q_B}{r_A} + \frac{q_B(r_T - k)}{r_A k} + \frac{G_A(R_T - k)}{r_A k}$$

$$= \frac{q_B}{r_A} + q_r \left[\frac{q_B(r_T - k)}{r_T k} + \frac{G_A(R_T - k)}{r_T k} \right].$$

The first term simplifies to

$$\frac{q_B}{r_A} = \frac{\left(\dfrac{B_T}{B_A} \right)}{r_A}$$

$$= \frac{B_T}{E_A}$$

$$= \frac{1}{r_{AT}},$$

where r_{AT} is defined to be a "blended ROE" consisting of the reported earnings as a percentage of the economic book value.

The determination of r_{AT} requires only a projection of B_T. By separating out this asset-based $1/r_{AT}$ term, the remaining franchise-based P/E is able to subsume many of the more fragile estimates—namely, the economic ROEs (r_T and R_T), the capitalization rate (k), and the growth equivalent (G_A).

The franchise P/E incorporates both the going-concern value of current book assets and the prospects associated with new investment programs. In this sense, it represents a total franchise value. The two terms of this franchise P/E are similar in form. Note that $(r_T - k)/r_T k$ and $(R_T - k)/r_T k$ have the look of franchise factors applied to q_B (the size of the economic book value denominated in units of accounting book value) and to G_A. Specifically, the "current" and "new" franchise factors are defined as follows:

$$\text{FF}_{CUR} = \frac{r_T - k}{r_T k},$$

and

$$\mathrm{FF}_{NEW} = \frac{R_T - k}{r_T k} \ .$$

These definitions suggest that the franchise factors might be combined into a weighted-average franchise factor applied to the total of all firm investments. In fact, the franchise-based P/E terms can be rewritten as $(\mathrm{FF}_{TOT} \times G_{TOT})$ where FF_{TOT} is viewed as a weighted-average *total* franchise factor applied to a *total* growth equivalent that represents the present-value magnitude of all firm investments—past and future.[9]

Combining the preceding results gives

$$\frac{P_T}{E_A} = \frac{1}{r_{AT}} + q_r \mathrm{FF}_{TOT} G_{TOT} \ .$$

For Firm D, r_A was 15 percent and q_B was 2. Thus,

$$r_{AT} = \frac{r_A}{q_B}$$

$$= 7.5 \text{ percent,}$$

and

$$\frac{1}{r_{AT}} = 13.33.$$

This value (13.33) is the asset-based component of the blended P/E (see Figure 10.12). To achieve a blended P/E of 18, the firm's franchise must provide the remaining 4.67 units of P/E.

In the new, total franchise framework, this incremental P/E is derived from r_T, R, and G_A, which permits calculation of q_r, FF_{TOT}, and G_{TOT}. For example, if r_T is 13 percent, R_T is 14 percent, and G_A is 3.2, then,

---

[9]It can be shown that Franchise-based P/E = $q_r \mathrm{FF}_{TOT} G_{TOT}$, where $G_{TOT} = q_B + G_A$, $\mathrm{FF}_{TOT} = (R_{TOT} - k)/r_T k$, and R_{TOT} is the weighted-average economic ROE; that is, $R_{TOT} = (q_B/G_{TOT})r_T + (G_A/G_{TOT})R_T$.

$$q_r = \frac{r_T}{r_A}$$

$$= \frac{0.13}{0.15}$$

$$= 0.87.$$

The present value of the firm's current and future investments can be expressed as

$$G_{TOT} = q_B + G_A$$

$$= 2.0 + 3.2$$

$$= 5.2.$$

The weighted-average return across all of these investments is

$$R_{TOT} = \frac{q_B r_T + G_A R}{G_{TOT}}$$

$$= \frac{(2.0 \times 0.13) + (3.2 \times 0.14)}{5.2}$$

$$= 13.6 \text{ percent.}$$

Using this value of R_{TOT} results in

$$\text{FF}_{TOT} = \frac{R_{TOT} - k}{r_T k}$$

$$= \frac{0.136 - 0.12}{0.13 \times 0.12}$$

$$= 1.04.$$

Finally, this franchise factor (1.04) can be applied to the total investment base of 5.2 and adjusted by the return ratio to reveal the required additional units of franchise-based P/E:

$$\text{Franchise-based P/E} = q_r \text{FF}_{TOT} G_{TOT}$$

$$= 0.87 \times 1.04 \times 5.20$$

$$= 4.67.$$

Thus, the firm's overall P/E of 18 can now be viewed as derived from two distinct sources: the asset-based P/E of 13.33 and the franchise-based P/E of 4.67.

Figure 10.13 shows that, of these 4.67 units, 1.11 units are attributable to the going-concern franchise and 3.56 units are from new investments. The dotted line in Figure 10.13 illustrates how the first 2 units of G_{TOT} (that is, q_B) bring the blended P_T/E_A up from 13.33 ($1/r_{AT}$) to 14.44. Observe that the slope of the line is $q_r \text{FF}_{TOT}$.[10] The next 3.2 units of G_{TOT} (that is, G_A) bring P_T/E_A up to 18. The slope of the final line segment is $q_r \text{FF}_{NEW}$.[11]

Summary

Because of the nature of accounting conventions, price/earnings ratios based purely on reported earnings and market prices can lead to misperceptions of true value. This chapter has shown how appropriate adjustments for the differences between economic and accounting variables can lead to insights into the conventional P/E. When earnings are significantly understated, a high P/E may simply reflect that understatement. In contrast, overstated accounting earnings may mean that only a dramatically large set of opportunities for above-market investments can "justify" a given P/E multiple.

The same type of analysis applies to the price-to-book ratio. When P/B is based on an accounting book value, a ratio value greater than 1 does not necessarily signify value creation. True value is created only when P/B exceeds the ratio of the book equity's market value to its accounting value. When it does, further value additions are attributable to an above-market economic return on current assets and/or a franchise premium on future

---

[10] $\text{FF}_{CUR} = (r_T - k)/r_T k = (0.13 - 0.12)/(0.13 \times 0.12) = 0.64$; $q_r \text{F}_{CUR} = (0.13/0.15) \times 0.64 = 0.87 \times 0.64 = 0.56$.

[11] $q_r \text{FF}_{NEW} = q_r (R_T - k)/r_T k = 0.87 \times (0.14 - 0.12)/(0.13 \times 0.12) = 1.11$.

Figure 10.13. Elements of the Total Franchise

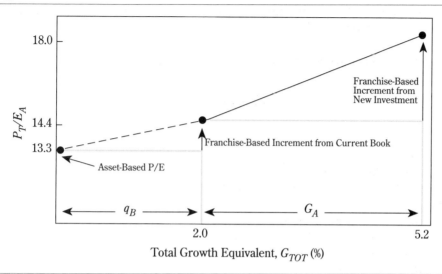

investment prospects.

Finally, the analysis showed how a firm's P/E multiple can be viewed in a total franchise framework. The virtue of this approach is its clear-cut delineation between the asset-based and the franchise-derived components of P/E value.

Appendix A. Derivation of the Franchise Factor Model

According to the standard dividend discount model, a theoretical stock price (P) is computed by discounting the stream of all future dividends (d) at the market rate (k). Thus,

$$P = \frac{d_1}{1+k} + \frac{d_2}{(1+k)^2} + \ldots + \frac{d_N}{(1+k)^N} + \ldots ,$$

where d_i is the dividend at time i.

If dividends are assumed to grow annually at a constant rate (g), then

$$d_i = (1+g)^{i-1} d_1 \qquad \text{for } i = 1,\ 2,\ 3,\ \ldots \tag{A.1}$$

and

$$P = \frac{d_1}{1+k} + \frac{(1+g)d_1}{(1+k)^2} + \frac{(1+g)^2 d_1}{(1+k)^3} + \ldots .$$

Summing this infinite geometric progression results in

$$P = \frac{d_1}{k-g}, \tag{A.2}$$

which is the standard Gordon formula. Note that the formula was derived without regard to the source of dividend growth.

The dividend growth is related to the firm's return on equity and to the growth in book value that results from retained earnings. To see this relationship, first note that the dollar dividend payout at time i depends on the firms' earnings over the period from time (i–1) to time i. These earnings are symbolized by E_i. The dividend payout is expressed as a fraction of earnings, the dividend payout ratio. Here, the dividend payout ratio (α) is assumed to be constant over time. Thus,

$$d_i = \alpha E_i .$$

The earnings are the product of the ROE and the book value at the beginning of the period (B_{i-1}). The ROE is assumed to be a constant (r), so

$$E_i = rB_{i-1} \quad \text{for } i = 1, 2, \ldots . \tag{A.3}$$

Because earnings are a constant multiple of book value, the earnings will grow at the same rate as book value. All earnings not paid out as dividends (that is, all retained earnings) add to the book value of the firm. Furthermore, for the moment, the assumption is that no other sources of additions to book value exist (for example, no new equity issuances).

The earnings retention rate is $\beta = (1 - \alpha)$. If B_0 is the initial book value, the book value at the end of the first year (B_1) is

$$B_1 = B_0 + \beta E_1 .$$

Similarly, B_2, the book value at the end of the second year, is

$$B_2 = B_1 + \beta E_2 .$$

With the use of equation (A.3), the book value at any time can be expressed in terms of the initial book value (B_0). For example, because $E_1 = rB_0$,

$$B_1 = B_0 + \beta rB_0$$

$$= (1 + \beta r)B_0 .$$

In addition, because $E_2 = rB_1$,

$$B_2 = B_1 + \beta r B_1$$

$$= (1 + \beta r)B_1$$

$$= (1 + \beta r)^2 B_0 .$$

Generalizing results in

$$B_i = (1 + \beta r)^i B_0 . \qquad (A.4)$$

As the book value grows, so do the earnings and dividend streams. From equation (A.3) and equation (A.4), it follows that

$$E_i = r(1 + \beta r)^{i-1} B_0 ,$$

and because $d_i = \alpha E_i$,

$$d_i = \alpha r(1 + \beta r)^{i-1} B_0 .$$

Finally, because $d_1 = \alpha E_1 = \alpha r B_0$,

$$d_i = (1 + \beta r)^{i-1} d_1 . \qquad (A.5)$$

Thus, βr is the sustainable rate at which book value, earnings, and dividends all grow. When comparing equations (A.5) and (A.1), note that βr and g are the same. That is,

$$g = \beta r$$

$$= (1 - \text{Payout ratio}) \times \text{ROE}.$$

Note that the Gordon formula (equation A.2) can be rewritten in terms of the initial earnings and the dividend payout ratio as

$$P = \frac{\alpha E_1}{k - g}.$$

Thus, the theoretical price/earnings ratio is

$$P/E = \frac{\alpha}{k-g}. \tag{A.6}$$

Table A.1 provides four examples (the four firms discussed in Chapter 2) of these pricing and P/E formulas. In all cases, the market rate (k) is assumed to be 12 percent.

Now, by algebraic manipulation, formula (A.6) can be transformed into the Miller–Modigliani formula. First,

$$P/E = \frac{\alpha}{k-g}$$

$$= \frac{1-\beta}{k-r\beta}.$$

Then, factoring out $1/k$ produces

$$P/E = \frac{1}{k}\left[\frac{k(1-\beta)}{k-r\beta}\right]$$

$$= \frac{1}{k}\left(\frac{k-k\beta}{k-r\beta}\right).$$

Subtracting and adding $r\beta$ to the numerator of the last term in brackets results in

$$P/E = \frac{1}{k}\left(\frac{k-r\beta+r\beta-k\beta}{k-r\beta}\right).$$

Carrying out the indicated division gives the Miller–Modigliani formula:

$$P/E = \frac{1}{k}\left[1 + \frac{\beta(r-k)}{k-r\beta}\right]. \tag{A.7}$$

In the absence of growth (that is, $\beta = 0$), the second term in the brackets vanishes and the P/E is the inverse of the market rate, regardless of the value of r. Thus, for example, if $\beta = 0$ and $k = 12$ percent, P/E $= 1/0.12 = 8.33$.

Therefore, both Firms B and C in Table A.1 have P/Es of 8.33 (the base P/E). If β is greater than zero but the return on equity (*r*) is the same as the market rate, the second term still vanishes and, again, P/E = 1/*k*. Thus, because *r* = 12 percent for Firm A, that firm also has a base P/E of 8.33.

Table A.1. Theoretical Stock Prices and P/Es for Firms A, B, C, and D
(market rate, *k*, = 12 percent; initial book value, b_0, = $100)

	Specifications				Resulting Values		
Firm	Payout Ratio (α)	ROE (*r*)	Retention Rate (β)	Growth Rate (*r*β)	Initial Earnings (rB_0)	Price [$(\alpha rB_0)/(k-g)$]	P/E [$\alpha/(k-g)$]
A	1/3	12%	2/3	8%	$12	$100	8.33
B	1	12	0	0	12	100	8.33
C	1	15	0	0	15	125	8.33
D	1/3	15	2/3	10	15	250	16.67

For the P/E to rise above the base P/E, the firm must have both growth and reinvestment at an above-market ROE. Growth alone is not enough. For Firm D, because β = 2/3 and *r* = 15 percent, the P/E is 16.67.

Additional insight into the nature of growth can be gained by rewriting equation (A.7) in terms of price and initial book value rather than in terms of P/E. Multiply both sides of (A.7) by *E* and replace *E* with rB_0 in the second term:

$$P = \frac{E}{k} + \frac{\beta rB_0(r-k)}{k(k-r\beta)},$$

or

$$P = \frac{E}{k} + \left(\frac{r-k}{k}\right)\left(\frac{g}{k-g}\right)B_0. \tag{A.8}$$

The first term in equation (A.8) represents the present value of a perpetual stream of unchanging earnings of magnitude *E*. In other words, this term corresponds to a firm's full-payout equivalent. The second term can be shown to represent the earnings impact of a series of new investments. The magnitude of these new investments is ($B_0[g/(k-g)]$). The factor [$g/(k-g)$] can be interpreted as an immediate percentage increase in book value. Thus, the present-value growth equivalent of all book increases (*G*) is defined as follows:

$$G = \frac{g}{k-g}.$$

The new investments (GB_0) provide perpetual incremental above-market earnings of ($r-k$). The present value of this perpetual stream is obtained by dividing $[(r-k)GB_0]$ by k.

Equation (A.8) can be rewritten in terms of the growth equivalent as follows:

$$P = \frac{E}{k} + \left[\left(\frac{r-k}{k}\right)GB_0\right].$$ (A.9)

The growth equivalent can now be shown to equal the present value of all future investments implied by the DDM model expressed as a percentage of B_0. Recall that B_i, the firm's book value at time i, is

$$B_i = (1+g)^i B_0.$$

The increment to book value at time i is symbolized by b_i and is equal to ($B_i - B_{i-1}$). Thus,

$$b_i = B_i - B_{i-1}$$

$$= (1+g)^i B_0 - (1+g)^{i-1} B_0,$$

or

$$b_i = (1+g)^{i-1} g B_0.$$

The present value (PV) of all such book increments is as follows:

$$PV[b_1, b_2, b_3, \ldots] = \frac{gB_0}{1+k} + \frac{gB_0(1+g)}{(1+k)^2} + \frac{gB_0(1+g)^2}{(1+k)^3} + \cdots$$

$$= \left(\frac{gB_0}{1+k}\right)\left[1 + \frac{1+g}{1+k} + \frac{(1+g)^2}{(1+k)^2} + \cdots\right]$$

$$= \frac{gB_0}{k-g}.$$

Thus,

$$\frac{PV[b_1, b_2, b_3, \ldots]}{B_0} = \frac{g}{k-g},$$

which is precisely G as defined previously.

Note that G is independent of the funding of the book-value increments; that is, the assumption that only retained earnings are used to fund new investments is artificial. If an opportunity to invest b_i and earn r exists at time i, this investment could be funded through the issuance of equity at a cost of k. The earnings on this new investment, net of financing costs, would then be precisely $(r - k)$.

Note further that the magnitude of the growth equivalent—not the specific timing of investment opportunities—is what matters. A different sequence of book increments $(b_1^*, b_2^*, b_3^*, \ldots)$ for which $PV(b_1^*, b_2^*, b_3^*, \ldots)/B_0$ is equal to G would have precisely the same impact on the theoretical price as the sequence of book increments implied by the constant-growth model.

As an example of the magnitude of growth implicit in the DDM, consider Firm D. Because $g = 10$ percent and $k = 12$ percent, the growth equivalent is 500 percent (that is, $0.10/0.02$). Thus, for this firm to sustain a P/E of 16.67 (see Table A.1), some sequence of investments must exist that, in present-value terms, is equal to 500 percent of the current book value of the firm. Furthermore, each of these investments must earn 15 percent. These extraordinary opportunities are reflected in the price through the present value of the excess returns on those investments, as illustrated in equation (A.9).

For Firm D, because $r = 15$ percent, $B_0 = \$100$, and $E = \$15$,

$$P = \frac{15}{0.12} + \left(\frac{0.15 - 0.12}{0.12}\right) \times 5.00 \times 100.00$$

$$= 125 + 125$$

$$= 250.$$

Thus, the value of the present earnings of $15 in perpetuity is $125 and the value of all future excess earnings is also $125.

To understand the impact of G fully, consider the P/E formula. Dividing both sides of equation (A.9) by E (that is, by rB_0), produces

$$P/E = \frac{1}{k} + \left(\frac{r-k}{rk}\right)G.$$

The first term, $1/k$, is the base P/E (that is, P/E = 8.33 when k = 12 percent). If the second term is positive, the P/E will be above this base level. If that term is negative, the P/E will be below the base P/E. The factor $[(r-k)/rk]$ measures the impact of opportunities to make new investments that provide a return equal to the firm's ROE. This factor is the franchise factor. Thus,

$$FF = \frac{r-k}{rk},$$

and

$$P/E = \frac{1}{k} + (FF \times G).$$

Because the growth equivalent is measured in units of initial book value (that is, G is expressed as a percentage of B_0), FF is the increase in P/E per "book unit" of investment.

Note that when $r = k$, the franchise factor is zero. This result is consistent with the previous observation that growth alone is not enough to affect the P/E. As r increases, however, the impact of growth on the P/E increases.

These results are illustrated in Table A.2. Consider, for example, the case of Firm D. Because r = 15 percent, FF = 1.67. Thus, an investment equal to 100 percent of this firm's initial book value (that is, $100) will lift the P/E by 1.67 units. An investment of 5 times book will lift the P/E by 8.34 units, just enough to bring it from the base P/E of 8.33 to its actual P/E of 16.67.

Table A.2. Franchise Factors for Varying ROEs
(with a 12 percent market rate)

ROE (r)	FF	ROE (r)	FF
12.00%	0.00	17.00%	2.45
13.00	0.64	18.00	2.78
14.00	1.19	19.00	3.07
15.00	1.67	20.00	3.33
16.00	2.08	50.00	6.33

Finally, note that, as r approaches infinity, the franchise factor levels off at the inverse of the (k) market rate. That is, no matter how large the ROE, with a 12 percent market rate, FF can never rise above 8.33. In particular, no matter how large the reinvestment rate, at least a 100 percent increase in book value is required to raise the P/E from 8.33 to 16.67.

Appendix B. Firm Valuation with Varying Investment and Return Patterns

An Investment Opportunity Approach to Firm Valuation

The development of the theoretical formula for valuing a firm's stock makes use of the following variables:[1]

k	=	market capitalization rate,
B	=	initial book value,
r	=	ROE (return on initial book value),
NPV_j	=	net present value at time j of a new investment made at time j, and
I_j	=	magnitude of investment opportunity at time j.

The earnings on initial book value are assumed to remain rB in perpetuity. Thus, this earnings stream contributes (rB/k) to the current value of the firm. The contribution of all new investments to firm value is the sum of the discounted NPVs of these investments. The present value (PV) of the firm can thus be expressed as follows:

$$PV = \frac{rB}{k} + \sum_{j=1}^{\infty} \frac{NPV_j}{(1+k)^j}. \tag{B.1}$$

Assume now that investment I_j provides payments $p_{j+1}, p_{j+2}, \ldots,$ at times $j+1, j+2, \ldots$ Then,

$$NPV_j = PV_j - I_j, \tag{B.2}$$

---

[1]This approach to valuation is based on Miller and Modigliani (1961).

where PV_j is the sum of the present values (at times j) of the payments p_{j+1}, p_{j+2}, ... That is,

$$PV_j = \sum_{i=1}^{\infty} \frac{p_{j+i}}{(1+k)^i}.$$

The payment stream provided by I_j can always be represented by a perpetual-equivalent return (R_{pj}) on I_j. For this representation to be valid, the present value of the perpetual payments must be the same as PV_j. Because the present value of the perpetual payments is found by dividing by the discount rate,

$$PV_j = \frac{R_{pj}I_j}{k},$$

or

$$R_{pj} = k\left(\frac{PV_j}{I_j}\right). \tag{B.3}$$

Combining equations (B.2) and (B.3) allows NPV_j to be expressed in terms of the perpetual equivalent:

$$NPV_j = \frac{R_{pj}I_j}{k} - I_j$$

$$= \left(\frac{R_{pj} - k}{k}\right)I_j. \tag{B.4}$$

Substituting equation (B.4) in equation (B.1) and rearranging terms allows P to be rewritten as[2]

$$PV = \frac{rB}{k} + \sum_{j=1}^{\infty}\left(\frac{R_{pj} - k}{k}\right)\left(\frac{I_j}{(1+k)^j}\right). \tag{B.5}$$

---

[2]This result is precisely the formula derived by Miller and Modigliani.

Observe that no assumption has been made in this general model about the source of financing for new investments. The financing could be internal, external, or a combination of the two.

The Franchise Factor and Present-Value Growth Equivalent

In the special case in which all new investments provide the same perpetual return (R_p), equation (B.5) becomes

$$PV = \frac{rB}{k} + \left(\frac{R_p - k}{k}\right) \sum_{j=1}^{\infty} \left(\frac{I_j}{(1+k)^j}\right). \tag{B.6}$$

The P/E can be found by dividing both sides of (B.6) by the initial earnings (rB). That is,

$$P/E = \frac{1}{k} + \left(\frac{R_p - k}{rk}\right) \left(\frac{\sum_{j=1}^{\infty} \left[\frac{I_j}{(1+k)^j}\right]}{B}\right). \tag{B.7}$$

The last term is the present value of all future investment opportunities expressed as a percentage of the initial book value. The factor $[(R_p - k)/rk]$ gives the impact on P/E of each unit increase in book value; that is, if the book value increases by 100 percent, the P/E increases by $[(R_p - k)/rk]$. This expression is the franchise factor:

$$FF = \frac{R_p - k}{rk}. \tag{B.8}$$

The growth equivalent is defined as

$$G = \frac{\sum_{j=1}^{\infty} \left[\frac{I_j}{(1+k)^j}\right]}{B}$$

and is interpreted as the present-value growth equivalent of all future investments that return R_p in perpetuity. This definition is motivated by the observation that an immediate investment of magnitude G that earns R_p in perpetuity will have precisely the same price impact as the complex stream of investment opportunities discussed earlier in the appendix. The P/E formula (equation B.7) can now be rewritten as

$$P/E = \frac{1}{k} + (FF \times G).$$
(B.9)

In general, different new investments will have different perpetual-equivalent returns and distinct franchise factors. The franchise factor corresponding to perpetual-equivalent return R_{pi} is symbolized by FF_i; that is, $FF_i = (R_{pi} - k)/rk$. The present value of all future investments with franchise factor FF_i is symbolized by G_i.

Under these assumptions, the P/E formula (equation B.9) can be generalized to encompass n distinct franchise factors, as follows:

$$P/E = \frac{1}{k} + \sum_{i=1}^{n} (FF_i \times G_i)$$
(B.10)

An example of the application of equation (B.10) is provided in the section of this appendix dealing with multiphase growth.

A Duration-Based Approximation to the Franchise Factor

In the previous section, the magnitude of FF was shown to depend on the size of R_p. Substituting the formula for R_p (equation B.3) into the formula for FF (equation B.8) gives the following formula for FF in terms of the present value of the payments on investment I:

$$FF = \frac{PV - I}{rI},$$
(B.11)

in which PV is computed at the market discount rate (k). That is, $PV = PV(k)$. Then, because the internal rate of return is the discount rate at which the present value equals the value of investment, $I = PV(IRR)$. Thus, the numerator in equation (B.11) is $PV(k) - PV(IRR)$.

The difference between these present values can be approximated by a Taylor series:

$$PV(k) - PV(IRR) = PV'(IRR)(k - IRR) + \ldots .$$

With D as duration and because, by definition, the modified duration is $-PV'/PV$, the Taylor series can be rewritten as

$$PV(k) - PV(IRR) = PV(IRR)D(IRR)(IRR - k) + \ldots .$$

An approximate formula for FF is obtained by substituting this formula in equation (B.11), approximating $D(IRR)$ by $D(k)$, and dropping higher order terms:

$$FF \approx \frac{D(IRR - k)}{r} .$$

Multiphase Growth

To understand multiphase growth, first consider the case in which the investment opportunity at time j is always the same fixed percentage (g) of the firm's book value at time ($j - 1$). For example, if $g = 10$ percent and $B = \$100$, the firm is assumed to have an investment opportunity at time 1 equal to $10 (that is, 10 percent of the initial book value of $100). After taking advantage of this investment opportunity, the firm's book value increases by $10 to $110 (110 percent of $100). The following year, another investment opportunity arises of which the magnitude is $11 (10 percent of $110). Pursuing this opportunity leads to a new book value of $121 (110 percent of $100). This pattern, which is illustrated in Table B.1, can be written generally as

Table B.1. Investment Opportunities and Book Value when Firm Grows at 10 Percent a Year

Time	Investment Opportunity	New Book Value
0	NA	$100.00
1	$10.00	110.00
2	11.00	121.00
3	12.10	133.10

NA = not applicable.

$$I_1 = gB,$$

$$I_2 = g(1+g)B,$$

$$I_3 = g(1+g)^2 B, \text{ etc.}$$

If this pattern of constant growth continues forever (recall Chapter 2 and Appendix A), then

$$G = \frac{g}{k-g}. \tag{B.12}$$

The analysis of multiphase growth, for simplicity, is restricted here to the case in which the investments $I_1, I_2, \ldots, I_n$ earn R_{p1} in perpetuity and all subsequent investments, $I_{n+1}, I_{n+2}, \ldots$, earn R_{p2} in perpetuity. Then, from equation (B.5),

$$\text{PV} = \frac{rB}{k} + \left(\frac{R_{p1}-k}{k}\right)\sum_{j=1}^{n}\left[\frac{I_j}{(1+k)^j}\right] + \left(\frac{R_{p2}-k}{k}\right)\sum_{j=1}^{\infty}\left[\frac{I_{n+j}}{(1+k)^{n+j}}\right]. \tag{B.13}$$

Dividing both sides of equation (B.13) by the initial earnings *(rB)* gives

$$\text{P/E} = \frac{1}{k} + (\text{FF}_1 \times G_1) + (\text{FF}_2 \times G_2). $$

Observe that this equation is the same as equation (B.10) with $n = 2$. The G_1 and G_2 growth equivalents are given by the following:

$$G_1 = \frac{\displaystyle\sum_{j=1}^{n}\left[\frac{I_j}{(1+k)^j}\right]}{B} \tag{B.14}$$

and

$$G_2 = \frac{\displaystyle\sum_{j=1}^{\infty}\left[\frac{I_{n+j}}{(1+k)^{n+j}}\right]}{B}. \tag{B.15}$$

The additional assumption is now made that $(I_j, j = 1, \ldots, n)$ is a constant percentage (g_1) of the book value at time $j - 1$. Furthermore, $(I_j, j = n + 1, n + 2, \ldots,)$ is taken to be a different constant percentage (g_2) of the prior year's book value. Thus,

$$I_1 = g_1 B,$$
$$I_2 = g_1(1 + g_1)B,$$
$$I_3 = g_1(1 + g_1)^2 B,$$

.
.
.

$$I_n = g_1(1 + g_1)^{n-1} B,$$
$$I_{n+1} = g_2(1 + g_1)^n B,$$
$$I_{n+2} = g_2(1 + g_2)(1+g_1)^n B$$

.
.
.

Using these expressions in equations (B.14) and (B.15) and summing the resulting geometric progression provides the following:

$$G_1 = \left(\frac{g_1}{k - g_1}\right)\left[1 - \left(\frac{1+g_1}{1+k}\right)^n\right] \qquad \text{if } g_1 \neq k$$

or

$$G_1 = \frac{ng_1}{1 + k} \qquad\qquad \text{if } g_1 = k \qquad\qquad\qquad \text{(B.16)}$$

and

$$G_2 = \left(\frac{g_2}{k - g_2}\right)\left(\frac{1+g_1}{1+k}\right)^n \qquad \text{if } g_2 < k. \qquad\qquad \text{(B.17)}$$

Because the series for G_1 was finite, no restriction had to be made on g_1. In contrast, the infinite geometric progression involving g_2 converges only when g_2 is less than k. Furthermore, as n approaches infinity, G_2 approaches zero and G_1 approaches G, as given in equation (B.12). When $g_1 = g_2$, G_1 and G_2 combined give the G of equation (B.12).

Consider the case of ten years of growth at 10 percent and growth at 5 percent for each succeeding year. If $k = 12$ percent, then equations (B.16) and (B.17) give the following:

$$G_1 = \left(\frac{0.10}{0.12 - 0.10} \right) \left[1 - \left(\frac{1 + 0.10}{1 + 0.12} \right)^{10} \right]$$

$$= 0.8244, \text{ or } 82.44 \text{ percent},$$

and

$$G_2 = \left(\frac{0.05}{0.12 - 0.05} \right) \left(\frac{1 + 0.10}{1 + 0.12} \right)^{10}$$

$$= 0.5965, \text{ or } 59.65 \text{ percent}.$$

Appendix C.   A Franchise Factor Formula for the Base P/E

Recall from Chapter 3 that, for a firm with n future investment opportunities, FF_i franchise factors, and G_i growth equivalents, the theoretical P/E can be expressed as

$$P/E = \frac{1}{k} + \sum_{i=1}^{n} FF_i G_i , \tag{C.1}$$

where k is the market capitalization rate and $1/k$ is the base P/E.

If a new investment of magnitude I_i is made n years from today, FF_i and G_i can be computed from the following formulas:

$$FF_i = \frac{R_i - k}{rk},$$

and

$$G_i = \frac{\left[\dfrac{I_i}{(1+k)^n} \right]}{B}, \tag{C.2}$$

where

R_i	=	perpetual-equivalent return on investment I_i,
r	=	return on equity (the perpetual return on initial book value), and
B	=	initial book value.

In spread banking, R_i can be expressed in terms of the net spread on borrowed funds (NS_i), the leverage multiple (L_i), and the risk-free rate (R_f); that is,

$$R_i = R_f + (L_i \times NS_i).$$

Now FF_i can be expressed as follows:

$$\mathrm{FF}_i = \frac{R_f + (L_i \times NS_i) - k}{rk}.$$

The P/E formula (C.1) can also be extended to include franchise factors for a firm's current book of business (B): Assume that the current book comprises m subunits. The size of each subunit (b_i) is expressed as a percentage of the current book, so that

$$\sum_{i=1}^{m} b_i B = B$$

and

$$\sum_{i=1}^{m} b_i = 1. \tag{C.3}$$

Now, define r_i as the ROE for subunit b_i. Thus, the current earnings (E) can be written as follows:

$$E = rB$$

$$= \sum_{i=1}^{m} r_i b_i B.$$

Consequently,

$$r = \sum_{i=1}^{m} r_i b_i. \tag{C.4}$$

That is, r is the weighted-average return on book equity, and the weights are the sizes of the subunits.

The value (P) of a firm has three components. First, if a firm has no growth opportunities and book equity capital earns k in perpetuity (that is, $r = k$), the capitalized value of current earnings is $kB/k = B$. Thus, in this case, the firm's value would be the same as its book value.

Second, if the current business provides a return that exceeds the k market rate, an incremental value (P_0) will exist. This P_0 is defined as the capitalized value of excess earnings on the current book equity (assuming that those earnings continue year after year). Thus, P_0 can be viewed as a franchise value associated with the *current* book of business.

Finally, if *future* opportunities with above-market returns exist that the firm can pursue, value has a third component, P_1, which is the net present value of all anticipated future earnings from new investments, or the franchise value associated with future investment opportunities.

Therefore,

$$P = B + P_0 + P_1,$$

and the price/earnings ratio is

$$P/E = \frac{B + P_0 + P_1}{E}$$

$$= \frac{B}{E} + \frac{P_0}{E} + \frac{P_1}{E}. \tag{C.5}$$

Note that multiplying both sides of equation (C.5) by E/B results in a formula for the price-to-book ratio in terms of the incremental P_0 and P_1 values. The price-to-book formula is

$$\frac{P}{B} = 1 + \frac{P_0}{B} + \frac{P_1}{B}.$$

This formula also shows that the premium to book is the sum of P_0/B and P_1/B; that is,

$$\frac{P - B}{B} = \frac{P_0}{B} + \frac{P_1}{B}.$$

Returning to the P/E, notè that because $E = rB$,

$$\frac{B}{E} = \frac{B}{rB}$$

$$= \frac{1}{r}. \qquad \qquad \text{(C.6)}$$

From the definition of P_0,

$$P_0 = \frac{rB - kB}{k}$$

$$= \frac{(r-k)B}{k}$$

and

$$\frac{P_0}{E} = \frac{(r-k)B}{k}\left(\frac{1}{rB}\right)$$

$$= \frac{r-k}{rk}. \qquad \qquad \text{(C.7)}$$

Adding equations (C.6) and (C.7) yields

$$\frac{B}{E} + \frac{P_0}{E} = \frac{1}{r} + \frac{r-k}{rk}$$

$$= \left(\frac{1}{r}\right)\left(1 + \frac{r-k}{k}\right)$$

$$= \frac{1}{k},$$

which demonstrates that the first two terms in the P/E equation (C.5), combine to produce the base P/E, $1/k$. The last term in equation (C.5), which is P_1/E, corresponds to the last term in equation (C.1); that is,

$$\frac{P_1}{E} = \sum_{i=1}^{n} FF_i G_i.$$

One can also express P_0/E in FF format by using equations (C.3) and (C.4) in equation (C.7) and rearranging terms:

$$\frac{P_0}{E} = \frac{\sum r_i b_i - k \sum b_i}{rk}$$

$$= \sum \frac{(r_i - k)}{rk} b_i.$$

With equation (C.2) as a guide, franchise factors for the current book of business are defined as follows:

$$FF_i^{(b)} = \frac{r_i - k}{rk}.$$

Thus, the base P/E can be expressed as

$$\text{Base P/E} = \frac{B}{E} + \frac{P_0}{E}$$

$$= \frac{1}{r} + \sum_{i=1}^{j} FF_i^{(b)} b_i. \tag{C.8}$$

The primary difference between formula (C.8) and the general P/E formula (C.1) is that, in the general formula, the term $1/k$ (the base P/E) has been replaced by the B/E ratio $(1/r)$. Using equation (C.5) produces the following expanded general form of the P/E formula:

$$P/E = \frac{1}{r} + \sum_{i=1}^{j} FF_i^{(b)} b_i + \sum_{i=1}^{n} FF_i G_i.$$

Appendix D. The Franchise Factor Model Applied to the Leveraged Firm

The analysis begins with an unleveraged firm and assumes that all returns are perpetual and net of taxes. The value of the unleveraged firm (V^U) is the sum of the firm's tangible value (TV) and its franchise value (FV); earnings generated by the current book of business are denoted by rB; the tangible value is thus the capitalized value of those earnings (rB/k); and the franchise value is the net present value of anticipated new businesses. If the earnings rate on new assets is R and the present value of all funds invested in franchise businesses is GB, the present value of these prospective earnings is (RGB/k). The franchise value then becomes

$$\text{FV} = \left(\frac{RGB}{k}\right) - GB$$

$$= \left(\frac{R-k}{k}\right)GB,$$

and

$$V^U = \text{TV} + \text{FV}$$

$$= \frac{rB}{k} + \left(\frac{R-k}{k}\right)GB. \tag{D.1}$$

The P/E is obtained by dividing the value of the firm by the earnings:

$$\text{P/E (unleveraged)} = \frac{V^U}{rB}$$

$$= \frac{1}{k} + \left(\frac{R-k}{rk}\right)G.$$

As previously, the base P/E and franchise factor are

$$\text{Base P/E (unleveraged)} = \frac{1}{k}$$

and

$$\text{FF (unleveraged)} = \frac{R-k}{k}.$$

Thus,

$$\text{P/E (unleveraged)} = \text{Base P/E} + (\text{FF} \times G). \tag{D.2}$$

The Leveraged, Tax-Free Firm

Now consider a leveraged firm (V^L) with a perpetual debt that is priced at par. In the absence of taxes, leverage does not change the firm's value (Modigliani and Miller 1958). Thus,

$$V^L = V^U.$$

The value of the leveraged firm's equity (V_E^L) is the difference between the total firm value and the value of debt; that is, $V_E^L = V^L - \text{Debt}$.

The firm's debt is expressed as a percentage (h) of the current book value of assets,

$$\text{Debt} = hB.$$

Thus,

$$V_E^L = V^U - hB. \tag{D.3}$$

The earnings are reduced by the debt payments (ihB), where i is the pretax interest on the debt, so

Net earnings $= rB - ihB$

$$= (r - ih)B. \tag{D.4}$$

Finally, the firm's earnings must be greater than its debt payments. Thus,

$r - ih > 0.$

The P/E is now obtained by dividing the value of the firm's equity by the net earnings:

$$\text{P/E (leveraged)} = \frac{V_E^L}{(r - ih)B}.$$

To express the P/E in terms of a leverage-adjusted base P/E and FF, V_E^L must first be expressed in an appropriate algebraic format. In equation (D.3), V^U is replaced by the expression given in equation (D.1) to obtain the following relationship:

$$V_E^L = \frac{rB}{k} + \frac{R-k}{k}GB - hB.$$

Interchanging the last two terms in this expression results in

$$V_E^L = \frac{rB}{k} - hB + \frac{R-k}{k}GB$$

$$= \frac{(r - kh)B}{k} + \frac{R-k}{k}GB. \tag{D.5}$$

The first term in equation (D.5) is the difference between the firm's tangible value and the value of the debt. If that difference is positive, $r - kh > 0$.

A formula for P/E is again found by dividing the equity value (equation D.5) by the net earnings (equation D.4); that is,

$$\text{P/E (leveraged)} = \frac{r - kh}{k(r - ih)} + \frac{R-k}{k(r - ih)}G.$$

An equity capitalization rate (k_E) is now defined as follows:

$$\dot{\kappa}_E \equiv \frac{k(r - ih)}{r - kh}. \tag{D.6}$$

If the debt rate (i) is less than the cost of capital (k), then $r - ih > r - kh$. Thus, $k_E > k$. Moreover, k_E increases with leverage.

With this definition of k_E, the P/E for the leveraged firm is as follows:

$$\text{P/E (leveraged)} = \frac{1}{k_E} + \frac{R - k}{(r - ih)k}G.$$

After a comparison of this P/E formulation with the P/E for the unleveraged firm (see equation D.2), the base P/E and the franchise factor for the leveraged firm can be defined as follows:

$$\text{Base P/E} = \frac{1}{k_E}, \tag{D.7}$$

and

$$\text{FF} = \frac{R - k}{(r - ih)k}. \tag{D.8}$$

With these definitions in place, the P/E can always be expressed as the sum of a base P/E and a franchise P/E. The franchise P/E is the product of the franchise factor and the growth equivalent, where the growth equivalent is unaffected by leverage.

The Weighted-Average Cost of Capital

From the defining equation for k_E (equation D.6),

$$(r - kh)k_E = (r - ih)k.$$

Thus,

$$(r - kh)k_E + ihk = rk$$

and

$$\left[1 - \left(\frac{k}{r}\right)h\right]k_E + \left[\left(\frac{k}{r}\right)h\right]i = k.$$

If k is assumed to remain constant, this equation indicates that k_E is determined from the weighted-average cost of capital. The weight $([k/r]h)$ will now be shown to be the percentage of total debt relative to the tangible value of the unleveraged firm:

$$\frac{kh}{r} = \frac{khB}{rB}$$

$$= \frac{hB}{\left(\dfrac{rB}{k}\right)}$$

$$= \frac{\text{Debt}}{\text{Tangible value}}.$$

Therefore, k_E can be interpreted as the cost of equity for a leveraged TV firm (a firm without franchise value). If the debt rate is assumed constant, the required return on equity (k_E) will increase with leverage so that k remains constant. This increasing equity capitalization rate can be viewed (in accordance with Modigliani and Miller) as a consequence of the fact that, as leverage increases, so does the riskiness of the remaining equity cash flows.

At first, it may seem surprising that, regardless of the extent of the franchise value, k_E is based only on the tangible component of the firm's full market value. In fact, these results are mathematically equivalent to computing a risk-adjusted discount rate (k^*) for the entire equity component of the firm's market value. Such a general approach would have led to precisely the same value of leveraged equity as obtained in equation (D.5). The definition of k_E effectively loaded all the financial leverage risk onto the TV component. Consequently, k_E will generally be larger than k^*. The advantage of the given decomposition lies in the simplicity it provides and the parallelism that results with the base P/E and FF for the unleveraged firm.

The Leveraged, Fully Taxable Firm

Consider now the effect of taxes. In contrast to tax-exempt firms, taxable firms will gain from leverage.

For simplicity, assume that the full benefits of the tax shield pass directly to

223

the corporate entity. If the annual debt payments are $(i \times \text{Debt})$, the tax gain is $t \times i \times \text{Debt}$, where t is the marginal tax rate. Because the debt is assumed to be priced at par, the tax wedge is $[t \times i \times \text{Debt}]/i = t \times \text{Debt}$.

The value of the leveraged firm is simply the value of the unleveraged firm plus the tax wedge: $V^L = V^U + (t \times \text{Debt})$. As before, the value of the leveraged firm's equity is the difference between the total value and the value of debt,

$$V_E^L = V^L - \text{Debt}$$

$$= V^U + (t \times \text{Debt}) - \text{Debt}$$

$$= V^U - (1-t)\text{Debt}.$$

Thus,

$$V_E^L = V^U - (1-t)hB.$$

The net earnings for the taxable firm are computed by reducing the earnings (which are assumed to be after taxes) by the *after-tax* debt payments:

$$\text{Net earnings} = rB - (1-t)ihB$$

$$= [r - i(1-t)h]B.$$

When comparing these formulas for the equity value and net earnings with similar formulas for the tax-free firm (equations D.3 and D.4), observe that the only difference is that h for the taxable firm always appears in combination with $(1-t)$. Consequently, the base P/E and the FF for the taxable firm will be the same as in equations (D.7) and (D.8) with h replaced by $[(1-t)h]$. That is, the taxable firm can be treated as if it were a tax-free firm with an adjusted leverage of $[(1-t)h]$.

Appendix E. The Effects of External Financing

This appendix briefly reviews how earnings growth in the dividend discount model derives from retained earnings and how external financing can lead to enhanced earnings growth. The appendix then demonstrates that external financing and premium investments lead to counterbalancing changes in a firm's tangible value and franchise value. Consequently, in the absence of surprises, price growth is predetermined, earnings growth and P/E growth offset each other, and the firm remains on its value-preservation line.

Growth Assumptions in the Standard Dividend Discount Model

The standard DDM assumes that a firm pays a dividend (d_1) one year from today and that dividends in subsequent years grow at a constant rate (g). If the discount rate is k, the stream of future dividend payments can be discounted to obtain the following price formula:

$$P_0 = \frac{d_1}{k - g},$$

in which P_0 is the initial price based on annual dividend payments made at year end.

Assume that the firm retains a fixed proportion (b) of earnings (E) and pays out the balance of earnings as dividends. In this case,

$$d_1 = (1 - b)E_1 \tag{E.1}$$

$$P_0 = \frac{(1 - b)E_1}{k - g}, \tag{E.2}$$

and

$$\frac{P_0}{E_1} = \frac{1-b}{k-g}. \qquad \text{(E.3)}$$

In the DDM, the basic assumption of a constant g and a constant b naturally lead to price and earnings growth at the same rate. To see why, observe that the second-year dividend is

$$d_2 = (1+g)d_1$$

$$= (1+g)(1-b)E_1$$

$$= (1-b)[(1+g)E_1].$$

Because dividends are always $(1-b)$ times earnings,

$$E_2 = (1+g)E_1 .$$

Dividends continue to grow at rate g, so the price at the beginning of the second year will be

$$P_1 = \frac{d_2}{k-g}$$

$$= \frac{(1+g)(1-b)E_1}{k-g}. \qquad \text{(E.4)}$$

Comparing equation (E.4) with equation (E.2) shows that the price also grows at the g rate,

$$P_1 = (1+g)P_0 .$$

With earnings and price growing at the same rate, the P/E will have a constant value over time (see equation E.3); that is,

$$\text{P/E} = \frac{1-b}{k-g}.$$

226

In the DDM, no provision is made for external financing. Instead, smooth growth is obtained by making two heroic assumptions: All investments are derived from retained earnings, and such investments provide the *identical* return (r) in *each future period*. If B_0 is the initial book value, then

$$r = \frac{E_1}{B_0},$$

or

$$E_1 = rB_0.$$

At the end of the first year, retained earnings (bE_1) are added to B_0; so,

$$B_1 = B_0 + bE_1$$

$$= B_0 + brB_0$$

$$= B_0(1 + br).$$

The second-year earnings are

$$E_2 = rB_1$$

$$= rB_0(1 + br)$$

$$= E_1(1 + br).$$

Because $E_2 = (1 + g)E_1$, $g = br$. Thus, in the standard DDM, book value, price, and earnings all grow at the same rate as a result of continual new investments fueled by retained earnings.

Growth in Earnings per Share with External Financing

This section develops a formula for the incremental growth in earnings per share (EPS) that a firm achieves when it sells n new shares one year from today and invests the proceeds of the sale in high-return projects. Assume that the firm initially has N shares outstanding and earns E_1 dollars per share in the first year. At year end, the firm retains and invests b times E_1 in projects that return R in all subsequent years. This "core" investment leads to incremental earnings of RbE_1 in Year 2 in addition to the base earnings (E_1). The corresponding core earnings growth (from Year 1 to Year 2) is

$$g_1(E) = \text{Core earnings growth}$$

$$= \frac{E_1 + RbE_1}{E_1} - 1$$

$$= Rb.$$

If the firm requires additional funds to take advantage of franchise investment opportunities that arise at year end, it can issue new shares priced at P_1. In a stable market, new share issuance alone will not change the stock price.

If n shares are issued at the beginning of Year 2, the total external funding will be nP_1. Per (initial) share, this funding can be expressed as follows:

$$\text{External funds (per initial share)} = \frac{nP_1}{N.} \tag{E.5}$$

The external funds can also be expressed as a proportion (b^*) of E_1:

$$\text{External funds} = b^* E_1 . \tag{E.6}$$

Equating (E.5) and (E.6) and solving for n produces a formula for n that will soon become useful:

$$n = \frac{Nb^* E_1}{P_1}. \tag{E.7}$$

Assume that the proceeds of the equity sale are invested so as to return R^* annually. Because these proceeds are received and invested at the beginning of Year 2, Year 2 will garner additional earnings of $R^* b^* E_1$ for each initial share.

Total EPS growth ($g_{TOT}[E]$) can now be computed. As a first step, convert earnings per share to total earnings:

$$\text{Total earnings (end of Year 1)} = NE_1$$

$$\text{Total earnings (end of Year 2)} = (N + n)E_2 .$$

There are three contributors to Year 2 earnings (E_2): base earnings, income from retained earnings, and income from externally funded investments; that is,

$$(N + n)E_2 = NE_1 + RbNE_1 + R^* b^* NE_1 . \tag{E.8}$$

Equation (E.8) can now be used to derive a formula for $g_{TOT}(E)$:

$$g_{TOT}(E) = \frac{E_2}{E_1} - 1$$

$$= \left(\frac{N}{N + n}\right)(1 + Rb + R^* b^*) - 1. \tag{E.9}$$

If no new shares are issued, the total earnings growth will be the same as the core earnings growth. That is, if $b^* = n = 0$, then

$$g_{TOT}(E) = Rb$$

$$= g_1(E).$$

When new shares are sold (that is, $b^* > 0$ and $n > 0$) and the proceeds are reinvested, $g_{TOT}(E)$ will increase if R^* is sufficiently large.

An incremental growth formula that eliminates the need to know the number of shares can now be derived:

$$\text{Incremental growth} = g_{TOT}(E) - g_1(E)$$

$$= g_{TOT}(E) - Rb.$$

Replacing $g_{TOT}(E)$ by the expression given in equation (E.9) produces

$$g_{TOT}(E) - Rb = \frac{N}{N + n}(1 + Rb + R^* b^*) - 1 - Rb, \tag{E.10}$$

and equation (E.7) can be used to eliminate the number of shares in equation (E.10):

$$\frac{N}{N+n} = \frac{N}{\left[N + Nb^* \left(\dfrac{E_1}{P_1} \right) \right]}$$

$$= \frac{P_1}{P_1 + b^* E_1}. \tag{E.11}$$

Equation (E.10) can be recast in a more revealing form by using equation (E.11) and then performing a variety of algebraic simplifications. The final result is the following formula:

$$g_{TOT}(E) - Rb = \left(\frac{P_1}{P_1 + b^* E_1} \right) b^* \left(R^* - \frac{(1 + Rb)E_1}{P_1} \right)$$

$$= \left(\frac{P_1}{P_1 + b^* E_1} \right) b^* \left(R^* - \frac{\hat{E}_2}{P_1} \right), \tag{E.12}$$

where

$\hat{E}_2 = $ Year 2 earnings without equity sales

$= (1 + Rb)E_1$.

The term $(\hat{E}_2/P_1)$ can be viewed as an "earnings yield threshold." Thus, for g_{TOT} (E) to be greater than Rb (that is, to have incremental earnings growth from the equity sale), proceeds of the equity sale must be invested at a rate of return greater than $(\hat{E}_2/P_1)$. This threshold will be attained in general for franchise investments for which $R^* > k$, because the earnings yield $(\hat{E}_2/P_1) \leq k$.

Formula (E.12) will now be applied to the franchise-value firm discussed in Chapter 7:

$b = b^* = 65$ percent

$R = R^* = 20$ percent

$P_0 = \$1,500$

$E_1 = \$100$

$g(P) = 9.67$ percent.

The result is the following:

E_1	=	$100
$1 + Rb$	=	1.13
$\hat{E}_2 = (1 + Rb)E_1$	=	$113
P_0	=	$1,500
$1 + g(P)$	=	1.0967
$P_1 = [1 + g(P)]P_0$	=	$1,645
$\hat{E}_2/P_1$	=	6.87 percent.

Because $R^* = 20$ percent and $b^* = 65$ percent,

$$\text{Earnings growth increment} = b^*\left[R^* - \frac{\hat{E}_2}{P_1} \right]$$

$$= 0.65 \times (20 \text{ percent} - 6.87 \text{ percent})$$

$$= 8.53 \text{ percent.}$$

The contribution of the 8.53 percent growth increment to $g_{TOT}(E)$ is diluted by the increased share base. This increased base is reflected in the first factor in equation (E.12). In the example, that first factor is

$$\frac{P_1}{P_1 + b^*E_1} = \frac{\$1,645}{\$1,645 + (0.65 \times \$100)}$$

$$= 96.2 \text{ percent.}$$

Thus, only 96.2 percent of the increment actually translates into increased total earnings growth.

Combining the results for this example gives

$$g_{TOT}(E) = Rb + (96.2 \text{ percent of } 8.53 \text{ percent})$$

$$= (0.20 \times 0.65) + (0.962 \times 0.0853)$$

$$= 0.13 + 0.082$$

$$= 0.212, \text{ or } 21.2 \text{ percent.}$$

The process can be summarized as follows:

- When $65 in retained earnings (65 percent of $100) is invested at 20 percent, the earnings growth is 13 percent, which adds $13 (13 percent of $100) to Year 2 earnings per share.
- When another $65 in investments is externally financed, the investment return is calculated as an incremental return over the earnings yield threshold. Dilution reduces that increment, so the additional earnings growth becomes 8.2 percent. This growth adds another $8.20 to the Year 2 earnings per share.

The final consideration is the change in the P/E that occurs from the beginning to the end of Year 1. The price/earnings ratio is calculated from the price per share at the beginning of the year and the earnings per share that accumulate over the course of the year. At the outset,

$$\frac{P_0}{E_1} = \frac{\$1,500}{\$100}$$

$$= 15.$$

At the beginning of Year 2,

$$\frac{P_1}{E_2} = \frac{\$1,645}{\$100 + \$13 + \$8.20}$$

$$= 13.57.$$

Thus,

$$g(\text{P/E}) = \frac{13.56}{15.00} - 1$$

$$= -9.5 \text{ percent.}$$

This combination of 21.2 percent earnings growth and a 9.5 percent P/E decline is consistent with 9.7 percent price growth because

$$g(P) = [1 + g(E)] \ [1 + g(P/E)] - 1$$

$$= (1 + 0.212) \times (1 - 0.095) - 1$$

$$= 9.7 \text{ percent.}$$

The 9.7 percent price growth characterizes all points on the value-preservation line that Figure 7.7 illustrated. Thus, external investment financing moves the firm along, but not off, the VPL.

Price Growth and the VPL

In the previous section, an example of external funding illustrated the following general principle: In a stable market, earnings growth and P/E growth always offset each other in such a way that a firm's price growth is independent of investment returns and the funding mechanism. In fact, the year-to-year price growth is determined by the firm's initial P/E and its retention policy. Consequently, the balance between earnings growth and P/E growth can always be represented as a point on a fixed value-preservation line.

This section offers a general proof of the preceding principle. The first step is to show how investing in premium projects increases the firm's tangible value and decreases its franchise value. The balance between these two value changes (that is, the franchise conversion process) is such that both the return on investment and the extent of external financing "drop out" of the calculation of price-per-share growth. The investment returns and the extent of funding do, however, have an impact on EPS growth. Because earnings increase while price growth does not change, a counterbalancing decrease must occur in the P/E.

Recall that stock price (P) is the sum of the tangible value (TV) per share and the franchise value (FV) per share. Initially, the stock price is as follows:

$$P_0 = TV_0 + FV_0. \tag{E.13}$$

By the end of the first year, TV and FV will have changed in accordance with their growth rates $g(TV)$ and $g(FV)$. At the beginning of the second year,

$$P_1 = TV_1 + FV_1;$$

that is,

$$[1 + g(P)]P_0 = [1 + g(TV)]TV_0 + [1 + g(FV)]FV_0 \, ,$$

and

$$1 + g(P) = [1 + g(TV)]\left(\frac{TV_0}{P_0}\right) + [1 + g(FV)]\left(\frac{FV_0}{P_0}\right). \qquad \text{(E.14)}$$

To simplify equation (E.14), another variable is introduced:

$$f = \frac{FV_0}{TV_0}. \qquad \text{(E.15)}$$

Combining equations (E.13) and (E.15) gives the following formulas:

$$\frac{TV_0}{P_0} = \frac{1}{1+f} \qquad \text{(E.16)}$$

and

$$\frac{FV_0}{P_0} = \frac{f}{1+f}. \qquad \text{(E.17)}$$

With equations (E.16) and (E.17), equation (E.14) can be simplified to

$$1 + g(P) = \frac{1}{1+f}([1 + g(TV)] + f[1 + g(FV)]). \qquad \text{(E.18)}$$

Finding $g(P)$ now requires substituting appropriate expressions for $g(TV)$ and $g(FV)$. The formula for $g(TV)$ was developed in the previous section for the general case in which investments are financed through a combination of retained earnings and new share issuance. These investments were shown to increase earnings and tangible value. In contrast, the new investments deplete the franchise value. To derive a formula for $g(FV)$, the total franchise value after one year is first needed:

Total FV (start of Year 2) = Time growth in initial FV
- FV depletion from investing retained earnings
- FV depletion from externally financed investments.

The FV depletion from an investment is equal to the net present value of the cash flows produced by that investment. Using this concept and the symbols defined earlier in this appendix and used in equation (E.5) results in the following relationships:

Total franchise value (start of Year 1) = $N \times FV_0$,
Total franchise value (start of Year 2) = $(N + n) \times FV_1$,

and

$$(N + n)FV_1 = N\left[(1 + k)FV_0 - \left(\frac{R - k}{k}\right)bE_1 - \left(\frac{R^* - k}{k}\right)b^*E_1\right].$$

Because $TV_0 = E_1/k$, this relationship can be expressed as

$$(N + n) \times FV_1 = N \times FV_0 \times \left([1 + k] - [(R - k)b + (R^* - k)b^*]\frac{TV_0}{FV_0}\right),$$

which provides the basis for a formula for $g(FV)$. Replacing TV_0/FV_0 by $1/f$ (see equation E.15) produces

$$1 + g(FV) = \frac{FV_1}{FV_0}$$

$$= \frac{N}{N + n}\left([1 + k] - \frac{1}{f}[(R - k)b + (R^* - k)b^*]\right)$$

$$= \frac{1}{f}\left(\frac{N}{N + n}\right)[f + k(f + b + b^*) - Rb - R^*b^*]. \tag{E.19}$$

Substituting formula (E.9) for $g(TV)$—that is, $g_{TOT}(E)$—and formula (E.19) for $g(FV)$ in the price-growth formula (E.18) results in

$$1+g(P) = \left(\frac{1}{1+f}\right)\left(\frac{N}{N+n}\right)[1+Rb+R^*b^* +f+k(f+b+b^*)-Rb-R^*b^*]$$

$$= \frac{N}{N+n}\left(1+\frac{k(f+b+b^*)}{1+f}\right). \tag{E.20}$$

Note at this point that both R and R^* have canceled out, which means that the price growth is independent of the return assumptions established previously.

Referring back to equation (E.11) and the fact that $P_1 = [1 + g(P)]P_0$, it follows that $[N/(N+n)]$ depends on $g(P)$ and it can be written as follows:

$$\frac{N}{N+n} = \frac{P_1}{P_1 + b^* E_1}$$

$$= \frac{[1+g(P)]P_0}{[1+g(P)]P_0 + b^* E_1}$$

$$= \frac{1+g(P)}{1+g(P)+\dfrac{b^* E_1}{P_0}} . \tag{E.21}$$

Substituting equation (E.21) in (E.20) leads to

$$1+g(P) = \left(\frac{1+g(P)}{1+g(P)+\dfrac{b^* E_1}{P_0}}\right)\left[1+\frac{k(f+b+b^*)}{1+f}\right]. \tag{E.22}$$

Next, equation (E.22) is solved for $g(P)$:

$$g(P) = \frac{k(f+b+b^*)}{1+f} - \frac{b^* E_1}{P_0}$$

$$= k - \frac{(1-b)k}{1+f} + \frac{kb^*}{1+f} - \frac{b^* E_1}{P_0}. \tag{E.23}$$

The last term in equation (E.23) involves the initial earnings-to-price ratio, which can also be written in terms of f:

$$\frac{E_1}{P_0} = \frac{k\left(\dfrac{E_1}{k}\right)}{P_0}$$

$$= \frac{k \times TV_0}{P_0}$$

$$= \frac{k}{1+f} \tag{E.24}$$

Using result (E.24) in (E.23) shows that the terms involving b^* (that is, the extent of external funding) drop out. The result is a formula for $g(P)$ that depends only on the retention rate and the initial P/E:

$$g(P) = k - \frac{(1-b)E_1}{P_0}$$

$$= k - \frac{1-b}{\left(\dfrac{P_0}{E_1}\right)}. \tag{E.25}$$

Equation (E.25) shows that the franchise conversion process does not affect price growth. This finding confirms that, even with external funding, price growth is simply the difference between market rate and dividend yield.

Chapter 7 demonstrated that

$$g(\text{P/E}) = \frac{1+g(P)}{1+g(E)} - 1.$$

Because the franchise conversion process increases $g(E)$ but does not change $g(P)$, this relationship indicates that any increase in $g(E)$ must be offset by a decrease in $g(\text{P/E})$. This statement defines the basic trade-off that determines the VPL for a given year.

References

Asikoglu, Yaman, and Metin R. Ercan. 1992. "Inflation Flow-Through and Stock Prices." *Journal of Portfolio Management* (Spring):63–68.

Bernstein, Peter L. 1992. "How Interest Sensitive Are Stocks? A New Look." *Economics and Portfolio Strategy.* New York: Peter L. Bernstein, Inc.

Bodie, Zvi, Alex Kane, and Alan J. Marcus. 1989. *Investments.* Homewood, Ill.: Richard D. Irwin.

Buffet, Warren E. 1977. "How Inflation Swindles the Equity Investor." *Fortune* (May):250–67.

Estep, Tony, and H. Nicholas Hanson. 1980. *The Valuation of Financial Assets in Inflation.* New York: Salomon Brothers Inc.

Financial Analysts Journal. 1985 (November/December).

Fruhan, William E. 1979. *Financial Strategy: Studies in the Creation, Transfer, and Destruction of Shareholder Value.* Homewood, Ill.: Richard D. Irwin.

Gordon, Myron J. 1962. *The Investment Financing and Valuation of the Corporation.* Homewood, Ill.: Richard D. Irwin.

Homer, Sidney, and Martin L. Leibowitz. 1972. *Inside the Yield Book.* Englewood Cliffs, N.J.: Prentice-Hall.

Keane, Simon M. 1990. "Can a Successful Company Expect to Increase Its Share Price? A Clarification of a Common Misconception." *Journal of Applied Corporate Finance* (Fall):82–88.

Leibowitz, Martin L. 1978. "Bond Equivalents of Stock Returns." *Journal of Portfolio Management* (Spring):25–30.

———. 1986. "Total Portfolio Duration: A New Perspective on Asset Allocation." *Financial Analysts Journal* (September/October):18–29, 77.

Leibowitz, Martin L., Lawrence N. Bader, and Stanley Kogelman. 1992. *Total Portfolio Duration and Relative Returns.* New York: Salomon Brothers Inc.

Leibowitz, Martin L., David Hartzell, David Shulman, and Terence Langetieg. 1987. *A Look at Real Estate Duration.* New York: Salomon Brothers Inc.

Leibowitz, Martin L., Eric H. Sorensen, Robert D. Arnott, and H. Nicholas Hanson. 1989. "A Total Differential Approach to Equity Duration." *Financial Analysts Journal* (September/October):30–37.

Miller, Merton H., and Franco Modigliani. 1961. "Dividend Policy, Growth, and the Valuation of Shares." *The Journal of Business* (October):411–33.

Modigliani, Franco, and Merton H. Miller. 1958. "The Cost of Capital, Corporation Finance, and the Theory of Investment." *The American Economic Review* (June):261–97.

Modigliani, Franco, and Richard A. Cohn. 1979. "Inflation, Rational Valuation and the Market." *Financial Analysts Journal* (March/April):24–44.

Rao, Ramesh K.S. 1987. *Financial Management.* New York: Macmillan.

Salomon Brothers Inc. 1990. *A Review of Bank Performance.* New York.

Solomon, Ezra. 1963. *The Theory of Financial Management.* New York: Columbia University Press.

Sorensen, Eric H., and Sergio Bienstock. 1992. *The Growth/Value Contest: A Growing American Tradition.* New York: Salomon Brothers Inc, October 2.

Standard & Poor's. 1992. *Analyst's Handbook.* New York: McGraw-Hill.

Stewart, G. Bennett, III. 1991. *The Quest for Value.* New York: Harper Business.

Stocks, Bonds, Bills, and Inflation, 1991 Yearbook. 1991. Chicago, Ill.: Ibbotson Associates.

Treynor, Jack L. 1972. "The Trouble with Earnings." *Financial Analysts Journal* (September/October):41–43.

Williams, John B. 1938. *The Theory of Investment Value.* Amsterdam: North-Holland Publishing.

Selected AIMR Publications*

The Modern Role of Bond Covenants, 1994 . . . . $20
  Ileen B. Malitz

Derivative Strategies for Managing Portfolio Risk, 1993 . . . . . . $20
  Keith C. Brown, CFA, *Editor*

Equity Securities Analysis and Evaluation, 1993 . . . . $20

The CAPM Controversy: Policy and Strategy Implications for
  Investment Management, 1993 . . . . $20
  Diana R. Harrington and Robert A. Korajczyk, *Editors*

The Health Care Industry, 1993 . . . . $20
  James Balog, *Editor*

The Oil and Gas Industries, 1993 . . . . $20
  Thomas A. Petrie, CFA, *Editor*

Execution Techniques, True Trading Costs, and the
  Microstructure of Markets, 1993 . . . . $20
  Katrina F. Sherrerd, CFA, *Editor*

Investment Counsel for Private Clients, 1993 . . . . $20
  John W. Peavy III, CFA, *Editor*

Active Currency Management, 1993 . . . . $20
  Murali Ramaswami

The Retail Industry—General Merchandisers and Discounters,
  Specialty Merchandisers, Apparel Specialty, and
  Food/Drug Retailers, 1993 . . . . $20
  Charles A. Ingene, *Editor*

Equity Trading Costs, 1993 . . . . $20
  Hans R. Stoll

Options and Futures: A Tutorial, 1992 . . . . $20
  Roger G. Clarke

Improving the Investment Decision Process—Better Use of
  Economic Inputs in Securities Analysis and Portfolio
  Management, 1992 . . . . $20
  H. Kent Baker, CFA, *Editor*

Ethics, Fairness, Efficiency, and Financial Markets, 1992 . . . . . $20
  Hersh Shefrin and Meir Statman

Investing Worldwide, 1992, 1991, 1990 . . . . $20 each

---

*A full catalog of publications is available from AIMR, P.O. Box 7947, Charlottesville, Va. 22906;
804/980-3647; fax 804/977-0350.

Order Form 023

Additional copies of *Franchise Value and the Price/Earnings Ratio* (and other AIMR publications listed on page 240) are available for purchase. The price is **$20 each in U.S. dollars**. Simply complete this form and return it via mail or fax to:

AIMR
Publications Sales Department
P.O. Box 7947
Charlottesville, Va. 22906 U.S.A.
Telephone: 804/980-3647 • Fax: 804/977-0350

Name _____

Company _____

Address _____

_____ Suite/Floor _____

City _____

State _____ ZIP _____ Country _____

Daytime Telephone _____

Title of Publication	Price	Qty.	Total
_____	____	____	____
_____	____	____	____

Shipping/Handling
- ☐ All U.S. orders: Included in price of book
- ☐ Airmail, Canada and Mexico: $5 per book
- ☐ Surface mail, Canada and Mexico: $3 per book
- ☐ Airmail, all other countries: $8 per book
- ☐ Surface mail, all other countries: $6 per book

Discounts
- ☐ Students, professors, university libraries: 25%
- ☐ CFA candidates (ID #_____): 25%
- ☐ Retired members (ID #_____): 25%
- ☐ Volume orders (50+ books of same title): 40%

Discount $_____

4.5% sales tax
(Virginia residents) $_____

8.25% sales tax
(New York residents) $_____

7% GST
(Canada residents,
#124134602) $_____

Shipping/handling $_____

Total cost of order $_____

☐ Check or money order enclosed payable to **AIMR**   ☐ Bill me
Charge to: ☐ VISA   ☐ MASTERCARD   ☐ AMERICAN EXPRESS

Card Number:_____   ☐ Corporate ☐ Personal

Signature:_____   Expiration date: _____

241